PENGUIN BOOKS

Looking for La Bomba

Richard Neill studied journalism at the London College of Printing. He has since lost all shorthand and his interviewing skills have not improved on a disastrous series of vox pops conducted outside Elephant and Castle shopping centre. By accident more than design, he began his writing career at the monthly wine magazine, *Decanter*, and despite an inability to spit into a spittoon without causing splashback, he managed (four years later) to convince the editor of the *Daily Telegraph* to swap the photo of their existing wine writer (Oz Clarke) with his own. For five years, Richard wrote a weekly wine column for the *Daily Telegraph* and in 1998 was voted Glenfiddich Wine Writer of the Year. To the despair of his mother (but your career!) and neighbours (but our free wine!) he resigned from the Circle of Wine Writers in 2001 and left for Cuba with a double bass and a yoga mat. Richard was last seen heading south through Patagonia in a VW Combi van.

Looking for La Bomba

The Cuban Adventures of a
Musical Oaf

RICHARD NEILL

PENGUIN BOOKS

PENGUIN BOOKS

Published by the Penguin Group
Penguin Books Ltd, 80 Strand, London WC2R ORL, England
Penguin Group (USA) Inc., 375 Hudson Street, New York, New York 10014, USA
Penguin Books Australia Ltd, 250 Camberwell Road,
Camberwell, Victoria 3124, Australia
Penguin Books Canada Ltd, 10 Alcorn Avenue, Toronto, Ontario, Canada M4V 3B2
Penguin Books India (P) Ltd, 11 Community Centre,
Panchsheel Park, New Delhi – 110 017, India
Penguin Books (NZ) Ltd, cnr Airborne and Rosedale Roads,
Albany, Auckland 1310, New Zealand
Penguin Books (South Africa) (Pty) Ltd, 24 Sturdee Avenue,
Rosebank 2196, South Africa

Penguin Books Ltd, Registered Offices: 80 Strand, London WC2R ORL, England

www.penguin.com

First published 2005

Set by Palimpsest Book Production Limited, Polmont, Stirlingshire
Printed in England by Clays Ltd, St Ives plc

For my
mum

Contents

Gracias

George, my agent, for believing in that idea I had

Tom Weldon, at Penguin, for saying yes

Rowland White, my editor, for taking what I sent him and turning it into something a lot more readable

Georgina and Christie for doing all the bits Rowland didn't

Tania, Braulio, Tanita and Liana for providing love, support and a wonderful home for a year

Everyone on Calle Santa Lucia for making me feel part of the *barrio*

Pastor, my inspiration and friend, for making music lessons so much fun

José Aquiles for letting me go on the other side of the glass partition

Sones de Oriente for allowing me to play with them

Carlos and all the gang at the San Agustín conga for letting a *pepe* inside the eye of the storm

Melian for showing me the beautiful Sierra Maestra

Rafael for teaching me to dance (a bit better than I used to)

All the musicians in Santiago who helped an Englishman look for his *bomba*

Prologue

In the winter of 1996, as a much-needed break from the rigours of being the wine correspondent for the *Daily Telegraph*, I took a two-week holiday to Cuba. I chose Cuba because the Cubana air tickets were cheap and everyone was saying you had to get there before Castro died. My knowledge of the country was as flimsy as my reason for visiting. I knew about the Bay of Pigs but without looking it up in the guidebook I couldn't tell you the specifics of what happened there. I was aware that Cuban athletes regularly won a disproportionate amount of Olympic medals, but I would have struggled to come up with a list of five famous Cuban athletes. As for my understanding of the Cuban Revolution – you could have written it on the back of the in-flight sick bag.

Despite, or perhaps because of all that ignorance, I ended up falling hopelessly in love with the place. The salt-encrusted Deauville Hotel on Havana's famous seafront drive, the Malecon, was just as chaotic and run-down as I had hoped it would be. The potholed streets, the smell of diesel and decay and sweat and alcohol, the sound of music pumping out of every passing car, the hustlers hissing at you from the shadows: it was everything the travel books and novels had suggested it would be.

I loved the fact that Havana was so badly lit you could see the night sky as clearly as if you were in the countryside, that the service in our hotel (in fact everywhere) was so bad it was almost professional in its rudeness and inefficiency, that there was no such thing as an unroadworthy vehicle, and that the concept of too much rum was anathema. Most of all, though, I loved the music, and my addiction to Cuban rhythm was firmly and finally cemented on one of our last nights on the island.

Returning to the Deauville after another arduous day testing the difference between three- and seven-year-old Havana Club rum, we were handed a message along with our keys. It was from our friendly concierge/fix-it man and the one-line, handwritten note simply announced, 'Los Van Van. 9pm. Palacio de la Salsa'. There was no mention of either ticket availability or prices. 'Who or what are Los Van Van?' asked my bemused-looking friend, Jason. 'The best salsa band in Cuba,' I replied confidently. 'Trust me, we have to get to this gig.'

I'd heard about Los Van Van while taking salsa classes in London. 'If you don't start dancing when you hear this, it's because you're dead,' our Cuban teacher had laughed while slotting in a CD for our first lesson. Whether he was right depends on your definition of dancing – my footwork was as clumsy as a deep-sea diver's – but by the end of the course I was a total Van Van fan. Named after a political slogan used by Fidel to rally the country's cane cutters in 1970 ('*los diez millones van van*' – 'the ten million tons are going . . . are going'), the group had been so successful for so long that they were sometimes referred to as the Rolling Stones of Cuban music. It was said that whenever they released a new single, the song title would invariably end up being incorporated into the street slang so beloved by Cubans. That was how popular they were. Going to a Van Van concert was an essential part of any crash course in Cuban culture.

Given all this information, you can understand our surprise (not to mention slight disappointment) to find, after rushing down to the Palacio de la Salsa and expecting to pay serious quantities of dollars to hard-nosed touts, there was absolutely no problem in getting in. The reason for such lack of interest was soon made clear. With tickets priced at 20 dollars, the potential audience had been reduced to tourists and prostitutes paid for by tourists: not exactly what I had in mind for my

Van Van initiation ceremony, but I wasn't missing out on this opportunity. We handed over the money, walked the gauntlet of hisses from women in various stages of undress, and with rum in hand took our places alongside the other sunburnt foreigners. Then, just as the lights went down and the first members of the band came on stage, something remarkable happened. The doors opened and a huge crowd of people burst into the auditorium. A Cuban friend later explained that the organizers always waited to sell as many dollar tickets as possible and then, at the last moment, switched to peso prices for the locals. In seconds, the entire three-tiered arena was a seething mass of bodies.

Until that night at the Palacio, salsa hadn't meant an awful lot to me. In fact, music in general hadn't meant that much to me. I bought CDs like everyone else. I went to the occasional gig like everyone else. But, to use the Star Wars vernacular, I had never felt the force. That all changed with Los Van Van. By the end of the first song I had been transported to a place I didn't recognize. Scotty had beamed me up and dumped me down in front of a group of fifteen men armed with an impressive variety of weapons of mass movement. I counted trombones, flute, maracas, electric bass, guitar, bongos, and an array of other percussive hardware I had never seen before. Against such an arsenal of rhythm, resistance was futile. Movement was inevitable. The ringleader was a tall black guy with a huge, luxuriant moustache and a large white Stetson on his bandanna-covered head. His shirt was unbuttoned down to the belly button and his trousers were tight enough to show everyone which side he preferred to dress. I recognized him from the CD covers and knew he was Pedro 'Pedrito' Calvo, a man whose reputation with the ladies was such that the band had apparently once written a song called 'El Negro No Tiene Na' ('The Black Guy Hasn't Got Anything'), a playful response to the rumours that Calvo had picked up a few sexual diseases from his many dalliances. He certainly wasn't denying he liked the opposite

sex – that was more than clear from his stage act. Even though
he looked like he could have been the sixth member of the
Village People, you were left in no doubt that the man was 110
per cent heterosexual. Halfway through the set, Calvo invited
a select group of female members of the audience on to the
stage and after lining them up in a row, persuaded each to perform (it took very little persuading) their sexiest hip-revolving
routine. Then, with the song still playing, the big man went
behind each woman, one by one, and to huge cheers and
applause allowed the scantily clad groupies to grind their bottoms into his groin area while he continued to sing the vocal
part. It was an astonishing performance, not least because he
somehow managed to avoid getting an erection. The man either
had incredible powers of control or he drank loads of bromide
tea before coming on stage.

Los Van Van played for over three hours and by the time we
got to the encores I was so totally under the spell of the music
that Fidel himself could have shimmied past me in a shell-suit
and I wouldn't have blinked. When it was finally all over and
the house lights came on again, I was overcome by an extraordinarily strong conviction. I had glimpsed the power a musician could wield and I wanted some of that power, badly. I had
witnessed the sheer crotch-thrusting pleasure of live performance and I knew that whatever it took, I had to find a way of
experiencing that pleasure too. Flat on my bed a couple of
hours later, ears ringing and feet throbbing, a pledge was made.
No matter what sacrifices it took and no matter the humiliation suffered, I vowed that I would go back home and take up
playing a musical instrument again. It was a *carpe diem* moment
of clarity, a cliché-bolstered vision of the future. 'One day,' I
promised myself, 'I will be the man who throws his bandanna
into the crowd.'

No one was more surprised than me by this revelation. In
the twenty-nine years that led up to that concert at the Palacio
de la Salsa, the true starting point to this sore-fingered odyssey,

I had shown absolutely no sign of any musical yearning, not a hint of regret at even failing to get past Grade 2 piano. Even so, it was another four years before I finally found the courage to buy a double bass and head off back to the Caribbean.

1. Childhood Scars and Air Guitars

'He makes a lot of noise,' was the closest Mrs Neill ever got to a cot-side compliment and I think even she soon accepted that any musical potential inside her elder son was buried so deep it would take a crack team of talent-sniffing Alsatians to find it. Making my debut with a high-pitched scream in the maternity ward of Amersham hospital (the only time in my life I can legitimately claim to have reached the high notes), I was, by genetic default I fear, a long-odds bet for an appearance in Young Musician of the Year. Born into a family tree whose various branches appeared to be notably bare of instrument-playing ability, it was clear that any scaling of musical heights was going to have to be achieved without the aid of any in-herited back-up. Getting to the top, or at least past base camp, would require hours of instruction, a lot of hard graft, and a financial support team accustomed to throwing daft amounts of cash at ludicrous challenges.

None of these three was in evidence during my early child-hood. That's not to say my parents wouldn't have sacrificed what cash was available had I shown signs of interest. But I hadn't so they didn't. When I was about four, we (we being my parents, younger brother, older sister, golden Labrador Splash, and me) moved from Buckinghamshire to north Derbyshire, twenty minutes' drive from the family steel business in Sheffield. For my sister it was probably not the dream move, but for us two young boys it was like arriving in a new adven-ture park. We had a massive garden with a stream at the bottom of it, lots of open fields to play in, a neighbouring farm with an owner who had a false leg, and a nearby wood that was too scary to enter on your own: all a young boy's favourite ingredients were there. When it rained and we were forced indoors, we'd go up to the attic and play with the Scalectrix or shoot model cars along long strips of yellow tracking. That attic was a special place. It was where I went to read my beloved *Commando* army comics, where I disappeared if I'd been told off for doing something wrong, and most important of all it was where I got my first introduction to music.

My parents had an old record player, one of those all-in-one jobs that opened up like a box with a single speaker at the front and a needle so worn that when it hit the record it was as if someone had thrown a bag of chips into a deep-fat fryer. I can't actually remember asking for it but my first record was 'I'll Be Your Long-haired Lover from Liverpool' by Jimmy Osmond. I was five years old when it came out and although I hadn't a clue what a 'sunshine daisy from LA' was, it didn't stop me bellowing out the words into my hairbrush. My other favourite was 'Hello Muddah, Hello Faddah' by Allan Sherman, a song about an unhappy summer camper begging his parents to let him come home. I didn't see the irony at the time but the lyrics proved to be particularly pertinent.

One day, when I was aged seven, without warning, my parents drove me to the other end of the country, dropped me off with a trunk-load of belongings and then disappeared down the drive without me. I can't even begin to describe the emotional trauma involved in this sudden relocation. My mum was the best mum in the world. She was the best cook, the best nurse and the best teacher all rolled into one. And my dad was the best dad in the world. He gave me pocket money and let me light the bonfire at weekends. Why would such loving people go and leave me behind in a strange place with 200 strangers, thirty whole M1 motorway exits away from home? What had I done wrong?

For the first two weeks, Caldicott Preparatory School felt every bit as bad as Allan Sherman's Camp Grenada. I had to cope with battered fish every Friday lunch, a head matron who seemed worse than the witch in *Hansel and Gretel*, and a weekly torture known as chapel service. But the crying only lasted for a couple of weeks. Like the end of Sherman's song, things eventually took on a brighter hue. I discovered sport, spud guns and the art of stealing bourbon biscuits, and by the time my parents turned up for the first weekend break, I couldn't wait for them to drop me off again.

Caldicott was where I made my first stab at reaching some sort of musical proficiency. Like most children, I graduated to piano by way of triangle and recorder but unlike most children, I never even made it to 'Chopsticks'. An unexpected dose of stage fright in my Grade 2 piano exam brought an abrupt end to my musical ambitions and to this day I still bear the emotional scars of being one of the few people to come to grief at this level without even playing a note.

Fortunately I was performing to an audience substantially smaller than the one that saw me fluff the high note on 'O Little Town of Bethlehem' at the school carol service, an event I still insist was caused by a mix-up with the cassocks that left me straining for air. In fact, only one person – my music teacher, Mr Freeman – witnessed what happened on the day of the exam in the winter term of 1978 in practice room number four.

There I was with Freeman squeezed in close beside me on one of those two-person piano stools that bring little boys in shorts far too close to their teachers. Wiping the sweat off my palms, I gave the foot pedal a couple of nervous taps and moved my hands into the customary hover position a couple of inches above the keys. 'In your own time, Neill,' came the instruction to my left, and staring straight ahead at a hostile topography of undulating crotchets and quavers, I breathed in and prepared to let rip – if such a thing is possible at Grade 2. Half an hour and it would all be over.

And still my hands hovered, and would have continued to hover had Mr Freeman not eventually interrupted and asked whether I planned to sit the exam before or after lunch. Call it nerves or a fear of being in a shoebox of a room with a man who resembled an adult Billy Bunter, but suddenly I had absolutely no idea where to put my fingers. It was like I had never sat at a piano before, and not even Freeman's admirable gesture of pointing out the first note could snap me out of the trance. Very few people fail Grade 2 piano and those who do usually find the trauma of failing too great even to consider giving it a second go. Like the actor who forgets his lines on opening night, I knew I couldn't bounce back easily from such a crushing defeat. So I took the only available option. I gave up music and switched to carpentry, throwing myself into the therapeutic task of making double-decker shoe-cleaning kit containers and elaborately grooved but totally unstable candle-stick holders.

Dented self-confidence aside, the piano incident wasn't actually a total disaster. Whatever my prep school prospectus might have tried to imply, the truth was that playing an instrument or even just showing an interest in playing an instrument was about as good for your classroom cred as admitting you quite liked Religious Studies. Boys who took up playing the cello were boys who didn't want to (or didn't have time to) follow that far more creditable path of self-improvement marked 'truancy', the path lined with the small dried blobs of pink blotting paper fired from a home-made Bic blowpipe. Boys who played cello never got around to discovering the terminal elasticity of a balloon filled with water and they definitely never used their set of compasses to pick holes in the elbows of their jumper just so that they could get really cool leather patches sewn on. By the time the toy companies began selling containers of green slime, I was, thanks to a schedule free of music lessons, at the peak of my creatively destructive powers.

At the age of thirteen I moved to Rugby School, an institution that appeared to have changed very little since Tom Brown's days. When I arrived in 1980, the old system of 'fagging' had still not been swept away. New school entrants were expected to act as unofficial slaves for the senior members of the house, polishing shoes, running errands, and generally learning to be subservient little underlings. My parents were spending thousands of pounds, and making enormous personal sacrifices, for their son to make endless cups of tea and learn about master–servant relationships. Bullying had been honed into an art form and my first three years were little more than a crash course in personal survival. Of the many physical forms of terror that were inflicted on the weaker boys the one I remember most was lamp-posting. This involved someone upturning your metal bed (while you were asleep of course) so that it (and you) ended up as vertical as a lamp-post. Head injuries were common and it happened so often to me that I learned to sleep with the pillow resting up against the metal bars of the headrest so that when the inevitable lamp-posting happened I at least had some sort of protection in place.

I hated Rugby and, like all the other weaker misfits, I disappeared into my own little world and waited for the bad times to pass. Music was an important part of that escapist act, and along with the rest of my Clearasil-using contemporaries I discovered a love and talent for a particular type of musical craft. Without a single lesson or practice session, in fact without even having to buy an instrument, I had soon managed to master air guitar, air drums, air bass and air keyboards. There was no piece of music too difficult to handle and no band that I wouldn't willingly play for at short notice. Phil Collins taken ill just before the important drum bit in the middle of 'In the Air Tonight'? No problem, we've got Richard Neill with his two plastic rulers and a set of empty Tupperware (a tuck-box full of my mum's cakes was another lifeline). Joe Walsh goes AWOL just as Don Henley sings the last line of 'Hotel California'? It's okay; our man is standing in on lead hockey stick. My greatest air-playing achievement – these were difficult times, you understand – was playing the entire eighty minutes of a Marillion concept album using a couple of Donnay rackets strapped together to form a perfectly strung, double-headed guitar. Back then I took my air-playing extremely seriously.

Of all the bands I grew to love in my teens, Marillion, a so-called progressive rock band generally acknowledged by *New Musical Express* readers to be 'pretentious Genesis sound-a-like bollocks', was the one that got me through the darkest moments. But, however embarrassing this musical phase now seems, the truth is I loved the band with a passion and considered their songwriter and lead singer, Fish, a lyrical hero. Listening to some of my Marillion albums today – for safety reasons I keep them under headphones – I admit some of the words seem a trifle grandiose, but back during those opening years of the 1980s, songs like 'Garden Party' and 'Chelsea Monday' were literature of the highest form. Fish was a poet, an angry anti-establishment wordsmith, and had I been asked to sit an O-level on the early work of Derek William Dick (Fish's real name), I would have scored a higher grade than the C I got for English Lit.

As for musicianship, for the serious air player Marillion offered the whole gamut of mime challenges. Incredibly con-voluted drum parts, lengthy swooping guitar solos, tricky key-board arrangements on one of those two-level synthesizers: this was a band that required an air roadie to set things up before a bedroom performance.

Yet those acts of note-perfect, fantasy fingerwork were as close to musical participation as I would ever get. Marillion might have been my antidote to the cruelty going on around me, but repeated listening did not inspire me to get back in a music room. It would appear that my decision to give up piano for nailing together bits of badly sawn wood had extinguished the musical starter flame, that flickering tongue of creativity required to ignite the instrumentalist inside us all. Music was a language I could admire, enjoy, even mimic, but evidently not master.

In an effort to apportion blame for my lack of musical contribution at Rugby, one of the more entertaining excuses I used
was based on a geography theory connecting behavioural activity to the environmental conditions in which a person lived.
Environmental Determinism, I believe it was called. Looking
back at those crucial formative years between thirteen and
eighteen, I now recognize that I was not living in a place or
indeed a time when music and musicianship were cherished.
During my five long years at Rugby School, the only time the
Kilbracken House piano was ever used by more than ten people in one week was when a food fight broke out and the
trusty old Grand stuck in one corner of the dining room unex-
pectedly found its lid being raised to provide shelter from flying
toast (jam on both sides, naturally) and ravioli.

And it wasn't just over-privileged, under-educated boys who
were showing no respect for music at that time; you only had
to listen to the radio for half an hour during the early Eighties
to see that the disdain for playing an instrument was not just
restricted to posh public schools. This was the age of New
Romanticism, of drum machines and over-produced bands
whose idea of a pre-gig warm-up was to plug in the blow-
driers. How could you possibly be inspired to become a musician when your team of available role models was led by Nik
Kershaw, Howard Jones and Simon le Bon? Sure, this musical
period had an influence. My wardrobe and hair gel bill took
the brunt of it.

If musical ambitions had been on the slide throughout school,
by the time I arrived at university they had retreated into a
state of dormancy that only a miraculous blast of inspiration
could have reversed. That blast never came. At Durham I studied
geography. Actually, that isn't entirely accurate. At Durham, I
drank a lot of beer and occasionally, when absolutely necessary,
I studied geography. Which explains why I scraped through
with a 2:2, traditionally known as a gentleman's degree but
more accurately, a lazy barfly's degree. Musical achievements?

Well, I did learn a huge variety of rugby songs but I'm not sure whether singing 'We're All Going Up Sunshine Mountain' and 'The Wreck of the Sloop John B' counts as either musical or achievements.

Post Durham, what little ambition I had (career, monetary, or otherwise) was immediately ditched in favour of adventure and the desire to see some of that geography I'd been learning about. In the summer of 1988 I flew into the northern Australian town of Cairns, wearing a ridiculous sleeveless denim jacket (an item I would never have dared wear back home) and carrying a brand-new rucksack that, despite my attempts to scuff and stain it at the airport, still screamed 'Novice traveller, come and get me!' to every scam artist around. My southern hemisphere awakening, while pleasantly tropical, was ruder than I expected. After being holed up in a single room in a dirty backpackers' hostel for three days, acute loneliness enhanced by the cheerful groups of scuba divers having a great time around me, I decided movement was less depressing than inertia. So I took a bus to Brisbane and went to look for a job at World Expo.

My first job was working behind the bar at a mock pub in the British pavilion. Eight hours a day, six days a week, I served 'Cornish Ale' to pissed Aussies while suffering hourly renditions of 'I've Got a Lovely Bunch of Coconuts' by a camp pianist with a bad cockney accent. It wasn't quite what I had in mind when I left England. Fortunately, escape arrived one evening in the form of two very friendly, very drunk cattle farmers from Queensland. A week later, with a brand new Akubra hat that looked as daft on me as the shiny pair of 100-dollar R. M. Williams boots, I found myself on a farm, or station to give its correct Aussie title, in the middle of the Outback. I don't think the Clarke family really needed an extra hand (and I'm absolutely certain they didn't need my untrained hand) but for their kindness and charity they were amply rewarded with enough new dinner-table anecdotes to last until the next useless labourer turned up. There was the one about the Pommie who couldn't roll up a barbed-wire fence, the one about the Pommie who needed three shots to kill a goanna sitting in a tree 10 yards away from him, and let's not forget the one about the Pommie who screamed at the sight of a large hairy spider under his bed.

After three months with hardened cattle men, I left the little town of Taroom with calloused hands, an Outback tan (white torso, brown limbs), and a habit of talking as if everything was a question? Farming was followed by three months washing dishes at a resort on an island on the Barrier Reef, four months working with a couple of ex-cons on a building site in Sydney, a month travelling overland to Perth, and then the long journey home.

Rather than fly straight back to London, I decided to take the slow circuitous route, via Zimbabwe and fifteen other African countries. During the seven months it took to get back to Britain, I managed narrowly to miss getting trampled by an elephant in Tanzania, suffered a week of acute diarrhoea in Uganda, spent a month trying to get across Zaire in the rainy season, and was refused entry into Algeria because Mrs Thatcher had turned back a bunch of Algerians attempting to enter Britain. This last inconvenience wouldn't have been so bad had the border post not been in the middle of the Sahara Desert.

The man who returned home after almost two years away was certainly not the same as the one who had left clutching a new rucksack and a W. H. Smith bag full of things that wouldn't fit in it. The man washing off months of grime in his sister's Fulham bathroom was more inquisitive, more self-assured, and a little bit wiser as to what went on outside the narrow confines of his cosy middle-class world. And thanks to Africa, in particular, he had got hooked on the buzz that came with getting into uncompromising situations in exotic locations, an addiction that would continue to bubble under the surface for years to come, threatening to surface whenever stability and a Corby trouser press looked just around the corner. While not the driving force behind my subsequent quest for musical achievement, this love of travel and putting myself in unlikely positions was certainly the kindling that helped turn the spark of an idea into a full career-ditching blaze.

For the next two years I drifted from one mindless job to another. I was a labourer for a landscape gardener, I worked in a showroom for a Docklands property development, and I even broke my no-suit rule by doing mundane office duties at my then brother-in-law's stockbroker business. Rumours that I was also seen on a Birmingham stage singing the Milkybar Kid song to a crowd of school kids are, I'm ashamed to admit, perfectly true. But those were desperate days, clinging to not so much a career ladder as a temporary job wobbly castle.

And then, by accident as much as design, a career of sorts arrived. I'd always liked the idea of being a journalist but had never had the courage to give it a go. Singing the Milkybar Kid song gives you courage. Fed up with drifting, I signed up for the postgraduate journalism diploma at the London College of Printing and began learning about news reporting, short-hand, page layouts, and the art of interviewing trauma victims for triumph-over-tragedy features – the most lucrative area of feature writing. As part of the thirteen-week intensive course, there was a compulsory period of work experience with a magazine or newspaper of your choice. Like all my other class-mates, I took the carpet-bomb approach and mailed a letter to just about every glossy consumer magazine in the book. A miserably small number of replies came back and the only two that showed any interest beyond the usual 'We have a week's vacancy next to the photocopier,' were the editor of *Decanter*, an upmarket glossy wine magazine, and someone who had just set up a new publication for lovers of soap operas, called (none too imaginatively) *Inside Soap*. In the end, I decided to give both a go and – in their own very different ways – both turned out to be extremely frightening experiences.

At the end of my first day at *Decanter*, I remember walking into the in-house tasting room and being confronted by the then head of Christie's wine department, Michael Broadbent, nosing his way through a formidable line-up of vintage champagnes. Sticking my curious but extremely ignorant snout in a glass, I recall reeling back and spluttering something along the lines of, 'This one's had it, Mr Broadbent – smells like old biscuits!' A frowning Broadbent strode over and stuck his own finely tuned proboscis into the rim of the offending sample. Within seconds he'd rattled out his own, rather more detailed verdict (fine mousse, buttery complexity and yeasty autolysis were definitely all in there somewhere), ending with the declaration, 'Excellent length!' I crept away vowing never to open my mouth unless spoken to.

Somehow, I survived the four weeks, and after a disastrous time at *Inside Soap* (I knew even less about soaps than wine) I was surprised and relieved to get an offer of a job as editorial assistant on 'the world's best wine magazine'. Of course, it was just meant to be a stepping-stone from which I would hop on to my original goal of award-winning investigative journalist writing worthy features on weird virus outbreaks in Central Africa.

But a year later, and wise to the fact that my editorial position involved very little writing and rather a lot of carving up roast beef for distinguished tasting panels, I decided the odds of me becoming the new Oz Clarke were lengthening with every week I stayed at *Decanter*. Keen to make my mark on the wine-writing world, I took out the nearest atlas and made a shortlist of countries that were making good wine but did not have any resident wine press to tell people about it. I needed a place that was on the cusp of a wine boom but at the bottom of the consumer-awareness charts. The year was 1993. After just two minutes scanning the world map, I had my destination.

'I'm going to Chile,' I said to my parents a few weeks later, a piece of news greeted with the same level of disbelief as my announcement that I'd turned up on the wrong day for my university interview. Where I saw the snow-capped Andes, wild Patagonian adventures, and beautiful dark-haired women about to inherit large profitable fruit plantations, they saw Pinochet, drug barons, and dark-haired women with a gringo's wallet in their hand. Fortunately, I had taken the wise precaution of handing in my notice before divulging the news, so disbelief and displeasure were forced into a corner where concerned support was the only way out.

Despite a wobbly first few months caused by my neglect to factor in the language barrier (I landed in Santiago with O-level Spanish and a bag of Linguaphone cassettes), the move proved surprisingly successful. Instead of being the guy that lined up the bottles at *Decanter* magazine, I became the guy that filed wine stories from Chile. Okay, so I was earning barely enough to pay for my growing Pisco Sour habit, but I was a journalist working in one of the most beautiful countries in the world and that was all that mattered. The dream lasted a year. That's the time it took for all the other wine journalists to twig that Chile and Argentina were nice places to visit. And that's the time it took me to get bored of writing about nothing else but the intense varietal character of Maipo Valley Cabernet Sauvignon.

I flew back to London, and thanks to being in the right place at the right time (and having a friend in the right place at the right time), landed a job as a restaurant reviewer at *Time Out*. This in turn led to a phone call from the editor of the *Daily Telegraph*'s Weekend section who, after commissioning a couple of trial columns, proved he was a risk-taker by offering me the job of wine correspondent for the paper. Knowing what I knew about the world's wines and knowing how many people read the *Daily Telegraph*, I actually considered doing the honest thing and saying, 'Thanks but no thanks.' After all, a bullshit artist can only bullshit so far before someone sniffs him out, and I didn't relish being ushered into Charles Moore's office to give an in-depth assessment of the latest Bordeaux vintage. I had been to the Médoc once and had set foot in only one French vineyard. Yes, of course I took the job.

As my thirtieth birthday approached, life had developed a rather nice Chardonnay glow. I had my own column in a national newspaper, a great social life, an unlimited supply of free wine to fuel it, and an endless string of invitations to visit vineyards around the world. Bar the absence of a lottery win and the unexpected arrival of Kylie at my door late at night, it was as close to the bachelor's dream ticket as you could get.

It was around this time that I went for that Cuban holiday, the time I saw Los Van Van play live and came out convinced that I had to learn to play a musical instrument. Of course nothing of the sort happened. I flew back home with a bag stuffed with Cohiba cigars, went straight to work on an article on why Malbec was the new Cabernet, and drifted back into the not exactly uncomfortable routine of wine tastings and press trips.

Then came the jolt that sent the whole charabanc off the rails. One dank grey November day, while visiting a food and wine show in Birmingham, I received a call from my brother that turned the good life upside down. My father had died. 'Mum found him in the garden,' said the quiet voice at the other end of the line. The full emotional impact didn't arrive until about six months later and, along with the delayed grief, came a bout of depression that left me struggling to care about anything, least of all another pithy 800-word story about the possibility of a rosé revival.

It took a wine trip to New Zealand in early 1998 to shift the cloud of self-pity and cynicism from my head. While the vineyards of Marlborough provided the backdrop to my exit from apathy and gloom, a bunch of old Cuban musicians were the unexpected providers of the accompanying soundtrack.

Somewhere on the way to the first winery visit, my friend Fiona, a fellow wine writer, pulled an unmarked tape out of her bag and slotted it into the car's cassette player. Seconds later, those beautiful opening chords of Compay Segundo's 'Chan Chan' filled my ears for the first time. 'This is great, who is it?' I asked while reaching to turn the volume up a notch. 'They're called the Buena Vista Social Club,' she answered, 'my husband gave it to me.' By the time we dropped the car off in Auckland ten days later, the tape was nearly worn through.

Like the vast majority of people who ended up buying the CD, I knew very little about *son*, the traditional Eastern Cuban music that made up most of the Buena Vista repertoire. But like everyone else I found it totally bewitching. Here was music that brought a smile to your face even if you didn't understand what they were singing about, a sound that seemed both novel and fresh and yet at the same time strangely familiar. And it took me straight back to that holiday, to the Palacio de la Salsa and Pedrito Calvo's ridiculous display of Cuban machismo. Those images became even sharper after watching the Wim Wenders documentary about the making of Buena Vista. If ever there was a film to make you want to return to Cuba, this was it. And as a trigger for deeply buried musical longings it was similarly effective. Watching these old men perform, the undisguised pleasure on their faces at having been given a second chance, I felt both ashamed at the fact that I'd given up playing an instrument so early but also encouraged that I still had time to restart what had been thoughtlessly abandoned. If Compay Segundo could do it at ninety-odd, why couldn't I?

To be honest, I expected these urges to disappear, just as they had previously with the distractions and pressures of weekly press deadlines, sensible reminders of mortgage payments and career paths. But they didn't. In fact as the weeks passed, the urge to do the unthinkable grew stronger rather than weaker. Unconsciously, I began glancing through the small ads for music teachers and instruments for sale. I went to far more gigs than normal and even broke my 'no going south of the river' rule a couple of times to go and see Cuban bands. I even started giving money to buskers.

Now, there are three ways your average thirty-something (with a cushy job that involves copious quantities of free wine) can deal with such behavioural tics. The first and most likely and sensible of the three would be to laugh at the stupidity of your dream and just get on with the day job. The second would be to buy a musical instrument and start taking evening classes until you got bored and reverted back to the first option. And the third would be to hand in your notice, buy a musical instrument and disappear to Cuba, thus removing the possibility of reverting to option one.

As 1999 rolled into 2000 and 2000 slipped into 2001, option three had moved from a long-odds bet to 5–1 favourite. Wine writing had lost its appeal. Apart from the diminishing joys of the endless marathon swill 'n' spit sessions and the increasingly large bills from my dentist's latest attempt to patch up the acid-stripped enamel, there was the numbing thought that if I kept it going for another ten years I'd look like one of the haggard, beetroot-nosed wine hacks you found mumbling incoherently on the back stretch of the Co-op winter tasting. Fear of jumping into the unknown was beginning to be outweighed by the fear of what I would become if I didn't.

Sometime during the first cold winter months of early 2001, I hit a particularly bad pocket of turbulence, a fold-your-tray-table-up and fasten-your-seatbelts moment when you accidentally tune in to Heart FM, and find you don't actually mind it. I was single, bored with work, far too familiar with the Marks & Spencer bung-it-in-the-oven range, and could find little reason (apart from the obvious financial one) not to give music the chance it had never had. The time had come, I decided, to put the ghosts of past piano exams to rest, to get beyond secretive air solos and singing to myself in the car. I wanted to see if I could succeed as an adult where I had failed as a child. It was time to ditch the excuses, find an instrument, and play.

2. Forgiving Instruments

Choosing the place where you want to play before you know *what* you want to play is probably not the accepted musical norm, but I knew I wanted to carry out my mission in Cuba before I'd even picked the tools (or rather, tool) to complete the mission. Apart from the obvious attractions of spending a year in one of the last remaining outposts of communism – an outpost thankfully located in warm Caribbean water rather than some bleak part of the Baltic – and finally getting my Spanish to a decent level of fluency, the combined effects of Los Van Van and Buena Vista sealed the deal. Here was a country renowned for the richness of its music culture, a place where toddlers could dance salsa before they could run and where even the garbage collectors announced their arrival on the street with a rhythmic percussion routine banged out on the side of the truck. I instinctively felt that this was the sort of training school (possibly the *only* training school) that would welcome in a musical Eddie the Eagle. The land of miracles they called it, and I was going to need plenty of miracles if I was ever going to realize my dream of standing on stage with a band.

Having targeted Cuba, the obvious place to go and study was Havana. A nice beach apartment, lazy afternoons hanging around the Egrem studios – scene of the Buena Vista recordings – followed by evenings sipping iced Daiquiris in one of Hemingway's old haunts. These were alluring images. Except, of course, Havana was far too easy and far too predictable a choice. And it was the wrong choice. If I wanted to learn to play an instrument in Cuba I knew I'd have to learn about the country's dominant music genre, *son*, and if I wanted to understand *son*, it made much more sense to go and live there and study the thing at its source.

Whatever the attractions of the capital, it was Santiago de Cuba, fifteen train hours to the east, that boasted the required musical pedigree. The mountains around Santiago were said to be the cradle of *son* and the city itself had been churning out great *soneros* ever since this traditional mountain music migrated to the city. Santiago was also the birthplace of other important musical movements like *trova* and *bolero*. And besides, it had a world-renowned carnival, the best rum, and a baseball team that had won the national championship for the last three seasons in a row.

Satisfaction at sorting out the location for my battle with crotchets and quavers was dampened somewhat by the realization that I still hadn't chosen a weapon to do battle with. A quick glance at the Cuban chapter of the *Rough Guide to World Music* left me with a scribbled list that included guitar, something called a *tres* (a six-stringed Cuban guitar which I was forced to strike off immediately for having the frightening words 'three sets of double strings' tucked into the description), percussion, piano, wind instruments and bass.

Flushed with the warm memory of thrashing Mum's Tupperware all those years ago, I initially edged towards the drumming option. And then, after the briefest of investigations, immediately backed off again. Cuban percussion, it appeared, was a discipline somewhat more expansive than just a pair of bongos and a few hollowed-out pumpkins. As I thumbed through a copy of Fernando Ortiz's door-wedging tome, *Los Instrumentos de la Música AfroCubana*, not only did it become clear why there was a livestock problem on the island (Ortiz should have called it 101 ways to get a noise out of stretched animal skin) but it was obvious that just selecting what to play could take up my entire year. However, not wishing to be accused of giving up without at least a try, I signed myself up on a weekend drumming course at the Ray Man percussion centre in Chalk Farm. My doubts that I had any hope of becoming Fast Hands Dicky were likely to be confirmed by a little practical experience. And they were. Four hours of African drumming (somewhat closer to flailing than drumming in my case) proved that had I been relying on jungle drums to communicate, those listening would have needed sub-titles. Drums, shakers, rattles, dangly metal thingies and cow bells – all were happily ticked off my shortlist as I closed the door on a now surprisingly deserted shop.

From the outset, piano had been ruthlessly cast aside on the grounds of excess emotional baggage (the ghosts of failed exams past were ones I wished to leave undisturbed), and guitar was similarly ditched after being deemed a boring choice by the friends I had dared consult. Which left me with a rapidly shrinking list of options topped by the wind section. Perhaps the boy who once managed to play the theme tune to *The Great Escape* using a comb, tracing paper and raw lung power could transform himself into the Clarence Clemons of mambo, the Kenny G of Cuban jazz (God help us)? But then again, perhaps he wouldn't. After a sober deliberation of all the huffing and puffing, not to mention post-performance, spittle-cleaning duties attached to this division of the orchestra, I was happily, if perhaps a little hastily, drawing a line through trumpet, flute, saxophone, trombone and anything else that required lip control and protracted gurning.

A somewhat rapid process of elimination left me staring at the one potential partner still standing on the other side of the music hall. Tall, big body, wide hips, deep voice, difficult to carry – not exactly my usual type but hey, you can't afford to be too fussy when the music's about to start and you don't want to be left blowing into two cupped hands. If I needed confirmation that we were destined to perform together, the response of the first friend to hear the news sealed it.

'Double bass is perfect for you,' affirmed Jeff, whose opinion I valued despite his complete lack of musical experience and an annoying habit of using my Camden flat as a public convenience before weekly Marks & Sparks visits. 'You're tall, you've got big hands and besides, they say it's a forgiving instrument,' he chuckled while going through his customary fly-buttoning ritual. Choosing an instrument on the grounds that you can get away with playing it slightly out of tune might seem a bit of a cop-out (not to mention a slur on the name of all great bass players), but from where I stood it looked an extremely sensible decision.

I'm sure if you asked other double bassists how they came to be partnered with their instruments, you'd get something a little more convincing. Something along the lines of 'My father was a bassist and his father before him', or 'It was left to me by my long-lost uncle'. Mine just didn't have the same ring of destiny to it. 'Well, I've got big hands and a friend of mine said it was a forgiving instrument.'

Still not totally persuaded, I bought a ticket to see the bassist from the Buena Vista Social Club, a man called Orlando 'Cachaito' Lopez. As an inevitable spin-off from the original album, almost all the key members of the band had subsequently recorded solo projects. Lopez had just released a new critically lauded album and was due to perform for one night only at the Festival Hall. I needed something more than just Jeff's approval. I needed an inspirational moment of some sort and I hoped this show would provide that moment. Lopez being a fairly low-profile member of the BV line-up and (let's be honest here) being a bassist, I hadn't expected a problem getting a seat near the front. Big mistake. 'We only have a few seats at the back,' said the man at the box office. 'But I'm studying double bass,' I pleaded, 'I need to be able to see his hands.' It was a pathetic if novel bit of grovelling and the ticket salesman was not impressed. 'Look, sir, do you want the ticket or not – it's all we've got.' I bought the ticket and two weeks later took my place at the back, right at the back, of the Festival Hall.

At 9 p.m. the lights went down and Cachaito walked out alone into the middle of the stage. After nodding shyly at all the applause, he took his gleaming double bass off its stand and, ear pressed to the neck of the bass, gently flicked his fingers across each of the four strings to check it was in tune. I know this because I was watching his every move through a set of binoculars I'd brought with me. When there was absolute silence in the hall, he began. Within ten notes, I realized why I had been forced into row X. Within another ten, I was silently saying thanks for getting in any row at all. For the next ten minutes we were treated to a virtuoso bass solo that involved plucking, tapping and slapping sounds off almost every part of the strings and woodwork. One minute he was playing a string instrument, the next he was playing percussion. Hands and fingers moved in a blur up and down the fingerboard. Notes were found where there shouldn't have been notes. Sounds were produced that weren't double-bass sounds. I, and I suspect most of the audience, had never seen or heard anything like it. By the end of this intro, the entire auditorium was on its feet and my vote for the double bass was almost in the bag.

Almost. A few doubts did still creep in over the next few weeks, particularly when I started doing some Internet research. From very early on I deduced that the door policy to the double-bass owners' club – like that for lawnmower racing and growing record-size marrows – was definitely oddball-friendly. Not content with the ample quantity of official alternative names for their woody goliaths – Bass Fiddle, Standup Bass, Contrabass, Contrabajo, Doghouse, to name a few – many owners felt such a pet-like attachment that they personalized their instruments with names like The Beast, Bubba, Stuffed Ostrich and (posted up by a Reverend Jon Paulus who I'm hoping is back on the medication) The Big Blonde with the Red G-string. Did I really want to join this clan?

The good news was that Jeff's prognosis about it being a forgiving instrument appeared to be accurate. Pretty much every punchline to every double-bass joke posted on the web involved highlighting the fact that hitting the exact note was not part of the bassist's job spec. Did you hear about the bassist who was so out of tune his section noticed? How do you make a double bass sound in tune? Chop it up and make it into a xylophone. Boy, those violinists can be a catty bunch.

Pulling myself away from a fascinating (if utterly irrelevant) technical study on bow hair, I returned to the main page of Bob Gollihur's hugely informative and ever so slightly worrying site and clicked on the Choosing an Instrument box. I had somewhat naively assumed that double basses were of a uniform size, as in large. But like the quantitative team at Starbucks, the people who made Bubbas and Big Blondes with Red G-strings preferred to confuse things by dealing in odd degrees of largeness. 'The standard full size bass is referred to as three-quarters size but the actual size of a three-quarters size bass is not standardized,' informed Gollihur. If I had any doubts about what sort of bass I should buy, this news helped firm them up considerably.

It has yet to be scientifically proven, but my own case study unequivocally verifies that the quantity of new information a musical novice takes on board has a direct and exponential relationship with the quantity of cheap Chilean red said tyro drinks directly after taking it all in. Brain-frazzled by Bob's tips on string heights, adjustable bridges, wolf-tone eliminators (a small metal weight you fix to your strings – not, as I guessed, a projectile to be aimed at unreceptive audiences), and some scary-sounding advice about 'deriving an intelligent fingering', I was forced to break into the nearest box of tasting samples and make uncommonly determined progress through a bottle of £2.99 Somerfield Maipo Cabernet.

Eventually, though, I knew there was only one real way I would find out whether the double bass was for me and that was to get off my backside and go and get my hands on one. Bullets had to be bitten, fences had to be jumped off, and more crucially, money had to be spent. The time had come to visit

Foote's, purveyors of fine instruments and assorted musical paraphernalia.

I'd walked past this famous central London store hundreds of times and often stood in front of the window display dreamily admiring the impressive arrangement of gleaming hardware. I often wondered how it managed to stay in business because there never seemed to be any customers inside. And now that mystery was finally cleared up. All the customers came and bought their instruments on one day in the year, the one day when it was rumoured a double bass would be rented out. The place was packed with people; all, I noticed, with the confident air of those who a) know what they're looking for and b) probably know what to do with it when they find it.

'Could you tell me where the double basses are kept?' I asked the assistant. 'Downstairs, mate,' he replied with a big smile. I soon found out why he was smiling. Positioning the least manoeuvrable member of the string family in a basement, access to which was evidently designed with only flute removal in mind, smelled suspiciously like a bad in-store joke. Sure enough, downstairs three shiny double basses stood at attention like well-buffed body builders, each with an incongruously dainty little price tag dangling from their tuning keys. To an untrained eye such as mine, they all looked exactly the same. The prices suggested otherwise. The first tag said £5,000, at which I broke shopping etiquette with an audible 'Bloody hell' and a rapid move on to number two. £2,500. Getting better but still nowhere near my budget. £2,400, said the final tag, refusing to take part in the reduction game and making no mention of discounts or special credit deals for the newly unemployed.

'Interested in the double bass, are we, sir?' came the voice behind the counter.

'Er yes, yes I am,' I stammered back like a man who's been caught out reading a top-shelf magazine, 'but I was really looking for something to rent.'

'I'm afraid we don't rent basses but we do have a buy-back deal on one.'

'A buy-back deal?'

'Yes, we'll buy the bass from you for slightly less than you bought it, as long as you sell it within six months.'

'Which of the three basses is it?' I asked, desperately hoping it wasn't the £5,000 model.

'Oh no, sir, it's not one of those. Wait a second and I'll bring it out for you.'

A fourth bass hidden in what I assumed was the 'not worth displaying' section was duly presented. The model in question looked as if it might have been delivered to the shop as a flat-pack. Pale, almost artificial-looking in skin tone, very shiny of complexion, light in weight, and (judging by my brief twang of a string) shallow and angular in voice – everything about it shouted second-rate.

'How much?' I asked.

'Six hundred pounds.'

'Six hundred?' I repeated, wearing a suitably pained expression.

'And we'll throw in a carrying case as well.'

Either they were being incredibly helpful or they hadn't seen someone mount those stairs with a bass for a while.

'Perfect,' I said. 'Can I take it today?'

'Certainly, sir.'

If I had sensed for a second that this was all proving to be far too easy, the thought soon vanished as, payments made and bass squeezed into carrying case, I attempted to leave the store. Using a technique somewhere between a sumo hug and a fireman's lift, I staggered up the stairs and threaded my way towards the exit looking like some sort of Billy Smart reject with prop but no costume. 'Good luck!' called one of the staff as I left the shop, a message that could have been aimed at the instrument as much as the purchaser.

There's a knack to carrying a double bass. Earlier that

morning I had made a point of reading page 11 of Barry Green's *The Fundamentals of Playing Double Bass*, where handy advice could be found on the important issue of Carrying Positions. Most ordinary instruments don't require detailed manoeuvring advice of the sort Barry divulged but then the double bass was no ordinary instrument. Standing at over 6 feet 6 inches in height and resembling some sort of antique piece of furniture on which someone has mistakenly stuck a scale model of a sus- pension bridge, it was, to use removal business terminology, a bugger to handle.

'Stand with the body weight on both feet, resting the side of the bass against the body,' suggested Green. 'Place the right hand in the position shown in Fig. 11a.' Fig. 11a showed a man in tails lifting his bass with the hips (the bass's hips) pointed to the front. 'Note the corner bout is between the first and second fingers and the palm of the hand is holding the side and the back of the bass simultaneously.' I noted it, along with the little 'Can I put it down now?' grimace on the model's face. Fig. 11b, meanwhile, revealed the far more laid back but potentially calamitous hips forward position.

All this was probably fine advice for the man wishing to move his double bass from one side of the Royal Albert Hall to another. But as I quickly discovered on my way home, it was totally inadequate for the brave soul attempting to nego- tiate his newly purchased piece of hardware through the London Underground during rush hour.

After being repeatedly bumped and bashed by train-chasing commuters – Barry's advice to 'recess the end pin before trans- porting' should have had an 'except on the Tube' proviso – I finally emerged into sunlight at Camden Town and struck out for home with spirit weakening and mutiny imminent. A cruel headwind ground me to a wheezing halt outside the Jazz Café and I was about to lay down the bass and have a lip-quivering moment when a man burst out of the box-office doors and nearly changed my buy-back deal to a buy-firewood deal.

Mistakenly assuming all instrument bearers are instrument players (a misunderstanding I soon learned to milk for all its worth), he apologized and said, 'Sorry, mate – you playing tonight?'

They say that Shackleton managed to motivate his frostbitten emaciated crew by making them believe they were brave explorers rather than unknowing participants in an experiment on long-term penguin eating. Tell us what we want to be seen to be, and the effects can be staggering. Hearing the words of this stranger, I glanced up proudly at the neon Jazz Café sign and replied, 'Not tonight' in a manner that suggested there might be a tonight in the future. Was it my imagination or had the wind suddenly dropped? And was that the sound of a choir drifting out of the normally silent church of Our Lady of Hal? The illusions didn't last long. Just as Shackleton's crew woke up to the icy reality of seal rashers every morning, I opened my front door and remembered I lived on the top floor of a liftless building.

3. Hip Power

'So how much practice are you doing?' asked Jennifer off the back of yet another butchered C major scale.

When your mum asks you how much you drink, you halve it. When your new music teacher asks how much effort you are putting in, you double it. And then add some. 'Oh, I don't know, a couple of hours a day I guess,' I replied.

Trying to avoid eye contact during lie delivery, I ended up staring at the wrong things: Jennifer's fluffy slippers. If ever footwear delivered a message, these two household softies were crying out, 'I'm not hiding anything from you, sonny, so quit the bullshit,' and with a deep sigh I beat an awkward retreat, sheepishly admitting, 'Actually, twenty minutes is nearer the mark.'

I had found Jennifer through an ad I'd placed in the classified section of *Time Out*. Not wishing to arrive in Cuba and be laughed at for not being able even to put my hands in the correct position, I chose to do a quick crash course before leaving. '*Double Bass Players: Journalist seeks tuition for Cuban music project. Ring Richard*,' said an ad that I assumed was vague and titillating enough to lure in a whole raft of curious musicians. Evidently, curiosity never killed the bassist. It took exactly twenty-three days to receive my first call and even then it took me some time to convince Jennifer I wasn't some deranged axeman who used strange classifieds to lure in unsuspecting victims.

From the moment I first turned up at her Kennington flat – wearing the weary expression of a man who has crossed London with a large piece of furniture – I knew I had struck lucky. Jennifer was a young American music teacher who taught in a local South London school. Classically trained, she had years of experience of working with children (a useful skill when dealing with lying adults like me), and she was very knowledgeable about Cuban music. More worryingly – for my focus on the task at hand – she was beautiful, funny, and unintentionally tactile when it came to illustrating hand positioning.

'I said I'd try and get you ready for Cuba, hon, but you've gotta help me do it,' she tutted in response to my pathetic admission to lying about practice duration. Ready for Cuba was a goal whose definition seemed to be in constant flux. What had started out as a not too optimistic 'basic handling skills plus ability to play a few scales and bass lines' had soon slipped to the more realistic 'handling skills and scales'. Now it was threatening to downgrade to 'basic handling'. Jennifer deserved better. From the start she had showed nothing but total belief in what I was doing and set about the onerous task of pre-battle training with a gusto that was inspiring. She knew she had to treat me like a child on the one hand – 'Okay, hon, you've got four strings tuned G-D-A-E, so just remember God Damned African Elephants' – but leave me with no illusions as to my grown-up task on the other. For example, on the subject of playing positions she showed me the two options (standing up or perched on a stool) and immediately took away the stool. 'Haven't you heard of machismo?' was her only response to my wounded 'But miss' expression. And she was right, of course. If I asked for a stool in Cuba, I would probably be laughed out of town.

Playing my first note in front of Jennifer had been a big moment. Just about anyone can pick up a guitar and pluck a couple of clean-sounding notes, but as I quickly discovered, the double bass is not kind to strangers. Jennifer suggested we start with the hardest note to play – a low F on the thickest, most cumbersome string of the four, the appropriately named 'Elephant' of the G-D-A-E line-up. I pushed down hard with the index finger of my left hand, gave the string a twang with my right index finger and yes, that was a vibratory noise of sorts, but more a groan of disapproval than a note. I gave the bass the same look I'd give a golf club after a badly shanked drive and fired off a couple of whinges at Jennifer. One: Is it meant to hurt your fingers this much? Two: How the hell are you meant to find the notes when there are no markers? 'Yes,' was the blunt answer to the former, while little slivers of carefully placed masking tape were the suggested temporary solution for the latter. To play a clear low F – commonly known as the half position – took me half an f-ing hour of torture. I left Jennifer's home that day numbed by the depressing realization that I was still only halfway towards reaching the first position.

A handful of lessons – far too widely spaced – later and the progress report was not heartening. The nearest I got to a bass-player blister was a slightly raw patch on the outside edge of my little finger, a position that hinted at a man who had definitely not yet derived an intelligent fingering. 'Let's see how those fingertips are coming on,' friends would say, and even after painful attempts to speed up the hardening process by way of nightly finger rubs with a Brillo pad, all I could show was a scary set of printless tips.

My visits to Jennifer's flat had by now taken on a familiar routine. At least fifteen minutes would be wasted on news and gossip before one of us (rarely me) would suggest it might be a good idea to tune in the bass. This we did together. Starting with the G-string, Jennifer would play the note on the piano, leaving me to tighten or loosen the appropriate string until my note sounded something like hers. 'Do you hear it?' she'd ask.

'What?' I'd reply, thinking I was missing out on some strange Kennington ambient noise.

'You're flat.'

'Oh,' I'd mutter, giving the tuning key a frustrated, over-generous crank that pulled me out of flat and straight into sharp.

Finally in possession of four strings sounding more like God Damn African Elephants than Flipping Crazy Asian Gorillas, I then ran down and up a few scales, followed that with some 'find the note' tests, before – warmed up and ready for action – launching with gusto into a couple of lines from the bible of bass tuition by Austrian Franz Simandl. In the interests of maintaining an honest record of events (those slippers had a strong effect), I feel obliged to point out that Simandl's pages had been modified just a tad. Over every single note, Jennifer had painstakingly written a number and a letter. The numeral indicated the number of fingers required by the left hand (one, two or four), while the letter pointed to the string on which these fingers should be placed. Short of wiring up the fingerboard with 'press here' flashing lights, this was the only way I could complete a line of Simandl's music at a speed where it still resembled music.

You could tell how much time was left in the lesson by the angle of my left arm. In the first half-hour it vaguely resembled the textbook position – upper arm perpendicular to body, forearm at right angle to upper arm – and by the end of our ninety-minute session it was a perfect copy of the 'Don't do this at home' droop. Back went the bass into its bag, out came the wallet, and with promises to 'work on those things', off I would trudge.

I know a DIY novice shouldn't blame his new Black 'n' Decker workmate but anyone could see the 'Buy-back Beast' (as it had quickly been named) and I were not bonding. I often left it out of sight in the hallway of my flat like an unwanted pet, refusing to allow it into the living room where its shiny Czech torso could reflect accusingly in the corner of the television screen. And when I did actually deign to play it, the connection felt as awkward and impassive as a dance with an ugly aunt at a wedding.

Acknowledging that we were not destined to spend a year in the sun together and aware that my July departure was approaching fast, I now faced a dilemma. Should I try to find another partner before I left and face up to the challenge of transporting it to Cuba? Or did I save myself money and effort by looking for a double bass once I was there? The image of me discovering an unloved Russian bass in someone's pig-ridden back yard did have a certain appeal, but the picture kept jumping to the reality of me trying to squeeze a decent note off a worm-eaten piece of Taiga pine better used for cooking the family pig. Option A got the nod.

The move from machine-made plywood monstrosity to hand-made, carved wooden beauty was one I knew would involve a significant shift in financial outlay. Those price tags in Foote's had not been encouraging, and I'd already guessed they were just the first rungs of a price ladder with unseen extension capabilities. The switch to the serious gear would also require the use of double bass specialists. I was going to have to deal with people who probably wouldn't look favourably on customers asking for 'something with a bit of character', or for that matter, a buy-back deal.

Thanks to Barry Green, I had at least familiarized myself with a few of the working parts by now. Given a diagram of a double bass, I could now stick pins on where the ribs, the F-holes, the sound post and the bridge were. I could distinguish the upper bout from the middle bout. I could even bore friends with my knowledge of raw materials. Hard wood like maple and sycamore for the back, soft wood like spruce or pine for the top. And if it was really necessary to end a telephone conversation quickly, I could casually mention that the average string length from nut to bridge was 41 inches.

Pointless detail I had plenty of. Practical buying tips I had none. I had read somewhere that, like quality wine, a well-made double bass improved with age. Its voice supposedly became richer and mellower as the instrument matures. But, sticking to the wine analogy, I had no idea whether a double bass had the playing equivalent of a peak-drinking period beyond which it hit a downward slope towards arthritic groans and moans. And how old was old? When did 'too young' slip into respectable maturity and maturity stumble into 'Don't touch it with a barge-pole' senility?

Browsing through a couple of luthier sites – a luthier being the technical name for a professional maker and repairer of string instruments – only seemed to cloud what was already very murky water. Like a certain other tradesman who insists on using a poncey French title (the one who opens bottles of wine and tells sir he is mistaken when sir tells him the wine is corked), the luthiers in question exhibited a similar fondness for employing geek speak as a means of intimidating the novice. A typical example of a 'bass on offer' notice went something like this. '*French, makers label X Jacquet, dealer's label Jerome Thibouville Lamy, circa 1860, full size, flat back with slight bend, black lines on ribs and black edges, original large brass/chrome machines, strong "tiger" flame maple back and ribs (stop 42" 107cm; back 45" 114.5cms).*'

Messieurs Jacquet and Thibouville could have been the Savoie *frites*-eating champions for all I knew. Was a slight bend a positive or a negative? Should I be concerned about black lines, and what on earth was that tiger stuff about? The only piece of information I understood – in fact it was so clear it thankfully made all the rest redundant – was the five-figure sum at the bottom: £13,500! Flipping Nora, Third World nations have equipped their entire national orchestras for that sort of money. And paid them a handsome annual salary.

'Our cheapest is around the £5,000 mark,' I was informed by Tony from the Contrabasse Shoppe, a purveyor of fine instruments whose use of 'olde englishe' had already warned me of rather more modern mark-ups. 'And at the top end?' I asked. 'We haven't really put a fixed figure on our most expensive bass,' Tony batted back, correctly sensing its precise coordinates were of no relevance to this caller. 'Go on, roughly what are we talking about?' I persisted. 'Somewhere close to a hundred thousand,' came the reply. That was roughly what I didn't have in mind. Thankfully, Tony was either very bored or vaguely amused at the prospect of further customer belittlement, because my request to come round and have a look was met with a 'Sure, I'll give you the address' rather than the expected 'Look sir, perhaps I can give you another contact.'

The shop turned out to be slightly less quaint than the name suggested. In fact, it was about as quaint as an upstairs flat close to Southwark Tube station. But if the showroom was less than salubrious, the goods on display made up for it. This was my first close-up view of some expensive equipment, and if there had been any wavering on my instrument choice, it ended right here in this room filled with sleek curves, chestnut-coloured hips and dark burnished backs. It was the best-looking fire hazard I'd ever seen. I walked down a line of fifteen bodies, exhibiting the sort of excited demeanour I imagine Hugh Heffner employs when inspecting interviewees for pool attendant. Like Hugh, I had no idea which one to choose. Unlike Hugh, I couldn't just take the whole lot.

'No two double basses are the same,' said Tony, humouring me with some redundant sales patter. 'Each one has a particular shape and a particular voice — that's what makes them such a good investment, each one is unique.'

'Investment?' I asked. 'You mean these things keep their value?'

'Put on value,' corrected Tony, who was definitely enjoying his little retail tease. 'Most of the double basses we were selling for seven grand two years ago are now pushing eleven.'

The thought of people buying basses for investment conjured up a sad image of unused instruments gathering dust in some rich banker's Islington loft, and I felt obliged to inform Tony that in my opinion a bass was for life not just for Christmas, or something to that effect.

We got to the end of the line and Tony pulled the last bass off the rack.

'This is the cheapest one we've got. Sixty-year-old German, lovely rich sound, five thousand pounds, do you want to try it?'

'No really, thanks Tony, it's a bit beyond my . . .'

'Go on, at least get to see what it sounds like.'

Bastard Tony, I know what you're up to, I thought while moving the bass gingerly into a playing position. Had I been a bassist, this opportunity to touch what I couldn't afford would have been gratefully received. A chance to take a lovely piece of German engineering for a quick run-around, see how the engine sounded, check out the handling around some of those tight rhythmic corners. But I wasn't a bassist. I was a man who wanted to be a bassist, and the difference between the two revealed itself in both the duration and quality of my test drive. With the utmost concentration and with Tony standing expectantly to one side, I made my way slowly down the only musical path I knew by heart – the first twelve notes of 'Stand By Me'. In car trial terms it was about as embarrassing as a jerky start followed by a stall just outside the showroom. To his credit, Tony managed a face-saving 'You probably need a bit more time with it,' but the damage had been done. Quickly putting the bass back where it belonged, I made my excuses, took a card and made a swift beeline for ye olde exit.

A little wounded of spirit and still bass-less, I rang up a friend of a friend who played double bass in a band. Rod listened patiently as I explained my quest for musical enlightenment and only laughed a little bit when I told him about the 'Stand By Me' moment.

'How can I tell if it's worth buying if I can't even play?' I finally put it to him.

His advice was blunt but practical.

'At the sort of prices you can afford you don't need to be too worried about small differences in sound quality. Just make sure you give it a good look over. The main thing is to check that it's solid structurally. You can find weak points by tapping it and make sure all the joins are well sealed. Other than that, you can only really go on instinct – you'll know the bass for you when you see it.'

Less than a week later, I was putting Rod's advice into practice in the upstairs room of a house near Maidenhead. Peter Tyler was a retired grain technologist adviser who now filled his days (and walls) making clocks and barometers out of violin faces. He also restored double basses in his garden shed. The good news was that Peter's prices started at my level – his cheapest was £580. The bad news was that it was a half-size Chinese double bass that was only playable by a man of Ronnie Corbett's stature. I had already been faxed a list of Rod's stock a few days earlier, so I knew that in the crucial £1,000–£3,000 bracket there was just one bass on offer, described in worryingly short shrift with the entry, '*German, circa 1930, swell back, machines on brass half plates, brown varnish £1,500.*'

Not wishing to look like a man with few options, I duly gave my parade-ground inspection, employing Rod's tapping instructions perhaps a little too rigorously at times.

'They're all in superb condition,' affirmed a concerned-looking Peter. 'What sort of price were you looking at?'

'Up to about three thousand,' I replied. Not a penny above £1,500, I thought.

That moved things along a bit faster. 'It's not really what I'd call an investment buy but there's still plenty of playing left in it,' he said, pulling out my only choice. It didn't take long to see why it had slid out of the investment bracket. Apart from it seeming skinnier of girth compared to the expensive beef-cakes further up the row, a detailed body search revealed more marks and patch-ups than on a secondhand Capri at Dodgy Del's car mart. On one of its flanks, a piece of wood had been slotted in to fill some past injury. Its back was covered in what looked like the sort of scratches and lacerations you'd find on the lid of an old school desk, and the front edges gave the description 'heavy scuffing' a good run for its money. Everywhere I looked, there were war wounds. A visible crack ran down the top left-hand side of its chest, another small square patch had been slotted in halfway down the fingerboard, and the end pin was a Heath Robinson affair made from a piece of wood you might have found discarded on the floor of a carpenter's workshop. Apart from all that, she was in perfect working order.

My habit of calling a bass 'she' rather than 'he' or indeed 'it' had come from reading *The Double Bass*, Patrick Suskind's one-man play about a frustrated double bassist. In it, the lead character alludes to his instrument's femininity, albeit in rather less than glowing terms. 'It's like a fat old woman. Hips far too low, waist a disaster, much too high up and still too wide, and then those narrow, sloping, rickety shoulders – enough to drive you round the bend.' I was somewhat less derogatory about the shape of a double bass's body, but on gender there could be little disagreement.

'She's seen some action,' I said before Peter could get the line in himself. 'Do you know anything about its history?'

'Nothing, I'm afraid. Picked it up in a sale in Bath with a load of other stuff.'

'Well, it looks like it could do with being played a bit.'

Remembering Rod's 'you'll know' advice, I gave it a fond stroke of the neck accompanied by the sort of expression you'd associate with someone who has just adopted a neglected mutt. Luckily, Peter was within earshot because I fear if he hadn't been I would have whispered, 'Don't worry, I'm getting you out of here.' It would be nice to think this was a Speke meets Burton moment but the truth was probably closer to Laurel accidentally bumping into Hardy.

I imagine Peter and his good wife drank a little more than their usual glass of off-dry hock that Saturday night. 'Got rid of old Scarface today, darling. Should have seen the man getting all gooey-eyed over her. Didn't even bother playing a note. Heading off to Cuba, he said.

'Even managed to flog him that old travel case. You know, the one with the dodgy hinges and no wheels.'

Peter's battered old flight case, a necessary investment if I wanted to arrive in Cuba with a functioning instrument, was an added bonus. Not only was it saving me a few hundred pounds (a brand-new double bass case ran to nearly £800), but now I would be travelling around with a piece of luggage that said 'working musician' rather than 'complete novice'. Badly scuffed, with various cracks patched up with gaffer tape, and yes, dodgy hinges, it looked like it had seen some serious airport action. There were even some torn 'Youth Orchestra Italian Tour' stickers on its heavily scarred chest. It had respect written all over it. Driving back to London, the neck of the fibreglass case poking dangerously out of the front passenger window like a breeze-seeking dog, I barrelled back down the M40 in high spirits.

Owning an instrument and beginning the learning process were important early steps towards my as yet unannounced goal of eventually standing on stage with a Cuban band. But there was one other vital piece of preparation for Operation Trojan Horse. I needed a disguise. Come the day of musical reckoning, I had to look the part even if I was unfit to perform. In short, I needed some sharp threads.

To pick up some fashion tips and check out the current Cuban look, I headed off one night to watch Orlando 'Maraca' Valle at the Jazz Café. Friends with a more intimate knowledge of the Cuban scene had informed me this young flautist was one of the country's most talented stars. 'And he's got a great bassist,' one added, as if my nights out had now regressed to nothing more than obsessive bass-gazing exercises.

Even before the band came on, I noticed something wasn't quite right. In the place where the big piece of wood should have been, there was nothing but a ridiculous-looking fingerboard mounted on a massive tripod. Had I neglected to hear some vital piece of instrument changeover news? Had double basses suddenly been given the cold shoulder, to be replaced by sexy little travel-friendly electric thingies? Once the band started playing – judgement by this stage had been skewed away from impartial by three pints of lager – I consoled myself with the knowledge that no matter how good he was (pretty shit-hot by all accounts), the bassist looked a right plonker. All this 'Honey, I shrunk the instrument' audition stuff might have been great at the airline check-in desk, but stage cred? Forget it, I was still with the big dog supporters' club.

On the fashion front, the view wasn't much better. Yes, there was definitely a look, and no, it was not one that could be constructed from the contents of my wardrobe. For a start, copious quantities of jewellery seemed essential – gold being the colour if not metal of choice, chunky the size order. I've never worn a medallion or an earring in my life and starting now would be to laugh in the face of public ridicule. As for clothing, my preference for natural fibres would be mocked by this bunch. Fabric selection in the Cuban camp was definitely synthetics-friendly, with a particular penchant for shirts with a noticeable sheen to them or at the very least a few sparkly bits to catch the lighting. Finally, gratuitous use of sunglasses and Kangol hats (worn back to front of course) was noted. This was not a scene I could sneak into with ease.

Back in the days when I wrote a drinks column for *Esquire*, I remember the editor – perhaps prompted by the sight of his less than sartorially on-the-ball contributor – telling me that every man should have a bespoke suit made for him at least once in his life. Despite my keeping the specific details of my suit collection (one grey John Lewis very last decade) to myself, the suggestion of a makeover story fell on deaf ears. 'Stick to the drinks, Richard, we'll sort out the fashion,' was the gist of his reply. Now, five years later and with me in need of a killer outfit, the editor's tailoring advice came back like a siren call pushing me into action. When the going gets tough, the tough go bespoke. Someone, somewhere was going to make me a suit.

Consulting the fashion section of one of my London Shopping Guides, I scanned down the list searching for someone with the experience, talent and cost-cutting skills to meet this task. One entry immediately stood out from the crowd. The name was Chris Ruocco and if his downmarket address (Kentish Town) and modest prices (starting from £450) hadn't convinced me, the short review next to his name did. 'Ruocco', informed the Guide, 'has a history of cutting suits to the most eccentric specifications. As tailor to the 1980s pop scene he has worked with Wham, Spandau Ballet and Sade.' Some specifics would have been good (like was he responsible for the Spandau tartan phase and what about those tight shorts in 'Wake Me Up Before You Go Go'?), but if I was looking for a bit of retro-edged flamboyance, this was my man. My only niggling concern was the last line of the review which quoted Ruocco as saying, 'Ninety-five per cent of my clients come with strong ideas of what they want.' Never mind, I thought, it didn't say he told the other 5 per cent to piss off.

Arriving at his small shop on Fortess Road – sandwiched like a misplaced filling between Instant Hire and Martin's Refrigeration – it would not be a gross exaggeration to say reality gave expectation a rather sharp slap in the face. Shaded by a grubby awning, the window display was either a masterful disguise to keep out passing trade or proof that Chris had lost the key to the access door twenty years ago. Taking stock of the motley collection of beige socks stretched over sawn-off mannequin feet, chequered sports jackets and rather frightening ties, I almost considered walking on. But the door was open and I didn't exactly have a long list of alternatives.

It was about four o'clock on a Friday afternoon and Ruocco – a short, athletic-looking man with a face that suggested a long Friday, possibly Long Good Friday – was busy measuring out material on a huge table in the front room. His undisguised annoyance at being interrupted implied that my window display decoy theory was accurate. 'Er, I'm looking for a suit,' I mumbled, eyes falling on a strange photograph of what looked like him posing in swimming trunks. 'Right place to look for one,' came the gruff reply. 'Know wot yer want?' Any lingering suspicions that the concept of 'the customer is always right' might not have filtered into Ruocco's retail manifesto now stopped lingering.

'Is that you?' I said, pointing at the swimmer, trying to broker some sort of pre-purchase rapport.

'Yeah. Used to be a boxer. Swim every morning to keep in shape – up at 'ighgate Ponds. Only the ice stops me.'

I'd never inspected a tailor's hands before but Ruocco's thick stubby digits looked more suited to ripping people's suits, not delicately sewing them together. I decided on the blunt approach. 'I'm looking for something light in weight and loud in colour, something that will be noticed on stage.' Ruocco said nothing. Presuming he hadn't quite understood, I tried to elaborate with a visual example he'd be familiar with. 'I was thinking somewhere between Kool and the Gang and Crockett and Tubbs.' Before I'd even got the word Tubbs out, he'd put his scissors down on the table and was reaching for a long pole leaning in the corner. 'Crockett and Tubbs – you know? *Miami Vice*?' I stammered, edging back towards the door. The men's department at John Lewis suddenly looked a much better idea.

'Got a nice bright blue linen,' said Ruocco, using what I had thought was a weapon to lever a roll of material off one of the higher shelves. 'And some nice paisley for the lining if yer like.'

'I'm not sure about lining. It's very hot where I'm going.'

'Got to 'ave a lining, son, or yer suit'll look a bleedin' mess!'

'Paisley sounds great!'

If I'd thought that bespoke was a byword for time-consuming, fiddly hassle (I had), that preconception was swiftly taken in a few inches. Ruocco wasn't going to let his tea go cold. After batting around some image ideas using his photo montage of previous customers – Go West, Eddy Grant, a signed snap of Kid Creole and the Coconuts – Ruocco took my measurements and then, retrieving his notepad, fired off a series of design questions. Number and type of buttons, style of pockets, width of collar, button or zip fly, belt hoops or side tabs, turnups or no turn-ups, single, double or no vent on the jacket? Maybe it was the metronome tap of Ruocco's pole, but for a man who didn't know what he wanted, my decisiveness surprised even me.

He said he'd have the suit ready in two weeks – a few days before my departure – and that I'd need to come back for a fitting to check all was hanging well. I paid him half his £600 fee, shook hands (ow!) and strode out not knowing whether I'd be coming back to retrieve a hybrid monster or a hotchpotch masterpiece.

Between then and now I had a pre-departure checklist of NASA proportions. Find someone to rent my flat, get flat in state in which it can be rented (major wine sample handout), ring bank manager and grovel, organize post redirection, ring PRs to take name off press lists (well, all except the ones that send nice wines), visit dentist . . . and so stacked up the practical drudgery of an exciting life change. Top priority, however, was given to the reminder written in bold on a bright yellow post-it note by the telephone: 'Ring airline about baggage.'

The first rumblings of impending excess baggage doom had started a month back when the salesman at Trailfinders had suggested I rang British Airways to warn of unusually cumbersome travel companions. I had heard of cello players booking extra seats for their priceless instruments but this was an option I could not even begin to entertain. Apart from the obvious financial implications of sitting next to my instrument, there was the more obvious problem of actually fitting a double bass into one of the cattle stalls at the back. And even if you could find a seat big enough in the plane (as upgrade blags go it was worth a try) there were still important safety implications to consider. Like, how do you get a double bass into the brace position?

'Charges for excess baggage vary according to the route you are travelling,' the BA representative announced in a tone that immediately took the grovelling option out of the equation. 'On some routes, there is a set per item charge and on others it is calculated on weight. Where are you going to?'

'Havana,' I replied, silently praying that the gods of over-weight travel were music lovers.

'I'm afraid that will be on a weight basis and the charge is twelve pounds per kilo – what does your instrument weigh?'

Not only had I not got the faintest inkling as to how many kilos HP was pushing when inside her protective case, I had no intention of wheeling her down to the weighing machine in Woolies to find out. HP? Sorry, I should explain. After various friends (the female ones mostly) said I couldn't spend a year referring to my partner as 'the wood', I, or rather we, came up with a shortlist of possible names. HP – as in Hip Power – got the judges' vote from a shortlist that included Woody, Big Ron (as in Ronseal Wood Protector), the Hipster and Scarface.

'Give me a minute and I'll ring you back with a figure,' I told the woman at British Airways. A quick call to Peter Tyler provided the information required in the form of a bill for a bass he had recently sent to New York. 'It was a slightly lighter case than yours,' informed Tyler, 'but I'd say if you call it thirty kilos you won't be far out.' I scribbled the number on a pad and with a few taps on the calculator was staring at a figure that tipped just over half the value of my own economy seat.

'You could try sending it freight,' he suggested helpfully, 'but you'd have to move fast if you want it to be in Havana when you arrive.' He gave me a number and wished me luck.

It turned out the freight company had only just reopened business with Cuba after their previous American parent company had been taken over by a German outfit. 'We don't have a representative there yet and we've recently had some bad experiences trying to clear things out of Cuban Customs,' came the less than convincing opening salvo of optimism.

'Well, what about the cost of getting it there?'

'Okay, let's see now,' was followed by the sort of ominous pause that suggests large incoming calculations. 'First of all you've got your £14.50 airline handling charge, then you've got £10 security X-ray, £20 for documentation, a charge of 10p per kilo for fuel, a £1.80 per kilo freight charge, a customs release fee in Cuba that could be anything between 100 to and 200 dollars, and then there's . . .'

'Actually I think I'll just take it with me on the plane,' I interrupted. Weighing up the small financial advantage against the potential bureaucratic hassle, the scales begrudgingly tipped in BA's favour. Suddenly, one of those silly-looking stand-alone fingerboards with collapsible tripod didn't seem such a stupid idea after all.

4. Excess Baggage

Reactions to my quest for musical enlightenment had, on the whole, been positive, perhaps even a little too positive.

My main employers, the *Daily Telegraph*, were disconcertingly supportive, and if there had been any doubts about the expend-ability of the newspaper columnist, they disappeared the minute I opened my leaving gift. A hasty whip-round one Friday after-noon had only managed to raise enough to buy a compilation CD of top hits to make love to ('It Only Takes a Minute' by Tavares was track number one) and a pen key-ring. After five years of gum-staining service, this was a sobering reminder of my value to the people at Canary Wharf.

Most of my friends – the ones that weren't receiving regular wine handouts every month, at least – said they thought it a brilliant move. A couple of the more sensible ones did ponder why I hadn't gone for option B – keep the well-paid wine job and take evening classes to suppress the musical yearnings. They had a point, but it was a point for an evening class type of per-son. My mum was understandably the most upset, but previ-ous experience appeared to have hardened her to the bizarre whims of her nomadic elder son, and after the initial shock had worn off – and I'd convinced her that Cuba was far safer than Africa – she did exactly what she'd done every other time I'd flown the nest. She immediately took responsibility for all my admin and the nitty-gritty details of going away for a long period of time. Things like sorting out insurance for HP and checking whether I could withdraw money on my credit card in Santiago. And then when the last couple of weeks turned into the last couple of days, she stoically helped me pack up the flat, tracked down a minicab firm with a People Carrier (the only vehicle capable of carrying my entourage) and booked me a hotel for my first night in Havana. All of which combined to leave me a sniffling mess when we finally said our goodbyes.

The enormity of the challenge I was embarking on didn't really hit home until I arrived at Gatwick airport. For weeks I'd been happily milking all the attention and kudos that comes from escaping the rat race with a gigantic lump of wood in tow. Finally, alone with said lump of wood, my daft escapade suddenly seemed, well, just plain daft. Thanks to the People Carrier, the first real challenge of luggage manoeuvring didn't begin until outside the airport terminal. Having paid the driver and found a porter to take my bags, I tipped the bass case on to its newly attached wheels and began to move towards the terminal building with my best Mariachi-style swagger. The fact that a) I was reversing and b) I clearly had no control over my 7-foot high piece of luggage did dilute the swagger somewhat. I believe the parting of the crowd was more a result of fear of impalement than respect for the owner.

A rapid inspection of the undercarriage confirmed my worst fears. Faced with a wheel-less flight case, I had been forced to employ my friend and DIY wizard, Colin, to transform immobility into mobility. Unfortunately, a combination of my inexplicably moronic decision to buy revolving rather than fixed-position wheels, the uneven surface of the case and Colin's hangover meant that I was now looking at two less than level attachments and a lump of fibreglass that moved as if possessed.

After nearly wiping out the back end of the Bogota check-in queue, I began my final approach towards the British Airways Havana-bound desks. Five metres out from my intended target, it quickly became apparent that I had made a gross miscalculation of safe stopping distances, and as the flight case arced off to the right, I realized a collision with a trolley full of film equipment was imminent. At the last second, one of the crew bravely jumped in the way to act as a human buffer and saved me from an interesting but not particularly welcome insurance claim. I apologized for my lack of control and after checking no damage had been done, joined the back of the queue.

'Good morning, sir, how many items will you be checking in today?' said a woman with a Teresa name badge.

I could see her eyes focusing on the flight case and it was hard to tell whether her smile was of the 'Oh goody, this'll be fun' or 'Ah bless, poor man' variety.

'Two bags and, um, this,' I replied, nodding my head backwards as if I was too embarrassed to admit we were travelling together.

Teresa did her obligatory keyboard-tapping thing and after tagging the two normal pieces of luggage told me to take the bass over to the over-sized baggage department to be weighed. 'Have a nice flight – we begin boarding at 10 a.m.,' she said, handing me back the tickets. No mention of charges. No requests for supervisors. Could it be that my pleading call to a friend who was one of the wine buyers for British Airways had worked?

Zigzagging the hips over to the other side of the hall, I approached a counter where two men were weighing a motley collection of golf bags and surfing gear. We heaved the case on to the scales and watched the two red digits whizz upwards and stop with a neat click at 31 kilos. 'You can take your hands off the handles now, sir,' said a man who had clearly witnessed more weigh-in tricks than Frank Warren. I released my hands and the right-hand digit started moving again. Upwards and onwards it nudged, eventually stopping neatly on 38 kilos, eight more than Peter Tyler's estimate. I stood staring at the 3 and the 8 and waited for a voice to ask, 'How would you like to pay for that, sir?' But still there was no mention of money, and not bothering to wait and watch the case slide out of view down the conveyor belt, I slunk off as speedily as an unsuspicious getaway permitted. There was, of course, still a strong possibility that HP would be used as a battering ram by the baggage handlers but that was out of my control. For now, I was happy in the knowledge that the rum budget had just received a healthy (and unexpected) injection of capital.

Ten hours later, I was doing it all again in reverse. As I and all the other tired passengers crept slowly towards Cuban Passport Control, the impression was not so much welcome back to Cuba as, we're allowing you in again just this once but it is with great reluctance and we want you out as quickly as possible. '*En esta taquilla, no se cobre ningún servicio,*' said the sign stuck to the side of the cubicle I had randomly chosen to stand in line for. Underneath, an English translation informed non-Spanish speakers, 'In this window all services are free.' Judging by the portrait of inflexibility behind the counter – even the colour of her nail varnish said, don't mess – I guessed it might save time if I didn't attempt to lighten the mood with a request for two big Macs, a large coke and a light massage.

After an unnerving ten-second stare at my face to confirm a positive match with the passport portrait and a thorough examination of the immigration card, a buzzer eventually sounded and I was allowed to push open a door and enter the real world, of baggage reclaim. Luggage was already slam-dunking out on to the conveyor belt, and fearful of what might be happening to HP on the other side of the wall, I approached a nearby official loitering with very little intent. '*Estoy viajando con un contrabajo* – I'm travelling with a double bass,' I explained, employing the sort of ridiculous Marcel Marceau hand-signal accompaniment beloved of the language-rusty. Five years in London had caused the jettisoning of a lot of vocabulary and the rusting up of my Spanish fluency. 'It's very fragile and I don't want it coming out on that,' I said, pointing at the conveyor belt. This provoked a rapid-fire unintelligible conversation into a walkie-talkie and a hurried exit through an unmarked door. Moments later another official appeared, one whose different uniform colour implied either a higher rank and a major language hiccup (with my accent there was a fair chance that *contrabajo*, the Spanish for double bass, could have been mistaken for *contrabando*), or an army official and news that HP had just been blown up having not been reclaimed within the necessary half-hour.

'Please describe your luggage,' said the man with eyes that warned of long delays and possible detainment in small windowless rooms.

'It's very big and it looks like, like . . . THAT!'

'That' happened to be HP's head poking ominously through the flaps of the baggage ejection orifice. As I launched into a futile sprint to prevent the rib-cracking (possibly neck-breaking) effects of the metre-high drop-off — silently praying for a sacrificial cuddly toy to come trundling around the corner in the nick of time — I knew I wasn't going to make it. Only the athletic efforts of two Germans prevented a nasty test of flight-case durability. You don't see Englishmen embracing Germans in public much, and judging by their reaction to my appreciative hug it was a first for them too.

By some miracle I managed to wedge the bass in an upright position on my trolley with the flat side leaning against the handle end and my dive bag acting as a counterbalance at the front. Edging blindly through the scrum of reps and relatives, I got my first taste of problem-solving Cuban style. A man with a taxi ID badge pinned to his shirt stepped forward, took a few seconds to weigh up what he was letting himself in for and, with the skill of a trained bodyguard, ushered me through the crowd and out into the muggy embrace of 90 per cent humidity. Now I'm sure somewhere in the double bass safe-handling manual there's a list of Dos and Don'ts and somewhere in the Don'ts column — between Don't Use Revolving Doors and Don't Tour in Cold Countries with Fuel Shortages — it says, Don't Ever Attempt to Transport Your Bass on the Roof Rack of a Lada.

Watching two men heaving the case on to the fragile frame of the car, I could feel myself being torn between Mr

Adventurous and Mr Sensible. Mr A thought this would be well worth seeing, while Mr S saw a multiple pile-up and a lot of broken wood. By the time the two fraying bungee cords emerged from the boot, Mr S had shoved Mr A out of the way and was asking for the bass to be taken down again. 'Thanks, but I think I'll wait for a bigger taxi,' I said, unhooking one of the cords and attempting to slide the case off the roof. 'There are no bigger taxis,' replied the driver. 'It's with me or nothing.'

A quick glance along the line of taxis verified this claim, and with great reluctance I opened the passenger door and said, '*Vamos* – let's go.' Ignoring my request to drive '*muy lento por favor*', we tore out of the airport – the head of the case visible and visibly oscillating in front of us – and sped towards the centre of Havana. At one particularly tight roundabout, the driver stuck his arm out of the window, grabbed one of the handles on the side of the case, and with a manic leer straight out of Jack Nicholson's photo album said, '*Todo bien, señor?* Everything okay, sir?' At any moment I expected the sound of snapping elastic and the sight of a bass flying off into a roadside poster of Che Guevara – a crime no doubt punishable by death. But we made it. Half an hour later, I was flat on my back in the hotel with HP's impressive bulk standing guard by the bed. My first night back in Havana and I was asleep (fully clothed) by ten o'clock.

The following morning, filled if not fortified by a breakfast that brought back unwanted memories of Bulgarian press trips, I took a walk around the city I had waited five years to come back to. Everything seemed immediately familiar. The thick tropical smells, the cacophony of street noise, old American cars, police on every corner ('There are more police here than Cubans,' a taxi driver had joked on that first trip), camel buses crammed with commuters, the constant barrage of attention as one huckster after another tried to sell you something. Havana, I was pleased to see, hadn't changed a bit.

I took a taxi down to the train station to buy my ticket for the Santiago-bound train leaving that night. I wanted to take the train partly because it was half the price of the internal flight but mainly because there weren't many trains left in the Caribbean and it sounded like a nice leisurely way to reach my final destination.

Cuba runs a dual transport system. For peso-paying Cubans, it is a study in the art of patience and discomfort. For dollar-paying foreigners, the only hardship is the price and the weight on your conscience. Cubans wanting to take the train down to Santiago first had to wait hours in a queue to get their name on to the waiting list, then, when finally given a place on the train (a three-day wait is normal), they were guaranteed to suffer a buttock-challenging marathon in conditions where sleep was as unlikely as a drinks trolley. For dollar-paying *extranjeros* like me, travelling on exactly the same train as the Cubans, a ticket could be booked (without queuing) on the same day of travel.

The train left on alternate days and there was one leaving that evening. 'Be here at five-thirty p.m. The train goes one hour later,' came the stern instruction after I'd handed over 50 dollars. 'And what about my double bass?' I asked. 'All large items must go in the separate luggage compartment and . . .' she paused to mull over some complicated mental arithmetic '. . . and you must pay twenty more dollars, please.' The ruthless extraction of hard currency hadn't changed while I'd been away.

With a couple of hours to go, I found myself killing time in a bar in Calle Obispo, the well-known catwalk for hustlers, pimps and prostitutes between Parque Central and Old Havana. A band in the corner of the room was playing a badly rendered version of 'Guantanamera' while a couple of middle-aged tourists were being fondled by two young leggy Cubans whose jewellery displays suggested booming business. I ordered a beer and sat down at a free table. It didn't take long to be approached – it never did – but since I was keen to practise my Spanish and it was my first day, I didn't offer much resistance when Juan Carlos introduced himself and pulled up a seat. Thanks to my last trip to Cuba, I was already attuned to the variety of dollar-releasing tales spun by Obispo's roving band of grifters. The child in need of vital medicines, the sure-fire bet on a baseball game, the vital extra 10 dollars to make up the balance to secure an exit visa, the fantastic restaurant that wasn't in any of the guidebooks; I'd heard them all. What, I wondered, would Juan Carlos try out on me?

He asked me how long I was staying in Havana and when I told him I was about to catch a train to Santiago, his face lit up and for an awful moment I thought he was going to tell me he was coming too. In hindsight, it did seem a little strange that a Habanero could be so enthusiastic about the great Eastern rival, but Juan Carlos's passion seemed genuine, and when I revealed I was planning on learning to play double bass, he got even more excited. 'Have you got paper and a pen?' he asked. I tore a page out of the back of my diary and handed it over with a biro. 'This is your lucky day,' he beamed as he began scribbling names and numbers on to the paper. 'I know lots of good musicians in Santiago and there is an old bass teacher friend of mine who you must meet – he's sort of retired and only teaches people who he really believes are serious about learning. Are you serious, *compay*?'

'*Muy serio*,' I nodded, sepia-tinted images of the wizened old double bass maestros sharpening with every gulp of beer. 'This is it,' I thought. Here was the lucky break I needed, the hand of fate that would turn my stab at musical advancement from wildly fanciful to plain old optimistic.

One minute I didn't have a single musical contact in Santiago, the next I had a list of names and numbers and a letter of introduction to my future teacher. We must have talked for about an hour and by the third bottle of beer, I was sufficiently pliable that when JC started telling me about the band he was playing in and the gig they could get if only they could afford to get some new strings for the bass player, a donation was inevitable. Here was a needy musician like myself, a needy musician who had generously handed out his friends' numbers to a complete stranger. Ten dollars seemed like a nice and necessary gesture at the time.

'They're all dead,' laughed the man sitting next to me on the train two hours later. 'You've paid ten dollars for a bunch of false phone numbers of musicians who died years ago.' It was clearly the funniest tourist scam he'd heard in a long while. Mightily embarrassed at how naïve I'd been, I hastily screwed up the piece of paper, reclined my seat and did my best impression of man sufficiently non-concerned to sleep. In truth, I was concerned for HP's safety.

At 5.50 p.m. I'd loaded her on to the oversized luggage compartment – a large wagon filled with fridges, mattresses, bikes, post bags and two goats (untethered). It didn't appear to have a door on one side and the two men sitting in beaten arm-chairs looked the sort who would sell everything to the highest bidder at the 3 a.m. stop in Las Tunas. More forms had to be filled in, yet more dollars had to be extracted (and reluctantly given), and unnerved by the knowledge that HP was by far the most valuable item being transported, I walked back down the platform less than convinced that my partner would be around when we arrived at Santiago in the morning.

By choosing to live in Cuba's second biggest city as opposed to its capital, I had, whether I liked it or not, taken sides in the age-old rivalry between the *Orientales* (the Easterners) and the *Occidentales* (the Westerners). The antagonism between the two main cities at either end was legendary, and as we rattled east into the growing dark, I remembered a conversation I'd had with someone from Santa Clara during my first trip in 1996.

According to this Santa Clareno (who could be considered a neutral of sorts since his home town sat roughly in the middle of the country), most Habaneros regarded Santiagueros as an unruly bunch of hicks who drank too much rum, spoke a dialect that no one understood, and (perhaps as a result of these first two traits) couldn't finish an argument without resorting to the rule of the machete. For their part, the Santiagueros believed Habaneros were condescending, untrustworthy and self-interested – the sort of people who didn't open their door to strangers and certainly wouldn't offer you something to eat unless you'd brought your own food.

Santiago's trump card in this urban contest (apart from its rightful claim to musical superiority) was, of course, its proud title. In 1984, the Council of State awarded it the distinction of 'Heroic City' and the Order of Major General Antonio Maceo – the country's highest military honour – in gratitude for the city's unwavering loyalty to the revolutionary cause. It was in Santiago that it all kicked off in courageous and spectacularly disastrous fashion on 26 July 1953. It was in Santiago that Frank País's largely student-based underground movement kept sticking thorns in Batista's side while Fidel's *barbudos* (bearded ones) were battling away in the Sierra Maestra, and it was in Santiago that the eventual victory was first celebrated. All of this was a source of enormous pride according to my guidebook.

The history books say that Christopher Columbus first entered the bay of Santiago on 1 May 1494, on his second voyage to Cuba. He can't have been very impressed – perhaps the mangoes weren't ripe enough for his breakfast – because less than twenty-four hours after arriving, he'd hoisted the mainsail and set off for Jamaica.

With the idyllic palm-fringed settlement of Baracoa eventually being chosen as the first Spanish settlement in Cuba, it wasn't until 1514 that Diego Velásquez and his crew of gold-hunting pals set up a small settlement on the eastern side of Santiago's large natural harbour. Velásquez named the town after the King of Spain's patron saint, St Jago. The '*de Cuba*' came some time later. Not, as I had originally presumed, to prevent early Spanish postal workers from sending packages to the wrong Santiago, but because up until 1751 the Eastern part of the island was divided into three regions called Bayamo, Baracoa and Cuba. The '*de Cuba*' bit related to the region in which the city sat, not the country.

The Spaniards didn't waste time in stamping their authority on their new subjects. Within ten years, pretty much the entire indigenous population of the Oriente had been destroyed either by self-mutilation – mass suicides were common – disease or, as in the case of the insurrectionist Indian warrior, Hatuey, from being burnt at the stake. By 1521, realizing that in their haste to remove the locals they had also inconveniently removed the entire labour force, the Spanish were obliged to bring in the first slaves from Haiti.

Life in the early days of Cuba's first capital wasn't exactly a bundle of laughs. Assuming you had managed to arrive without having all your possessions stolen by pirates, you then had to survive the hurricanes, earthquakes and fires. The latter proved the greatest hazard, with one carelessly started blaze after another sweeping through the city. Add all that to the food shortages and tropical diseases and you can understand why the population wasn't exactly booming in the sixteenth century.

When it became apparent that Cuba wasn't going to be the gold mine the Spanish had hoped for, the metal detectors headed on to South America, and Santiago was left to the whims of eager Catalan businessmen. Labour-intensive industries like copper mining, sugar cane, coffee and cotton led the economic boom, and the city soon became a major centre for the slave trade. Boats of slaves coming in, boats stuffed with saleable goodies heading out – it was only a matter of time before the highwaymen of the sea pitched up to grab a share.

For anyone wanting a career in pirating and sea-born violence during the sixteenth and seventeenth centuries, Santiago de Cuba was the place to come for work experience. Between around 1530 and 1700, a journey by boat along this Eastern coast was only worth taking if you were keen to rid yourself of possessions and take a walk from the high plank. The French, the Dutch, the British all made various attempts to take the city or at least scupper a few Spanish galleons in the bay, and by the time the Dutch Corsario Cornelius Jules gave it a go in 1635, the local residents had had enough. Petitions were drawn up to build some decent defences and in 1638 the military engineer Juan Bautista began work on a fort at the mouth of the bay. Clearly, the man didn't test out his cannon-firing angles very well because in 1662, the English naval captain Christopher Myngs sailed in with twelve ships and 2,000 men, destroyed the fort and took the city with ease.

The Spanish managed to wrest it back and once in possession, proceeded to spend vast sums on its defence. Not only did they restrengthen the El Morro fort, they put cannon emplacements on the other side of the bay's entrance, constructed a ring of heavily armed garrisons around the city, and even built a gunpowder factory on an island in the bay. This still wasn't enough to put off the Brits – at war with Spain during the 1740s – who sent a force of 4,000 men to try to take what they still considered to be the main strategic base in the Caribbean. Thinking a land attack would give them an element of surprise, they anchored further down the coast at a bay now famous for being a small corner of the United States – Guantanamo Naval Base – and headed off at a confident quick march towards Santiago. They never made it. A combination of fatigue, dissension in the ranks and attacks by local guerrillas caused a humiliating retreat. Vice Admiral Edward Vernon sailed home with his tail between his legs and Prime Minister Robert Walpole got the sack. Not to be deterred, the British returned a few years later, this time trying the capital and this time succeeding. For eleven months in 1762, they occupied the city of Havana and the capital of Cuba briefly moved back to Santiago.

During this period, the Eastern city grew rapidly thanks to huge European demand for tropical products like coffee, tobacco and sugar. Plantations were springing up everywhere and by 1792, slaves made up 29 per cent of the province's population.

In the first two decades of the nineteenth century, an average of 3,000 slaves were coming through Santiago's port every year. Despite Spanish fears that they would outnumber whites, interbreeding meant that the city's racial and social hierarchy had soon blurred way beyond plain blacks, whites and mulattoes. In his book *La Isla de Cuba*, Hippolyte Peron described the colour divisions in nineteenth-century Santiago as being unbelievably complex, his own categorization including whites, those who passed as whites, mulattoes, criollos, grifos (whatever they were), cuarterones (ditto), and negroes. He even divided the Spanish into two groups, noting the differences between those who had come to the city out of curiosity or by chance, and those who had come simply to make money. Both, he admitted, were equally arrogant.

It wasn't clear whether curiosity or greed drew the Bacardi-Mazos to Santiago, but no one could have guessed that this family of Catalan drapery salesmen would end up creating one of the most powerful business empires in the world. After quickly finding his feet in his adopted city, Don Facundo Bacardi used a 6,700-peso loan to set up a haberdashery store on Calle Enramadas in November 1843. The business started well, enough to set up another shop in nearby El Cobre and register the new family company, Bacardi y Cia. Then it all went pear-shaped. A ten-year economic slump between 1850 and 1860 left the Catalans with a lot of unsold buttons and a very ropey balance sheet. Copies of legal documents from the time showed that Facundo owed his wife 10,000 pesos and in 1855 the company – facing debts of over 17,000 pesos – was forced into liquidation.

Facundo was not one to let a few losses get him down, however. As a side arm to his general store in the centre of the city, he bought an old Coffey still from an Englishman called Mr Nunes and – thanks to the timely arrival of a nice little inheritance – set up a small liquor outlet in June 1862. Again, his timing wasn't good. Just as the business was getting going, the Ten Year War started and Bacardi found his key market dying (literally) all around him. But he and his business survived, and when one of his rums won the medal of honour at a competition in Philadelphia in 1873, he knew things were on the turn. Facundo and his talented chief rum taster, Enrique Schweg Chassin, had made the shrewd decision of creating a new, lighter, smoother style of rum to replace the harsh throat-burning version of old. It worked. Other medals were won in Madrid, Paris and Chicago, and by the time Facundo Snr died in 1886 the company was making profits of over 30,000 pesos a year.

The rest is the stuff of commercial legend. By 1936, the company had opened distilleries in Mexico and Puerto Rico and their storage tanks in Santiago alone were able to hold over 5 million gallons of distillate. They had a brewery, an ice-making factory, a bottle-making plant, and their own rail wagons to distribute liquor in Cuba. Their white rum became so successful around the world that the brand was almost perceived as being a rum style in its own right.

Then came the revolution and nothing was the same again. The Bacardi family left for the United States, while their Santiago distillery, their Hatuey brewery, their beautiful Art Deco head office in Havana and all other family property were transferred to State ownership. Over the last forty-odd years, the Bacardis have battled (often successfully) to bring political pressure on Castro's Government, and although they have not distilled a drop of their rum on the island for over forty years, the brand continues to play on its Cuban heritage for marketing purposes.

'*Señor Nail! Señor Nail!*' said a voice in my ear. I awoke to an eerily silent and dark carriage, a bright torch in my eyes and a man demanding to know whether I owned a double bass. '*Señor Nail, el contrabajo es suyo, no?*' came the more urgent request. He turned the torch away from my eyes for a second, allowing me to glimpse a face that sadly bore a striking resemblance to one of the two shifty characters from the baggage compartment. Horrible images flashed before me: in particular, one that involved two well-roasted goats gently revolving over the burning embers of HP. I'm sorry to have to admit I lost it at this point, 'it' being my ability to travel with a double bass for over forty-eight hours and keep a humorous outlook on the proceedings. What little was left of a stiff upper lip began to melt into jellied defeat – witnessed, I'm ashamed to say, by a small girl sitting opposite who probably still suffers nightmares about torches and whimpering foreigners. Like Dorothy in the *Wizard of Oz*, I just wanted to click my heels three times and have all this disappear.

'Yes, it's mine,' I sighed in frustration, 'what's happened to it?'

'Señor Nail, you must come with me now,' was all he would offer.

The good news was that HP had not been stolen. The bad news was that there was a problem with the baggage compartment and I was going to have to do the unthinkable and move her to another carriage. Apparently, we'd been stuck in Camaguey for two hours, so my neighbour, Jorge, had long since disappeared, and with everyone else asleep there was nothing for it but to risk having my bags stolen while I sorted out the bass. The bleary-eyed caravan of excess baggage owners (goats thankfully in full bleating order) traipsing down the side of the train with their belongings was a sorry sight. Almost, but not quite, as sorry as the sight of a cursing Englishman successfully illustrating the correct procedure to slip a disc and have a hernia at the same time.

The rest of the night – what little was left of it – passed without incident, and three hours later than scheduled – and an awfully long time since I set out from Camden – we slowly shimmied our way through the ring of hills surrounding Cuba's second largest city. After passing nothing but kilometre after kilometre of flat green carpets of sugar cane since dawn, it was a relief to see the first contours of the Sierra Maestra, its thick coat of tangled tropical foliage spiked with tall palms poking out like comical punk giraffes. At the penultimate stop before our destination, a crowd of accommodation touts boarded the train to try to snap up some business among the weary foreigners. With a room already booked in a state-licensed *casa particular* (homes converted into bed and breakfast accommodation) and in less than generous mood after my disturbed night, I turned down wave after wave of card-pressing teenagers with a polite but firm, '*No, gracias.*' I'd read about Santiago's reputation for persistent wheeler-dealers ('*jineteros*', as they were known) and these guys were an impressive advance party. Saying no to one offer merely triggered a suggestion of something else from the next one in line. If you didn't want a *chica* or a *cabaña* on the beach to spend quality time with your *chica*, then maybe you'd need a box of cigars, some illegally caught lobster, a bottle of cheap Havana Club, a musical instrument, or a vintage Oldsmobile to tour the city. It won't take an American invasion to teach Cubans about the dynamics of a free market economy – the spirit of capitalism is already there.

As we finally pulled into the station – the second wave of *jineteros* visibly milling around on the platform – I wished I had the anonymity that came with dark skin and a couple of live animals as luggage. For once, however, the double bass provided a useful hassle-evasion device. By the time I'd walked down to the back of the train to collect HP – and spent another fifteen minutes looking for the flimsy luggage receipt I'd scrunched into an unrecognizable ball – the station had emptied.

Eventually staggering out of the Arrivals hall, the first thing I noticed, after the intensity of the heat, was Santiago's welcoming aroma. If the smell of baked bread is the way to clinch the sale of your house, positioning the railway station next to a rum distillery must be the top tip to sell your city. The air was thick with inviting wafts of Christmas pudding, caramel, raisins and brown sugar. Right across the road stood the oldest rum distillery in Cuba, built in 1868 by the Bacardi family, nationalized in 1959, and still home to over 42,000 barrels of what the marketing department could now legitimately tag 'a revolutionary style of rum'. Its station-facing wall had been decorated with a giant mural depicting young Fidel, weapon raised in defiance, alongside a mother with gun and baby. Underneath was the message, 'Santiago de Cuba: Rebellious Yesterday, Hospitable Today, Heroic Always'. Had I been in slightly better condition, I'd have been tempted to respond to this with a mighty Austin Powers-style 'Yeah, baby!' but all I could manage was a 'Bugger me, this sun's hot!'

The second thing I noticed was the lack of transport, or to be more precise, the lack of transport for a foreigner. In a move to prevent dollar-paying visitors from trying a sneaky cost-cutting exercise, the Cuban authorities had made it illegal for peso forms of transport to take us tourist types. Up above, gliding on the thermals in lazy circles, black vultures scanned the ground for their lunch. I imagined the short story in the foreign news round-up:'An Englishman is recovering in hospital today after surviving seven days without food and water out-side a Cuban railway station. Ambulance staff that picked up his vulture-pecked, dehydrated body later received heavy fines for illegally transporting a foreigner.' It wasn't illegal to use a peso-operating phone, but possessing neither the appropriate coinage nor a trustable companion to watch my luggage while I went in search of some, I was forced to sit it out and hope a solution would present itself. Which, after much howling and arm-waving, it did. Spotting the two empty Bicitaxis riding past the station, I managed (after much price haggling) to per-suade Raul and Abel to risk a large fine and take me and every-thing else to my *casa particular*. A Bicitaxi was a three-wheel, pedal-powered vehicle designed to carry two passengers, or in exceptional circumstances, a double bass and a large amount of luggage.

Raul asked me where I wanted to go and I pulled out the Casa Tania business card a friend had given me in London.

Under the owner's full name, Dr Tania M. Garcia Terrero, it listed the address and along the bottom (in English), 'Hot water for 24 hrs, Aircondition [sic], Downtown'. Evidently, round-the-clock hot water was not the norm in Santiago, although in a place where cooling off was going to be a number one priority, the words '24 hour ice availability' would have been a much better sales pitch.

Passing back the card, Raul brought out a coin and flicked it up in the air. Abel called out something and once the coin had landed he gave a delighted yelp. He'd won me instead of the luggage. In any other country it would have looked a ridiculous sight, but riding amidst the motley derby that was Santiago road traffic, we received barely a second glance. Along the main drag that skirted the docks, I saw horse-drawn carts, trucks loaded with vast blocks of rapidly melting ice, a motorbike with a passenger sitting side-saddle and carrying a large cake, various makes of vintage American cars, and a Moscovich – the poor man's Lada – with a bed tied to the roof. A Bicitaxi with the neck of a double bass sticking out of the side looked almost normal in this company.

Eventually, we turned off the main drag and headed up a steep hill towards the cathedral. The two drivers got off and manually shifted their chains on to a wider spoke. A group of children were playing football on the road with an old ballcock, and a volley of unintelligible friendly heckles greeted our brief invasion of the pitch. The slope then became so steep that, out of necessity more than charity, I dismounted and helped to push. Radio Bemba, the Cuban gossip network, must have been transmitting news of approaching three-wheeled comedy because people ahead were now coming out of their houses to watch. Abel was sweating so much his threadbare singlet was completely transparent, and Raul was making an ominous wheezing noise. I asked if he was okay and he just grinned, patted his chest and said 'Asthma.' The vultures continued to circle above us.

And then – just as I feared Raul might expire – I heard someone call out my name. '*Es el bajista, mami!* – It's the bassist, Mummy!' shouted a little girl leaning on a rail a couple of metres above my head. A few seconds later, I was surrounded by various family members, most of whom managed to mask their shock at seeing such a vast quantity of luggage with smiles and kind words. 'We thought you'd gone to another house,' said a woman with a head full of hair-clips. It was Tania, the boss of the *casa* and owner of the voice I had struggled to understand on various long-distance phone calls. She looked very pleased to see me.

The first few hours in my new home went by in a blur of introductions, instructions and room reorganization. Official room-renting forms had to be signed the minute I stepped in the door, house rules given, shower-operating instructions listened to but not necessarily followed, and strange tropical fruits devoured with relish. Oh yes, and the obligatory tired-person, big-whopper faux pas had to be delivered. Finally standing on the roof terrace, surveying the incredible 360-degree vista of clay-tiled rooftops, rolling mountains, and an eerily boatless bay, I pointed at an ugly plume of smoke belching out of the industrial complex in the distance and said something to Tania along the lines of, 'What a pity someone had to spoil your view.' She just smiled back politely and said, 'That's the oil refinery – my husband works there.' Doh!

5. Flat Pigs and Nincompoops

Despite some initial nervousness on my part about moving into a house with number 101 on its front door, Tania's *casa* proved to be a lucky find.

In estate-agent speak the exterior frontage displayed original colonial features with signs of some structural decay. In reality, four slowly eroding columns – one held up by the electricity wires – were all that was left of the original façade, making the front of the house look more like an ancient temple ruin than a habitable mansion.

But once inside the door, it was as if the front had just been a clever disguise to fool the chattering neighbours. The interior was not only vast but had bags of charm. Built around the turn of the nineteenth century, there were all the design features a homesick Spanish colonialist would have wanted: high ceilings, enormous wooden doors (the front one still on its original hoop hinges), tiled floors, a cool, shaded central courtyard and even an Arabic-style underground water chamber to supply that European fetish for cleanliness in the face of sweaty adversity. Most important of all, for a latter-day Englishman whose own pores had flicked into the permanently open position, its long corridor design meant that even in the most stifling conditions, you could count on some sort of breeze funnelling through the building.

My original intention had been to stay here for a couple of weeks and then find something a bit more independent – a place where a man could pluck strings to his heart's content without causing psychological damage to those unused to daily Simandl torture. But as I quickly discovered, extracting yourself from the welcoming clutches of a Cuban family was like trying to untangle yourself from a relationship with someone prepared to do almost anything to make the relationship work. It wasn't that they were actively preventing me from moving elsewhere. Theirs was a far more subtle technique of emotional manipulation.

Day by day I could feel myself being carefully tied down by a web of kind gestures and good intentions. For example, ever since my arrival, Tania's husband, Braulio, had been investing enormous amounts of time in modifying my room. Every electrical whim was catered for with an ingenuity that bordered on the potentially lethal. To generate enough power to get my hair-clippers to work, he managed to create a Heath Robinson adaptor device that connected with the air-conditioning unit, the only appliance with sufficient voltage to power my Remington scalp shredder. To heat the water for my shower (the round-the-clock hot water promised on the business card), he'd concocted the sort of terrifying arrangement of wires, switches and running water that wouldn't have looked out of place in the basement torture rooms of military dictators. It didn't inspire much confidence when he gave stern instructions to turn the water on first then flick the switch, not the other way around. Mind you, Cuban voltage was sufficiently low that a pre-breakfast electrocution probably wouldn't kill you, just leave you shaking like Stevens for a few hours.

No, to leave all this would have been a personal insult to his DIY prowess, not to mention a danger to the local grid if he'd been forced to try unwiring it all. Nothing was a problem and any potential problem was nothing. When I apologized for the noise I was making with the bass (and it was definitely still noise rather than music), they said that having a musician in the house might help stimulate the girls into taking up an instrument. Were they deaf? Even my nationality worked in my favour. In their unofficial league table of European visitors, the Brits were considered the most *simpatico*, the

Germans the most undemanding, the French the fussiest, and the Italians a law unto themselves and their unbridled libidos.

With an easy exit looking increasingly unlikely, I then made the fatal mistake of letting my curiosity get the better of me. One afternoon I asked Tania how she had started the business. Not a good move. Spared the details of how she had struggled (and was still struggling) to get things going, I could perhaps have maintained some semblance of emotional detachment. But the afternoon we sat down and collectively unloaded a decade's worth of pent-up stress was, in hindsight, the beginning of the end of my plans to find alternative lodging.

Among the many contradictions that litter Cuban life, property rights are particularly hard for outsiders to get their head around. While a large percentage of the population can rightfully claim to have their own home, nobody has the right to buy or sell their property. There are no estate agents (another unsung triumph of the Revolution) and the only speculative practices relate to predicting whether you'll ever get out of your parents' place. If you want to change locations you can do a swap with another house – assuming you can find some-one who likes your place as much as you like theirs – but to actually get your home in the first instance you must play the ultimate game of patience. It's either a long wait for a State-supplied apartment or an even longer wait for the family pad to pass into your hands. One last alternative – one that pro-vided Tania with a large house just five minutes from the central square and cathedral – is to befriend a family-less widow and look after her until she dies.

When old Josephina eventually died and the house passed into Tania's name, the young doctor knew this was her big chance to improve her family's standard of living. The Government's policy of allowing select Cubans to rent out rooms – selection depending on whether your house was in an 'acceptable' neighbourhood and you (the owner) were a good Party supporter with no black marks next to your name

– meant that she now had a potential access to dollars. And dollars were everything in peso-earning Cuba. To buy cooking oil, you needed dollars. To buy soap, shampoo, toilet roll and detergent, you needed dollars. An average Cuban salary – the peso equivalent of 15 dollars per month in Tania's case – would hardly fill a shopping bag in a dollar store.

So with the house in her name she got to work. First she sold all her grandmother's jewellery to fund the repair of the house, then took out a 3,000-peso loan from the bank to pay for the rental licence, and after the various inspectors had checked it was tourist-worthy, opened up for business in the summer of 1999. Like all the other guesthouse owners in Santiago, Tania had to pay a fixed 100-dollar tax every month (regardless of rental income) and after her first month without a single tourist, she started to panic. Down to her last 30 dollars, she was forced to take a gamble. A bus from the oil refinery was going to Havana, and after using part of the loan to print out some business cards, she used Braulio's contacts to get a free ride and spent the rest of her money persuading the driver to stop off at every town along the way. From Bayamo to Santa Clara, the refinery bus wove its way through the countryside – the other passengers presumably wondering why their driver needed so many long toilet stops – with Tania visiting scores of other *casas particulares* and dropping off cards wherever she went.

It was a shrewd move. Travellers who stay in these private houses tend to pick up recommendations along the way, and within a week of that journey, a Canadian family had turned up at the door of 101. They stayed for five nights, and at 25 dollars a night Tania had just enough to pay the following month's 100-dollar tax and the bills.

With two young girls to look after and a full-time job as a doctor in a cancer-screening clinic, it wasn't a great surprise to hear she had recently developed an ulcer. 'I make enough to buy things for the girls and make sure we eat well, but there is a lot of stress,' she admitted. It wasn't hard to understand the measure of her joy at seeing me arrive that morning.

Any lingering feelings of guilt about leaving 101 over-wired and at the mercy of randy Italians aside, the real reason I wanted to stay was because it felt the right place to be. I had an enormous room in a lovely old house with a roof terrace, boasting probably the best view in Santiago. And I had good company. After living alone in a small London flat for years it was a strange (but strangely enjoyable) experience to be sharing a big space with an eclectic cast of characters.

Tania and Braulio made for a fairly typical Cuban couple. She met him while on a medical assignment at the oil refinery. 'Within a month he told me I had to marry him or else we would have to fight,' laughed Tania, remembering Braulio's less than delicate proposal technique. She didn't want to fight but did want children, so they got married. She loved music and dancing and going out. He loved falling asleep in front of the television. She ran the house. He tinkered away on his rusting Moskovich and made sure at least one rocking chair was constantly in motion. It was a mismatch glued together by the practicalities of running a guesthouse and a mutual love for two adorable children.

Their two little girls were complete opposites. Liana, seven years old and the younger of the two, was a chubby little ball of energy whose cries of '*Tengo hambre, mami* – I'm hungry, Mummy!' would signal the start of the day and the 5 p.m. return from school. She was also, unintentionally most of the time, the queen of the one-liners. When the giant front door jammed one day and Tania said it was a job for a couple of men, I had quickly offered to assist. 'But Richard,' chirped Liana, 'you're not a man, you're a journalist.' Her older sister, Tanita, was the beauty of the family, a painfully shy nine-year-old whose looks brought a regular procession of hopeful schoolboys to the house. She wanted to be an actress and declared with an unnerving certainty that when she performed on stage for the first time she wanted '*nuestro comandante en jefe* – our commander-in-chief' to be in the front row of the audience. And if I thought that was a scary comment, an incident on the street a few days later made me even more suspicious of what was being taught in the classroom. Bumping into some sort of extra-curricular school outing one evening – the children still dressed in their neat red and white uniforms – I was given a resounding chorus of '*Ajo, cebolla, los yankis para la olla.*' The English translation – which didn't quite have the same nursery-rhyme bounce to it – was, 'Garlic, onion, the yankees into the cooking pot.' It beat 'Frère Jacques', I suppose.

Both girls had an attitude to schoolwork that British kids (and adults for that matter) would probably find totally incomprehensible. They left the house at 7.15 a.m., and if Braulio had problems getting the Moskovich started, Tanita would get into a right old flap, dialling up the speaking clock every two minutes and making pained expressions at her mother, Marcela. When I asked what she was getting so worried about, she told me that children who arrived late were sent back home. Try implementing that rule in England and you'd have an empty school on the first day. In the evenings after dinner, the two would do their homework until at least ten o'clock. Even taking the lack of alternative entertainment out of the equation, I have never come across children who worked so hard or with so much enthusiasm.

The other half of the family – Tania's parents and two brothers – lived a couple of doors down the road but spent much of their time helping run 101. Marcela worked at the wonderfully named Museum of the Underground Struggle – Revolutionary museums, I soon discovered, were a major employment provider in the Hero City – and then spent the rest of the time trying to increase my waist size and fix up her two sons, Antonio and Carlos, with suitable girlfriends. Antonio was my age and worked as a part-time security guard at El Morro, the seventeenth-century Spanish fort at the mouth of the bay, while Carlos got occasional work distributing the gas tanks that better-off Santiagueros used for cooking. With me, the two talked about nothing else but Hollywood films and travel. Their father, Manuel, was a journalist for the local weekly paper, *Sierra Maestra*, and as the job would suggest, he was an unyielding Fidelista. In his opinion – which was cast in well-set concrete – Cuba had the only real democracy in the world and the only truly free press. At first I did try to engage in open debate, but it was as futile as trying to persuade an Aussie that sport doesn't really matter.

I liked his newspaper, though. Compared to the dire content of the national organ, *Granma* – invariably found in a crumpled and soiled state in the bin next to public toilets – *Sierra Maestra* was a much brighter read and even made the odd stab at veiled criticism. My favourite bit was called *Camara en la Calle* – Camera in the Street. A journalist was sent out to take a snap of some public grievance, usually another vast hole in the road that was now full of water and being used as a public swimming pool, and alongside it answers would be demanded from the State department responsible for fixing it. The following week there would be a letter, in this case from the Water Board, explaining that since the hole had started before the water main burst, it was a problem for the road maintenance people. Week after week, evidence of a crumbling city mounted up, and week after week the officials' often hilariously lame excuses would be filed.

The final two members of the family were Chiri the dog and a mad black cat that only came down from the roof at mealtimes. If they opened all the cages at Battersea Dogs' Home and left out food laced with Viagra, the results might reflect the four-legged blends on display in Cuba. In Chiri's case a random coupling had given him the head of an Alsatian, the body of a Corgi and a tail that curled up like one of those Arctic-bound huskies. Apart from the mental confusion caused by this odd genetic cocktail, Chiri also suffered from myopia and sexual frustration, a lethal combination for the cat who, on three occasions, had to make a dramatic escape from an unwelcome (and potentially very uncomfortable) canine advance. When he couldn't find the cat, he released his tension by chasing and killing cockroaches. If any of us caught sight of one of these regular invaders, a shout of '*Vamos*, Chiri!' would cause a mad scampering of paws and a blur of fast-moving fur. His technique was crude but effective. He just gobbled up the cockroach in his mouth, shook his head vigorously, and then spat it out on the patio to a generous round of appreciative applause.

My first week in Santiago was spent destressing and acclimatizing – the oppressive heat and humidity being my top excuse for doing bugger-all. Sitting in an undulating bowl surrounded by a heat-trapping ring of hills, Santiago seemed better suited to ripening tomatoes than providing a dwelling-place for humans. Every day, the TV weather map showed the predicted temperatures for the country, and every day there were invariably two thirty-something figures in bright red down in the right-hand corner; one for Santiago and the other for its twin oven, Guantanamo, an hour's drive down the coast. Women walked the streets with colourful sun-blocking umbrellas, while those without filed along the shadowed side of the road like fugitives desperate not to be exposed. The *panuelo* – a small towelling flannel for neck- and brow-wiping duties – was the essential pocket accessory. Men cooled off by rolling T-shirts above their rice-bloated bellies. Dogs never stopped panting. Fans whirred away all day. Top lips remained permanently beaded. It was sauna life without the relief of a cold plunge pool.

I took my body's advice and remained as immobile as possible. I read a lot, took siestas that made a mockery of the term 'afternoon nap', ate mango after mango and sat on the roof watching towering white bouffants bruise into grey-black Afros, the early evening thunder routine rumbling away like distant detonations. For anyone wanting to write a thesis on the development and disintegration of the anvil-topped cumulo-nimbus, the roof of 101 would be highly recommended for field research. Santiago was where clouds came out to play. It was the Club 18–30 of upwardly mobile water vapour.

Occasionally, when my conscience got the better of me, I made some exploratory stabs at Jennifer-less musical self-improvement. The good news was that HP had survived the journey without any signs of injury. In fact, she sounded a far happier bass. Maybe it was the acoustics of my room (it certainly wasn't a change in the quality of the player), but I swear that the move from dry, temperate Maidenhead to hot, humid Santiago had brought out a richer timbre in her voice. Bored with ploughing through Simandl's turgid exercise routines – the man needed some laughing weed – I tried breaking into the first pages of *The True Cuban Bass*, a teaching manual for Cuban bass lines that I'd picked up off the Internet.

'A magnificent book which will bring all bassists closer to authentic Latin music,' said the first quote I had read. 'For the intermediate or professional bassist, this is it!' said the fifth one down, which I hadn't. It came with a couple of CDs and like one of those language-learning courses, the idea was, 'You listened, you read, you played'. In my case the reality was rather different. I listened, I frowned, and I pressed rewind. Even when I did finally manage to match up the track on the CD to the appropriate piece of music in the book, the combination of the speed of the music and the fact that my music-reading was still at the 'All Cows Eat Grass Bales' level, meant that it took a week to get past page 2.

Keen to begin the more pleasurable part of my education (field research in local music venues), I began spending most of my evenings in the company of a cold Mayabe beer listening to live music in the Casa de la Tradición on Calle Rabi. This was just an old wooden house with a small bar made of upturned rum barrels, photos and posters of musicians on the

walls, and a few rocking chairs and tables for those not dancing. It felt like a Bacardi ad without the cliché. And being Cuba,
without the Bacardi of course. The bands played in one corner
of what would have been the living room, usually performing
a mixture of traditional *son*, *boleros* and salsa. Trying to pick up
visual tips from the double bassists wasn't easy. Without the
benefit of amplifiers they had resorted to boosting the sound
by standing in the corner, facing their instruments against the
wall like naughty children. From what little I could see from
this rear view, however, very little attention was being paid to
correct arm and hand positions. Most gripped the neck with
their palm flat against the back of the fingerboard, and – sorry,
Barry – dangled their left elbow at an encouragingly can't-be-
bothered angle.

For a dollar you could sit and listen to hours of male-oriented
lyricism (love affairs with rum, women and the mountains
seemed to be the top song subjects) while watching Lycra-
bottomed *jineteras* loosening up their stiff-hipped, money-belted
sugar daddies. As a partnerless male in this situation, I was forced
to master a form of rapid eye movement that reduced the
possibility of catching a *jinetera*'s eye. In Santiago, where sex
tourism was clearly rife, a single misplaced glance could be
taken as a come-on, and short of wearing black robes and a
dog collar – and even that might backfire if they thought it
was God's night off – there was almost no way of avoiding the
charms of women whose interest in bulges in pockets went no
further than your wallet.

The promise of sex hung in the air like cheap scent. The
way the Cubans danced, the way they examined the opposite
sex as if doing a thorough X-ray scan, all that open flirtation
in the street. Hardly surprising, I suppose, in a country where
intercourse was both the freest form of expression, the cheapest
form of entertainment, and (in many cases) the most lucrative
form of work. In Cuba, young girls had usually mastered a
suggestive hip-gyrating dance routine before they'd even started

school, and on turning fifteen, would celebrate their *quince* (the traditional coming-of-age party that dates back to colonial times) with a photograph album that invariably included provocative Lolita-style swimsuit shots. Sex was legal at the age of sixteen, but according to Cuba's national Centre for Sex Education, most Cuban girls were sexually active by the age of thirteen. In a society as sexually permissive as this, the idea of a bunch of Cuban men getting excited about seeing a sex scene on a cinema screen would seem faintly ridiculous. Yet that is exactly what I witnessed the night I paid my first visit to the Cine Cuba, one of the oldest of the crumbling movie theatres in Santiago. Going to the movies hadn't been top of my must-do list, but not being in a position to claim a full diary or indeed a conflicting engagement of any variety, I had agreed to join Antonio who wanted to see a film starring the dark-eyed Spanish beauty, Penelope Cruz.

We bought our 1-peso tickets from the little kiosk in the entrance and walked, or rather felt our way, into a pitch-black auditorium. Unless Ms Cruz was starring in the trailer as well as the main feature, it seemed that we had mistimed our arrival. I pulled Antonio back out and told him we should wait for the next showing. He then explained that the film was on a continuous loop and that we could watch the rest of the film now and then stay and watch the bit we'd missed afterwards. 'You're joking, aren't you?' I laughed. 'No,' he replied, sounding a bit miffed that I'd dragged him out of the auditorium, 'it's what everyone does here.' The number of people filing in suggested he wasn't making it up. 'Do you mind?' persisted Antonio. 'It's just that if I wait for the next performance I'll be late for my night shift.'

Ninety-five per cent of the time there are good reasons why we don't watch the second half of a film first and then the first half, second. But there is that other 5 per cent – films like this extraordinarily bad corset-popper – where it really makes no difference at all. Normally, I would have been moaning about the blurred picture quality, the regular jump in frames and the subtle but effective dislocation between soundtrack and picture. But with this film, it lifted an already atrocious production into almost cult status. As soon as the first sex scene appeared, it was clear the plot hadn't been top of the audience's mind. A cacophony of wolf whistles and what I took to be the Cuban equivalent of 'Go on, my son!' filled the auditorium with such unrestrained gusto you might have thought someone had just scored a home run. Boisterous heckling I can deal with, public masturbation at close quarters I cannot. A movement in the corner of my eye made me turn my head and there, just two seats away, was a man with his hand down his trousers rigorously spanking the monkey with an expression that suggested it was too late to pass the tissues. I told Antonio I had seen enough and headed for the exit. 'Did you see what that guy was doing?' I protested, once safely outside. He nodded with embarrassment and admitted it was a bit of a problem. 'That is why so few women come to watch films here.' I never did go back to the Cine Cuba.

Carnival – one of the deciding factors in my choice of Santiago over Havana – was now only a few days away, and all around the city, bamboo and palm-leaf kiosks were being hastily erected. Down along the wide avenue called Victoriano Garzón – where the main parade of floats, dancers and conga bands was due to pass in front of a panel of judges – there were tiers of metal benches either side of the street and a special Cristal beer enclosure for dollar-paying foreigners. Every day the sounds of an approaching party got louder: the shrill siren of Chinese cornets, the low explosive thumps of conga practice in distant *barrios*, and the unavoidable pre-slaughter screams of fattened pigs. For some reason, the latter were most audible at about 8 p.m., just after the daily edition of *Mesa Redonda*, a TV programme where five panellists bravely attempted to create a discussion out of unanimous political agreement. Every night, barely five minutes after presenter Randy Alonso had made his customary signing-off speech, the first squeals would begin. Revolutionary fervour, political frustration, or a desire for fresh liver on the dinner table – one of the three must have been causing the punctual slaughter.

In the most recent issue of *Sierra Maestra*, the city's mayor had announced the arrival of carnival by asking for 'a happy, well-ordered party in which solidarity is to be projected' and a week free of 'any bloody deed or violence'. Unfortunately, his words lost a little of their resonance by being next to a story about the predicted alcohol consumption for this year's event: 30,000 cases of bottled beer, 270,000 cases of bulk beer, 4,000 cases of bottled rum, 9,000 cases of bulk rum, and 15,000 litres of cocktail. The only thing likely to be projected in this scenario would be a lot of misdirected urine. Bloody deeds seemed extremely likely.

A visit to the Museum of Carnival confirmed that concerns over rowdy behaviour were not a new phenomenon. All through its long history, the event had been littered with acts of subversion, indiscipline and drunken irresponsibility. The orgy of alcohol and stretched Lycra that was today's week-long shindig began life over 200 years ago as a series of street parades on the so-called 'Day of Kings'. Slaves were permitted to tag along and celebrate with their own imported forms of music and dance, with the use of costumes and masks allowing blacks and whites their one opportunity to intermingle and enjoy a mixed-race party without fear of persecution or (in the slaves' case) a good whipping.

In the early years, it seems this arrangement depended largely on the King's sense of humour in any particular year. In 1795, His Majesty prohibited the costumed party animals known as '*los mamarrachos*' (literally, 'the messy ones', but sometimes translated more entertainingly as 'the Nincompoops') because of the 'moral damage' they were causing. 'In view of the disorder that is noted with the *mamarrachos* on the days of San Juan, San Pedro and Santa Ana,' announced the royal messenger, 'in which unfortunately some revellers drink for the pleasure of getting drunk – causing accidents and confusion among the classes – a ban on such entertainment is to be imposed.' The Nincompoops doubtless went home and stuck a few more pins in their anti-monarchy dolls.

In 1815, the parades were banned again, this time due to the nannyish belief that indecent songs, '*dichos picantes*' ('saucy sayings') and improper dress were likely to insult certain parts of the community. 'Any pleb or coloured person caught wearing ridiculous clothes will be condemned to serve one year of public works,' came royal orders, clearly oblivious to the often laughable dress sense of the King himself. This on-off relationship continued through the nineteenth century, with politics never straying far from the party. In 1871, a number of Cubans were detained for making a huge caricature of the defeated Spanish General Martinez Campus, parading it through the streets to delighted cheers from the non-Spanish participants.

Early European visitors to Santiago – particularly the carnival virgins among them – often found this raucous, rum-fuelled event extremely intimidating. In his book *The Pearl of the Antilles*, the English painter Walter Goodman described the cultural shock of witnessing his first carnival in 1864. Deciding to watch events unfold from the safety of his balcony, the Englishman was reluctantly dragged into the party when a parade of masked revellers spotted him and diverted into his house. Apart from the annoyance of having all his beloved imported English beer polished off in seconds, he then got into a very English flap when a beautiful mulatto girl in an elaborate costume started dancing provocatively with him. Believing, as many Europeans at that time did, that provocative mulatto girls carried diseases and that tobacco smoke was an effective disinfectant, Goodman spent the next two hours attempting to chain-smoke his way out of her attentions.

Gradually, the carnival became more commercial, until in 1948 it finally lost its soul to big business. A millionaire called

Pepin Bosch created the committee for *La Gran Semana Santiaguera* (the big Santiago week), whose responsibilities, apart from milking off a nice cut from the profits, included the onerous task of judging the beauty contest and selecting a carnival queen. Old black and white photographs from that time showed the gratuitous promotion of Bacardi and its beer brand Hatuey. Back then, the famous bat symbol – today only visible as an eroded motif on the pillars of the company's old office on Calle Enremadas, itself now a dilapidated sock-making factory – was everywhere. Post-Revolution, the new communist carnival struggled (for obvious reasons) to deliver the same glitzy jamboree. No more Bacardi floats and sponsored parades. *Adiós* to gastronomic extravagance, expensive costumes and committees of wealthy businessmen. And, in a move that was as well received as news that Christmas was being cancelled, the authorities decided there would be no more beauty queens. In 1961, the organizers decided that from thenceforth, in accordance with revolutionary principles (it isn't made clear which particular principle was being adhered to but presumably it was an anti-monarchy clause), the beauty queens would now be called 'stars of the carnival'. During the so-called Special Period of the early Nineties – when the collapse of the old Soviet Union caused Cuba to suffer its worst economic crisis – the annual event was temporarily disbanded. Apart from the obvious lack of funds, the regularity and duration of power cuts meant the use of microphones and amps was virtually impossible. The irony was bitter. At a time when the population most needed a party, the party was cancelled. Cubans I had spoken to said the carnival today was a pale imitation of the pre-Special Period days. 'It used to go on for up to two weeks, everyone wore masks and costumes, and all the best Cuban bands came and played,' one of my neighbours told me. 'Now, it's just a lot of dead pigs and flat beer.'

They were right about the pigs. Judging by the number of full body roasts I counted on my first night of carnival, livestock numbers must have been reduced to a few ageing sows and the odd underweight piglet. Sitting flattened and roasted on metal trays – ears and tail singed to a crisp, eyes closed and legs outstretched as if in a death leap – they looked like victims of a nasty steamroller accident. The meat was served up with little ceremony and no thought for hygiene. Bits of mostly fatty matter were shoved unceremoniously inside a bread roll with a couple of slices of limp cucumber and a squirt of chilli vinegar. The alternative forms of sustenance were the Cuban version of a pizza – discs of floppy bread smeared with tomato and a few globs of cheese-coloured substance heated up in charcoal-fired metal drums – or little paper cones filled with *chicharrones*, the crisp, fat-soaked skin of the pig the British call crackling. To wash all this down, people stood in line to fill up giant plastic beakers with lager served from large metal tanks. I joined one such queue and paid 10 pesos (about 30 pence) for half a litre of beer. Just one sip and I understood why people were necking it back with such speed – allow this stuff to warm up even a fraction and you'd be facing a tough drinking assignment.

The highlight of the carnival was the *desfile*, the nightly parade of floats and dancers, and I was immediately faced with the foreigner's dilemma. Should I go and pay a couple of pesos to sit in the Cuban section – the cheaper option but one that required joining a queue of M25 tailback proportions – or hand over 5 dollars and sail straight into the tourists' section, perfectly positioned right opposite the judges' podium? My conscience said the former was the correct option, my patience (or lack of) headed towards the 5-dollar bill. With minutes to go before the start and a full bladder weakened by the sight of queueless toilets inside the tourist enclosure, the conscience didn't have a hope in hell. Carlos looked mortified when I told him how much our two tickets had cost and I could see he felt very uncomfortable about sitting in, as he called it, the *pepe* section. Among the variety of names I'd heard Cubans using for foreigners, the most common in Santiago were '*pepe*' (it came from the brand of jeans once worn by many visitors) and '*yuma*'. Yuma was apparently the name of a town in Arizona that appeared regularly in American Westerns shown on Cuban TV in the Seventies. It was now used to describe the United States, Americans, or just foreigners in general.

A burst of fireworks – a very quick burst – signalled the start of the show and a cavalcade of police motorbikes rode up and down the strip a couple of times to clear the way. First came the dancers from the Santiago Tropicana – all giant feathers, wire nipple covers, and costumes that did not require the question, 'Does my bum look good in this?' – followed by various folkloric groups, conga bands, and men running around with giant *It's a Knockout*-style heads. The conga bands got the biggest reaction. Each *barrio* – names such as Los Hoyos, San Agustín, San Pedrito, Paso Franco written on their banners – had a team of drummers led by someone playing the Chinese cornet. This instrument was said to have been brought to Cuba by Chinese labourers, but to me it looked and sounded more like the thing used to get cobras out of baskets than anything you'd associate with the Orient. The player certainly seemed to exert the same hypnotic power as a snake charmer, effortlessly transforming even the most conservative of bystanders into hip-gyrating, arm-waving extroverts. You could tell by the energy of the performances and the reaction of sections of the crowd when their *barrio* filed past that there was big neighbourhood pride at stake. The metallic ring of the percussion section – three men hammering different-sized brake drums – was so infectious that at one point even the judging panel, momentarily forgetting their neutral observer status, got up and started the famous conga shuffle.

As each group of participants reached the main stand, an announcer bellowed out an introduction into a microphone. Well, at least he did until there was an ill-timed power cut that killed his voice, removed most of the lighting and caused mass

confusion as the organizers couldn't decide (or indeed announce) what to do. In the end, the threat of a nasty pile-up
forced them to continue, the compere resorting to a loud-hailer
to inform the judges which group they were judging. By the
time the floats arrived – lights and buttocks flashing in equal
numbers – we had been in our seats for over four hours, and
Carlos was by now on intimate terms with a couple of Chilean
girls. The *pepe* section wasn't so bad after all.

On our way home we passed by an outdoor disco near to
101. A vast stack of speakers had been positioned across the
road and a DJ was perched on a raised platform, a box of
cassettes at his side, and a young assistant with a torch helping
him find the required tracks. The volume was such that the top
speakers were threatening to vibrate off the stack and yet I
spotted at least three old dears rocking away on their porches
as if nothing untoward was happening. All of a sudden, the
music changed, a huge roar of approval went up, and a sea of
couples moved into what can only be described as the rear
entry position. The women lowered their heads, stuck their
bottoms up, and proceeded to grind their backsides in seduc-
tive circles into the crotch area of their male partners. It was
exactly what I'd seen happen to Pedrito Calvo on stage at the
Palacio del Salsa five years before. The men, holding the women
by their waists, gave their best demonstration of the pelvic thrust
while grinning inanely and shouting encouragement to their
friends. 'What do the words mean?' I shouted in Carlos's ear.
He looked like he'd just walked into a large delicatessen. 'Take
her from behind,' he yelled back. No lyrical subtleties there
then. It wasn't so much dirty dancing as musical humping and
over the course of my year in Cuba I came to see it as an
anthem for young bored Cubans. In a country with little or
no room for dissent, this hugely provocative display of sexuality
was defiantly performed out in the open for all to see. 'They
can't stop us shagging,' seemed to be the message.

The rest of the carnival passed in much the same way. For

seven days, the disco up the road never stopped – even at ten in the morning the DJ was still there playing to a few stragglers – and for seven days Tania and all the other doctors in the city dealt with a regular procession of walking wounded. Carnival was a time of celebration but it was also a time of excessive drinking and score settling, often with the aid of a machete. According to the word on the street, at least seven deaths had been reported during the week. Then on the eighth day, the music stopped, the beer wagons were towed away, the DJ climbed wearily down from his post, and having spent night after night sharing beer cups and sipping from communal rum bottles, almost the entire population retired to bed with what everyone seemed to be calling '*gripe de la fiesta* – party flu'. You had to admire a place that diverted blame for over-indulgence on to an official party sickness.

6. The Man from Crackling

'There's someone to see you,' said Tania, knocking on my door one afternoon. It was siesta time, a sacred period of ceiling gazing when cold calls generally set off protracted gnashing of teeth. 'He says he's here about the double bass.'

I knew Cubans moved fast when dollars were in the offing but this was incredible. I had only been back from the music school half an hour – it being the logical starting point to look for a teacher – so even by Cuban standards this first rapid-response unit had broken all records. The visitor waiting down the hall couldn't have been more than seventeen or eighteen years old, somewhat younger than I had in mind for my musical Obi-Wan Kenobi. He was carrying an impressive bundle of music in his hands and came dressed in what must have been his smartest interview shirt. Strangely, he was neither sweating nor out of breath.

'Hi, I'm Ernesto,' he announced in English, quickly adding, 'I'm a bass player,' as if that were the magic password.

There followed an awkward pause during which both of us mentally rummaged for small talk and I became momentarily distracted by the length of his fingers. They were the longest sets of digits I'd seen in a long time – it was as if they'd been given an extra joint. After years of dedicated research, Cuban scientists had finally managed to create a genetically modified bass player.

'You didn't waste time,' I offered eventually, watching him nervously hide his hands behind his back.

He looked totally baffled. 'What do you mean, I didn't waste time?'

'Well, I only asked about a teacher this afternoon.'

'But I'm not a teacher.'

Now I was the one feeling awkward. 'So you're here for something else?'

'I'm studying double bass. I just came to have a look at your bass.'

He made it sound like I was hiding an exotic pet. In Britain, if a total stranger popped round to your house and asked if he could have a look at your trombone, you'd probably trick him into the garden shed, padlock the door and immediately call the police. But this was Cuba, where unannounced visits were as much the custom as the open-door hospitality, so blocking off the predicted rabid attack by Chiri, I threw my European distrust out the door and took Ernesto to my room.

I can still remember my expression the Christmas I took away the dustsheet covering a brand-new silver Chopper (in its day, the Ford Capri of the bicycle world), and Ernesto did a fine impression of it (my expression, not the Chopper) when he caught sight of HP. 'It's beautiful,' he sighed, trailing his enormous digits down her heavily scarred side with just a little bit too much intimacy. He explained he was in the middle of a four-year course at the music school and that there were twelve double bass students and only one bass between all of them.

'It's a terrible Russian thing,' he grumbled, starting instinctively to tune in the four strings in mid-conversation. I could see he was doing it by harmonics, a technique I had seen Jennifer demonstrate a few times but one that frankly stood little chance of being employed in the Neill warm-up. Tuning by harmonics involved lightly touching two adjacent strings at different points to achieve the same pitch and therefore a comparative means of note setting. Unfortunately, it required a delicate touch, a good ear, and the ability to get at least one of the strings in tune as a reference point to tune the other three. A battery-powered tuner, on the other hand, simply involved twisting the tuning keys until a flashing red light became a flashing green light. I don't think I need to tell you which option appealed to my strong belief in tonal precision.

Spotting a Charles Mingus CD lying on my desk, Ernesto's eyes lit up a second time. 'You like jazz?' he asked.

The CD had been a leaving present from a thoughtful friend – Mingus being a double bass legend of some repute – but the pitiful truth was I had only brought it along for exactly this situation; to garner double bass cred when visitors like Ernesto popped around. Jazz did nothing for me at all.

'No, I'm not a big fan, Ernesto,' I answered, unable to maintain the deceit.

He gave me a look that suggested I'd just proclaimed the Cuban female derrière to be not all it was touted to be, then took the CD out of its case, slotted it into my machine and pressed start.

'I've played with Herbie Hancock,' he announced out of the blue, quickly familiarizing himself with HP's fingerboard while making strange accompanying noises and mouth movements to the first track of *Ming Dynasty*. Ungenerous as it seems right now, the one thing I wanted to familiarize myself with was my bed. Hastily making some excuse about suffering from low salt levels, I gently retrieved my instrument from Ernesto's hands and suggested he popped round another time. I didn't exactly say '*Mi bajo es tu bajo*' but I did say that if he couldn't get hold of the school bass at a crucial time, mine was always available. Oh, and I lent him Mingus.

Maybe, in hindsight, that was being a bit too friendly. At almost the same time the following day, Ernesto was back at the front door, this time with a music stand, some CDs, music books and (oh no) a bow. I had somehow unwillingly adopted a musical puppy. By the third visit he'd plucked up enough courage to ask me to demonstrate my own ability. Reluctantly taking the bass from him, I assumed the playing position and racked my brain for a simple line from *The True Cuban Bass*. 'Wrong, wrong, wrong!' clucked Ernesto before I had even touched a string.

'Hold on, Ernesto, I haven't played a note yet,' I protested. Being shown up by a boy half my age was not part of the bass-sharing plan.

'Forget playing, just look at how you are holding the bass. You mustn't be frightened of it. It's just a piece of wood.'

It's just a piece of wood? Who was he kidding? It might have all the 'ah' appeal of a friendly elephant, but I knew this dumb piece of wood was actually a lethal weapon shaped into an ingenious dumb piece of wood disguise. Apart from its well-documented ability to inflict nasty doses of GBH, it also had the capacity to cause untold humiliation and leave self-confidence hobbling around on crutches for years to come. Frightened of it? I was bloody terrified of the thing.

But he was right, of course. I needed to start from the beginning again. If I couldn't hold it correctly, how could I begin to entertain notions of playing it correctly? After three weeks of faffing around avoiding the issue, finding a teacher was now an urgent priority.

In the end, the search for the chosen one proved far shorter than I could have hoped. The day after Ernesto's blunt appraisal, I bumped into a couple of musicians in Parque Cespedes. Actually they bumped into me, deliberately. Santiago's central square – named after Carlos Manuel Cespedes, the poet and plantation owner famous for emitting the first cry for Cuban Independence (though how you proved who shouted first beat me) – was the city's hub of hustle and hassle. Bordered by the cathedral, the Casa de Diego Velásquez, the Town Hall and the under-staffed, over-starred Casa Grande hotel, it was a magnet for tourists and those who lived off them. In the corner nearest the hotel sat the Rastafarian clan, a strange, ganja-less, Cuban sub-species of dreadlock wearers who spent their days trying to master highly elaborate handshake procedures before hooking up with foreign women. Then there were the non-Rasta *jineteros* who worked solo or in pairs and who managed to ply their trade despite the presence of at least two policemen on every corner. There were also beggars and buskers, men selling Che Guevara coins, and illegal taxi touts offering cheap rides to the beach. That was the daytime park life. After dark, lit by a grid of lamps that were so bright it felt like social night in an outdoor interrogation centre, the scene changed to a bizarre mix of innocence and vice. On one side of the square you'd have children being given rides in miniature goat-pulled carts while on the other, groups of prostitutes sat like patient fishermen, hoping to reel in a prize *pepe*.

I had deliberately chosen the 6–7 p.m. time slot, a short window of disturbance-free opportunity between the disappearance of the day shift and the arrival of the night crew, a time of bearable temperatures and soft evening light before the retina burners were switched on. Sitting down on one of the outside benches, I opened up the old Santiago guide Tania had given me and began to read something about superstition. Apparently, Santiago was the most superstitious city in Cuba. If they weren't paying respects to their chosen *santo* – the Afro-Cuban cult of *santería* being the Oriente's most widely practised faith – they'd be queuing up to leave gifts for the Virgin of Charity at the nearby shrine of El Cobre. This was a city where almost every house kept a glass of water to appease the spirits of the dead, where a cactus was believed to keep away evil, and where a sprig of leaves (from a *vencedor* tree) tucked behind the ear was the favoured protection from witchcraft. My scepticism was clearly noted, because the powers that be suddenly delivered a couple of peace-disrupting *trovadores* who completed their mission with an extremely ragged rendition of 'Chan Chan'. As soon as they finished the song I passed over some change and tried to prevent a likely segue into 'Guantanamera', another busker favourite, by asking whether they knew of any good double bass teachers.

'*Como no!* Of course!' said the one with the guitar and the terrible teeth. 'Come with me and I'll introduce you to someone.'

Through the recent purchase of a secondhand mountain bike – essential for negotiating Santiago's roller-coaster topography – I had already learnt about the financial baggage attached to the words 'I'll introduce you to'. It worked like this. If A passed on business to B, B would be obliged to pay A a proportion of his earnings, even if all A had done was given B's name to a tourist. While I admired the inherent honesty and camaraderie in the system, I didn't get such a kick out of the expense – prices were undoubtedly skewed upwards to take account of commission losses.

Together, we walked over to the Casa de la Trova, the most famous music venue in town, where from 11 a.m. until the early hours of the following morning, every day, 365 days a year, you could listen to live music for the price of a rum and coke. Originally a tiny smoke-filled café where local musicians came to sing for their drinks, the newer, bigger, more tourism-oriented Casa had little atmosphere and very poor acoustics. The big, high-ceilinged room had a small raised stage at one end, rows of uncomfortable wooden seats and a line of giant grilled windows that brought in a welcome breeze but also a less desirable barrage of street noise and diesel fumes. It was still an hour before the evening session was due to start and, apart from a lone *tres* player tuning up in one corner, the only other sound was the incessant call of a peanut seller whose repeated whiney announcement of '*Mani, mani, mani*' kept cutting in like some annoying heckler.

We walked past the stage and into a brightly lit back room where a man was putting a padlock around the neck of a battered-looking bass. He was wearing a black Guinness cap back to front so the words 'Good for You' filled his forehead. This was the musicians' warm-up area. There was a fading rota on the wall, a dirty-looking chilled water container with a plugless wire hanging off one side, a couple of chairs and an old publicity poster for Compay Segundo on one wall. Four battle-weary double basses stood to attention in the four corners of the room, each with either a chain or a bicycle lock hanging like a medallion around its chest. Portrayed in black and white, the scene would probably have taken on a moody poignancy – a perfect CD cover for another Cuban All-stars spin-off. Live and in colour, it just seemed rather sad.

As I guessed, the man in the cap was the person I was meant to meet. He introduced himself ('*Soy Pastor Panes*,' he beamed) and informed me he was the bassist and director of a band called Sones de Oriente. Pastor was as dark as the drink advertised on his cap. He had a small head of bowling ball roundness, an infectious grin, bloodshot, puckish eyes, and an endearing habit of biting his bottom lip when he was thinking. His hands (was it me or did all bassists stare at one another's hands?) were shockingly ugly. Short, stubby fingers, bits of peeling skin everywhere, visibly calloused tips, and nails beyond the skills of even the most talented manicurist. They looked like the hands of a masonry worker, not a musician.

The bad-toothed busker did the necessary commission-guaranteeing introductions and then Pastor and I sat down to talk. Either as a response to my undisguised interest in digital detail, or perhaps as a welcoming ritual for arriving bassists, he immediately asked me to show him my hands. 'Let's have a look at your fingers,' he chuckled with obvious relish.

I hesitantly put them forward for inspection, palms face down in a pathetic attempt to conceal the truth. Turning them over, he gave the fingertips the briefest of touch-tests and instantly let out the sort of high-pitched snort of astonishment I imagine a rugby coach would make if he discovered his prop forward had asked for some moisturizing cream. It was a humiliating exposure of my L-plate status.

'I've never met a bassist with such soft hands,' he finally wheezed, moist eyes requiring a dab from a sweaty flannel.

'I'm not a bassist,' I excused myself, a temporary sense of humour failure bubbling close to the surface. 'That's why I'm here in Santiago. I want to be a bassist.'

'So you have two weeks to learn?' laughed Pastor, assuming he had another rushed holiday case on his hands.

'No, I've come for a year.'

'*Un año?*'

'*Si, un año.*'

Somewhere underneath the Guinness cap, a mental calculation was quickly made and the figure that emerged provoked a grin that Pastor attempted (but failed) to rein in. We looked at each other and there was an instant mutual understanding of the situation. I knew that he knew I was a potential gold-mine and he knew that I knew what he was thinking.

'How much do you know?' he asked.

'Very little,' I replied, deciding the bullshit approach was going to get me nowhere.

From 'very little' it was a short step to a full spare-no-details confession, and I felt a cathartic release as each brutal layer of truth emerged. For starters, I spilled out the admission that holding the bass the right way had yet to be mastered. I mentioned my lessons with Jennifer and how little there was to show from them (my fault more than hers), confessed to an inability to practise longer than twenty minutes, and professed to have a major problem with Simandl.

'Who?' asked a very puzzled Pastor.

'Simandl,' I repeated slowly.

Still facing a blank and not equipped with the necessary vocabulary to elucidate on dull Austrians and scary teaching manuals, I did a quick bowing impression and raised my eyebrows as if to imply, 'Classical nonce – don't waste your time on him, mate.' Finally, despite fears of setting off more high-pitched noises and theatrical eye-dabbing, I told him that my goal was to stand on stage with a band and play in front of an audience marginally larger than the one next door.

Silence. Not even a stifled snigger. Pastor just smiled, patted me on the shoulder and said, 'Okay, can we go for a beer now?' I took that as a green light – for giving me lessons, if not for my ambitious stage plans. He suggested his regular drinking haunt, and we walked across the road to a little peso-paying place called La Cocinita. There was a thick red rope across the door and a man in an old Goodyear mechanic's shirt theatrically unclipped it to let us in. Quite why such a door policy was necessary was unclear. It was just a shabby little place full of Cubans eating fried chicken, with a bar at one end serving the local Hatuey beer for 10 pesos a bottle. Maybe the rope was to keep the foreigners out.

Pastor seemed to know everyone inside La Cocinita and it took a lot of '*Hola compays*' and '*Qué bola aceres?*' before we could sit down. The Santiaguero style of greeting took some getting used to. '*Compay*', the abbreviated version of *compañero*, was the standard male-to-male salute, although to fit in on the street you really needed to master the Afro-Cuban '*Qué bola acere?*' a rapidly spoken refrain ('How's it going, mate?') that foreigners – like myself – found almost impossible to deliver with either accurate pronunciation or conviction. Draining half his beer in a couple of greedy gulps, Pastor dug out a scrap of paper from his bag and scribbled down an address and a map. He told me we would begin tomorrow and that his fees would start at 10 dollars per lesson, reducing to 8 dollars after the first week and 5 dollars after the first month. A little confused by this unusual price system, I interrupted to ask why there wasn't just a fixed rate. His answer was typically Cuban in its logic. 'The more lessons you have, the cheaper it gets – I'll be happy because you're having lots of lessons, you'll be happy because they cost less.' I begrudgingly admitted it did have a certain rationale. He said that if I was prepared to work hard and submerge myself in Cuban music there was no reason why I couldn't play in the Casa de la Trova before my year was up. Then, having let this triumphant blue-suited image dangle in front of me for a few seconds, he abruptly reined in the fantasy with a big balloon-bursting 'but'. 'But of course a lot will depend on whether you've got *la bomba*.'

'*La bomba*?'

'Yes, *la bomba*.'

'What's *la bomba*?'

'It's what you've got inside here,' he said, prodding his finger at my chest. And with that, he drained the rest of his beer, stuck another filterless *Negro Puro* cigarette between his lips, and with a shake of my hand and a cheery '*Hasta mañana, compay!*', he was off and out the door.

Putting Pastor's instructions safely in my wallet, I returned to my beer and sat and listened to the house band. A quartet was playing something I recognized from a Cuban compilation tape I had bought recently. Even though I couldn't fully understand the meaning of the lyrics, the song and the performance had a powerful effect. It was just four men lined up along one wall of a dingy bar, four men with a violin that was missing a string, a beat-up guitar, a set of cheap bongos and some maracas. And yet (I admit the combination of beer and my being alone might have aided them slightly), they were managing to bring goose bumps to my skin. Here was a simple lesson in the fine art of Cuban *son*, and the foreign student at the front was totally transfixed.

No one knows exactly where and when the first notes of *son* were struck, but most people agree that it grew up in the isolated rural settlements of this mountainous Eastern corner of Cuba sometime during the nineteenth century.

It was the local *campesinos* of this area, the *guajiros* as they were known, who started it all off when they began playing homemade instruments at family get-togethers known as *gateques*. According to Cuban writer and music historian Helio Orevio, the term *son* not only referred to music but also to dancing, partying and a general atmosphere. *Son* was a social thing. It was how you let your hair down in the mountains.

The earliest Cuban *soneros* would have sat down with a bottle of rum and some imported *bacalao* (the first *tres* guitars were made from the boxes the salted cod was packed in) and sung songs about rural life. Originally, the only three instruments were the *tres*, bongos and *guiro*, the latter being a hollowed-out dried gourd with grooves cut into the side – a sort of vegetable scraper. A short while later, an early form of bass instrument arrived. It was called the *botija* or *botijuela*. Someone discovered that if you made a hole in the side of one of the empty clay containers used to bring olives over from Spain, and blew into it, you could make a resonant, low-pitched tone. The pitch could then be adjusted by moving your hand in or out of the mouth of the jar. These earliest bass lines would have been nothing more than a repeating two-note pulse, and had I been undertaking my musical quest in the 1860s, I could have been playing with a band as soon as I'd finished a jar of olives. No sore fingers, no worries about scales, just plenty of puff and a few well-timed burps from eating too much.

The next bass instrument was a bit trickier to play. The *marimbula*, sometimes known as a thumb piano, was a slave instrument brought over from the Congo. It was nothing more than a hollow wooden box with a line of metal tongs down one side. The player sat on the box – in my book any instrument that doubles as a seat should be applauded – and plucked the different-toned tongs while also striking a percussive beat on the side of the box.

Son perfectly encapsulated the island's rich blend of cultures. Not only did it fuse African instruments (the bongo and *marimbula*) with Spanish imports (the guitar) and Cuban inventions (the *clave, guiro* and *tres*), it also cleverly interwove African rhythms and call-and-response-style vocals with Spanish *decimas* (ten-line verses). On paper, this music of the mountains looked like the perfect ambassador for cross-cultural harmony. Out on the street, it struggled to break through the racist barriers that segregated the country in the early 1900s.

Perceived by the ruling elite as being Negro music, *son*'s early forays out of its Eastern homeland were not well received by the largely white authorities in Havana. Playing permission was rarely granted to *son* performers, and illegal *son* parties were initially the only places where you could hear it in the capital. Eventually, though, its popularity couldn't be stifled any longer. Like the double bass, a musical Trojan Horse that had helped black Cuban players get into white dances because of the instrument's association with classical 'white' music, *son* managed to achieve the same goal simply off the back of its unstoppable musical appeal. People of all races loved its lyrical inventiveness as well as its very danceable rhythm.

Often, *son* was used as a form of Speakers' Corner. It lived off improvisation, and by using the rich Cuban language that ran parallel to Castilian Spanish, songwriters managed to vent political sentiments, often without the Spanish authorities even twigging they were being made fun of. More often, though, it was simply a means of observing and celebrating Cuban life. You might hear a song about the sweet *guarapo* (cane juice) that the *macheteros* drank at harvest-time, about the beautiful Indian-faced women of Bayamo, or even something as mundane as trying to find your trousers when you wanted to go out. One of Miguel Matamoros's many *son* compositions was a song called 'Mi Ropa', all about the annoyance of having his favourite clothes ironed just when he wanted to wear them.

Without doubt one of the most prolific and talented songwriters ever to come out of Santiago – he wrote over 200 songs – Miguel Matamoros helped put *son* on the world music map. Born on 8 May 1894 in Calle San Herman, Matamoros began playing the guitar at the age of eight. By the time he was fifteen, he was so good that bands were asking him to play with them. The music didn't pay much so Matamoros had to fit it in between other jobs. He was a telephone line repairman, a miner, a carpenter, and, for while, a labourer on Facundo Bacardi's country estate. One year he was 11,000 feet underground digging out copper in the famous mines at El Cobre, the next he was working on the bottling line at the rum distillery. In his spare time he played in a group called the Trio Oriental, joining the rich baritone voice of Siro Rodriguez – a black-smith who helped make the iron crosses that still sat on top of Santiago's cathedral – and the talented guitar and *tres* player Rafael Cueto. Cueto had joined the trio by chance when the regular guitar player, Alfonso de Rio, failed to make it to a concert in Havana. Such was the sublime combination of three perfectly matched voices, catchy guitar chords and extraordinary songwriting talent that discovery by a major label was inevitable. Playing at the Teatro Aguilera in Santiago one night, they were spotted by an A&R man for the American record label RCA Victor, who immediately signed them up and took them to Camden, New Jersey to record their first album. At the time, Matamoros was working as a chauffeur for a business-man called Bartolome Rodriguez, and without telling him anything, he simply took extra holiday leave and headed off for the biggest two weeks of his life. The day after he returned, he was back behind the wheel as if nothing had happened.

About three months later, Miguel was driving the boss to work, and as always the route took them past a famous record shop called La Dichosa – The Fortunate One. On that particular day there was a large queue outside the store.

'Go and see what's happening,' said Rodriguez to his driver, so Matamoros left the car, chatted to someone in the line, then came back to the car window and relayed the news that a new American release had arrived at the store. Rodriguez got out his wallet and passing Matamoros enough money to bribe his way past the queue, told him to go and buy a copy. The new arrival was, of course, none other than the New Jersey recordings made by Matamoros and his Santiago trio, and the next morning the amazed businessman presented his moonlighting driver with a letter of redundancy and a cheque for 100 pesos. 'I don't think you'll be needing to drive me around any more,' were his parting words.

That was the start of a hugely successful musical career with the trio eventually expanding into a larger *septeto* format. They toured extensively and their combinations of traditional *son* with *boleros* and *trovas* found a huge market throughout Latin America. On 10 May 1960, they gave their last performance on a TV show called *Jueves de Partagas*. The first time the three of them had played together was 8 May 1925 – at Matamoros' thirty-first birthday party – so they'd stuck together for an amazing thirty-five years. Even in death, they had an uncanny sense of timing. Miguel died in 1971, Siro in 1981, and Rafael in 1991.

The retirement of Trio Matamoros didn't mean the end of *son* but it did mark a steady decline in its popularity and expo-sure outside Cuba. For most of the latter half of the twentieth century *son* remained isolated on the island, heard only by adventurous travellers or people with very old eclectic record collections. Then, in 1996, the British producer Nick Gold came to Cuba on a quest to fuse traditional Cuban *son* with guitar music from West Africa. With the help of Juan de Marcos Gonzalez, founder of the *son* revival group, Sierra Maestra, he gathered together some of the best old Cuban *soneros* from the 1950s, while at the same time organizing for a group of Malian musicians to come to Havana to provide the African half of the fusion. As fate would have it, the Malians lost their pass-ports when applying for Cuban visas, and with studio time already booked, Gold, de Marcos and American collaborator Ry Cooder decided to go ahead and record a bunch of classic songs with the Cubans who had already turned up. The Buena Vista Social Club – the name came from an extinct dancing club in the Havana suburb of Buena Vista – became the sur-prise hit of 1997 and went on to win a Grammy in 1998. Word of mouth, good marketing, and the effect of the Wim Wenders documentary helped sell millions of copies of the first CD and subsequent spin-offs. BVSC didn't just put Cuban *son* back on the map, it put Cuba back on the tourist map too. Thousands of people booked holidays on the back of those grainy shots of lovable crooners singing into old-fashioned microphones, and rusty old motorbikes with sidecars weaving in and out of the potholes.

Most Cubans I spoke to seemed fairly ambivalent towards the Buena Vista phenomenon. The first record had only been released in Cuba a year before I arrived and most local musicians who knew about the success of Ibrahim Ferrer, Compay Segundo, Ruben Gonzalez *et al.* seemed to find it amusing that a type of music that had never gone out of fashion in Cuba, music that had been around for two centuries, had suddenly been put on a pedestal by the world's music critics. On the subject of the film – which many Cubans hadn't seen yet – they generally had two comments to make. One, they said it wrongly portrayed Cuba as a very sad, melancholic place (which it most certainly wasn't) and two, they (the Santiagueros) found it mildly irritating that a documentary about *son* and *soneros* contained absolutely no footage of the part of the country where it all came from.

The odd grumble aside, there appeared to be very little envy or bitterness directed towards those lucky few musicians who had been plucked out of obscurity and handed fame and fortune. On one of my first days in Santiago, I spotted Eliades Ochoa, the cowboy hat-wearing guitarist from Buena Vista, stepping out of an old Lada near the Casa de la Trova and chatting happily to a bunch of people outside. According to a musician I spoke to a few minutes later, Ochoa hadn't changed a bit, and local people respected the fact that this hugely talented musician, after years of playing every night in this humble Santiago venue, had finally managed to hit the big time. More than anything, though, they loved the fact that Ochoa (now a very rich man with his own recording studio in his house) had not deserted his roots. He still lived in the city and he still walked the streets and chatted to his old friends as if nothing had changed. And he was even using some of his newly acquired wealth to help his fellow musicians. The upcoming Festival of Trova, an annual event that showcased the best *trovadores* from around the country, was being directed and partly funded by Ochoa.

The morning after my meeting with Pastor, thoughts of learning to play *son* were briefly put to one side as a more pressing concern took precedence; getting to Pastor's house without becoming the latest road-kill statistic. Even after only a couple of trips on the bike I had concluded that a two-wheeled journey across Santiago was more life-threatening than flying Cubana on Friday 13th. The two main stationary hazards were the potholes – some deep and old enough to support whole ecosystems in their dark depths – and the slippery stretches of disused tramlines that had to be crossed at a particular angle to avoid an uncontrollable skid. Among the mobile dangers there were motorbikes that turned their engines off on downhill sections, thus turning themselves into inaudible kamikazes, dogs that took territorial behaviour to new bike-chasing, ankle-gnawing levels of doggedness, trolley pushers setting up impromptu trading stalls willy-nilly, and pedestrians with a blithe disregard for pavements. If one or all of those didn't get you, then the diesel fumes certainly would.

Pastor lived in Chicharrones, and as you'd expect from a neighbourhood named after crispy bits of pig skin, it was considered to be one of the less safe *barrios* for a foreigner to visit. Tania's worried expression gave the impression I was heading straight into Santiago's Bronx wearing a 'Vote for Bush' baseball cap. The ride to Chicharrones (or Crackling as it became known) was an uphill, sweaty killer that required a humiliating dismount on a steep section going past the main children's hospital. Watching other bicycle riders whizz past me, I could see I was approaching the challenge with completely the wrong game plan. Exhibiting cheery disregard for hospital entrance etiquette, young boys on gearless Chinese bikes were taking on the slope Cubano-style, hanging on to the back of trucks with one outstretched arm attached to the bumper, the other trying to balance their now high-velocity Oriental imports.

It was probably only a couple of kilometres as the vulture glides, but Chicharrones felt and looked like another world. Most of the houses were simple concrete affairs with metal slats for shutters and corrugated iron roofs held down with stones and other bits of urban flotsam. As I cycled past, people stared at me in a way that suggested tourist sightings were rare, an assumption backed up by the complete absence of police in the neighbourhood. There were virtually no cars on the roads, which was just as well because they didn't appear to have been designed or maintained with cars in mind. Pastor's street was so steep that even with both brakes fully engaged, I had to descend in criss-cross skier fashion to avoid over-running and having a nasty accident at the T-junction at the bottom.

Pastor's was by far the best house in the block, possibly in the entire neighbourhood. For a start it had been painted – a sure sign of incoming dollars – and with its bright white coat and large first-floor terrace (a luxurious waste of space for a Cuban) it stood out like a proud, neat castle in a scene of jerry-built chaos. Outside the neighbouring house, two men were methodically cutting up plastic containers into tiny pieces using a sort of homemade hand-held chomping device. They kept a steady metronome pace and didn't bother looking up as I walked past.

I followed Pastor's instructions and climbed up the stairs to the first floor. The door was ajar and when I knocked a voice in a back room shouted for me to come in. It took a minute to adjust to the volume of the living room. Floor-to-ceiling nylon curtains lined every wall, the floral pattern so disdainfully loud it actually seemed to shimmer if you stared hard enough. From a large plastic gravel-filled urn sprouted a bright bunch of fake roses, petals speckled with impressively realistic plastic water droplets. Two large ceramic elephant piggybanks – one labelled P, the other R, both with large money-excavating holes in their heads – stood on guard next to an artificial Christmas tree seven months past its put-away date. There were a couple of rocking chairs, a large TV and a hi-fi system whose digital display was flashing out a dazzling exhibition of 'Look at me' showmanship. Not content with the standard level of wattage, Pastor had surrounded the original machine with other speakers of varying shapes and sizes, some tipped on their sides to fit into the jigsaw. The table it was on bowed ominously beneath the weight. I was nosily checking out the many photos of Pastor in man-with-bass poses when he padded through wearing nothing but shorts and a pair of flip-flops. 'You Englishmen really are punctual,' he announced as the clock on the wall whirred into action with an impressive electrical chime routine. He waited patiently for the last of ten metallic bongs to finish and then asked whether I'd like coffee. I said yes.

'*Cubano o Inglés?*'

'What's the difference?'

'One has a lot of sugar, the other not so much.'

'*Inglés* will be fine.'

'What are those guys doing outside?' I called while check-ing out Pastor's double bass.

'The ones breaking up plastic?'

'Yeah.'

'They're recycling. They collect old plastic crates, chop them up, melt it down, and turn it into beer mugs. You should have seen them before carnival. They had three guys out there full time.'

Walking back into the living room, he handed me a small glass filled with very dark coffee. One sip confirmed that *Inglés* had been the right choice. It was shockingly sweet.

'First I want to show you something,' Pastor said, slotting a video into one of two machines. He pressed the remote control but nothing but a thin white line appeared across the centre of the screen. Cursing quietly, he gave the top of the TV a couple of unhealthily hard slaps and on the second thump a picture miraculously appeared.

The video was a recording of a party in someone's back

yard. A beaming Pastor suddenly appeared in the picture and shouted something unintelligible, perhaps a suggestion that the cameraman stopped zooming in on his wife's bottom. Fastforwarding the tape, he stopped at a point where a group of foreigners arrived at the house.

'These are my Dutch friends – they have a part-time band in Holland,' chirped Pastor. 'Bass, bongos, guitar, *clave*, maracas – I taught them everything.'

I had an ominous premonition about what was coming next and sure enough, a few more forward skips and we were watching the five Dutchmen – each now holding a different instrument – breaking into the first bars of 'Chan Chan'. I stifled a groan, partly in reaction to the song they had chosen ('Chan Chan' overload was taking hold), but more because they sounded annoyingly good. I now knew what Scott must have felt like when he finally arrived at the Pole only to discover a flag in the ground and piss marks in the snow. I'd come all this way – sacrificed a career, invested in a bespoke suit, travelled thousands of miles – only to find I'd been pipped to the post by a bunch of cocky-looking holidaymakers from a country whose contribution to world music could be written on a Rizla paper. It was a devastating blow. All dreams of seeing a 'Pastor's Plucky Pepe' headline in the local newspaper had just been crushed. The damned Dutch had beaten me to it.

Perhaps sensing the slight cloud of despondency now hanging over his new student, Pastor stopped the tape and with an encouraging slap on the back confided that I could definitely play better than the bassist I had just seen.

'He had big problems with Cuban rhythm,' he confessed with a conspiratorial grin, 'he didn't have *la bomba*.' I wasn't sure whether this was meant to be a source of encouragement or just a subtle hint that many lessons would be required.

Talking of which, the first one began in somewhat unconventional fashion with me scampering around Pastor's roof in search of bricks. The logistics of bass transportation meant that

I had left HP at home and was faced with undertaking lesson one on a strange Russian piece of pine with no end pin. This wouldn't have been a problem if I'd been a man of Pastor's 5-foot 11-inch stature – his eye-line measured up perfectly to the top of the fingerboard – but being some four inches taller, I was forced to elevate my new partner with some unused construction material. Not a textbook method of learning to play, but one that with suitable spin I knew could be used to impress audiences in years to come. 'Neill learned bass the hard way, propping his instrument up on loose bricks.'

Content that the top of the fingerboard was now at his student's eye-line rather than shoulder-line, Pastor suddenly disappeared into the kitchen and after much rummaging around, returned with a large chopping knife. 'Show me your left-hand position,' he demanded, gently tapping the blade against the side of his bare leg. This definitely wasn't in the Barry Green book.

Placing the tip of my thumb on the back of the fingerboard, I curved my hand round so that the four fingers came to rest on the G-string. 'That okay?' I asked nervously. '*Más o menos*,' came the answer. Or rather, '*Maomeno*' since Pastor's version of 'more or less' came out stripped of its S's and blurred into a single word that sounded more Chinese than Spanish. 'More or less' seemed to be the standard judgement of quality in Pastorland. Everything I did in subsequent weeks and months was, infuriatingly, '*más o menos*', no matter how well executed. Repositioning my hand a little, he then took the knife and placed it at the top of the fingerboard with the blade flat against the wood and the sharp edge pointing down.

'I don't ever want to see that thumb poking around this side – if it comes round, this is what will happen.' He slid the knife down the side of the bass, guillotine fashion. 'Thumb comes round, thumb goes,' he repeated, the melodramatic threat being somewhat weakened by the fact that the executioner's wrist was modelling a rather elegant woman's watch.

'Nice watch,' I said.

'It's Rosalina's.'

'Rosalina?'

'My wife, Rosalina.'

'Do you always wear her watch?'

'No, I'm just borrowing it while . . . look, can we get back to the lesson please?'

'Sure.'

The thumb of the left hand, he demonstrated, should slide up and down an imaginary middle line but without exerting any pressure. Illogical as it sounded, he assured me that a bass player should still be able to play notes even if thumbless; an encouraging thought, given my almost certain confrontation with the knife, but one that sniffed just a little of teacher exaggeration. A quick demo by Pastor sadly proved otherwise.

With the knife still at the ready, he then asked me to play a few notes with my right hand. The technique I had developed over the course of my early trials in London involved twanging the strings (perhaps not the right technical term but definitely an accurate description of what I was doing), using my index and middle fingers pinned together as one. Said digits were angled downwards so that they were almost parallel with the strings. 'Where did you learn that?' queried an impressed-looking Pastor. At last, I was doing something right.

'From people I've seen playing double bass in jazz bands,' I said, chuffed to have at least copied something correctly.

'Well, forget jazz and get rid of that habit.'

He told me to imagine I was holding a baseball in my right hand and then to transfer that hand position to the bass.

'Use two fingers and imagine those fingers are walking across the strings. Friction not traction is what you're looking for.' I gave it a go and as expected, '*Más o menos* – More or less' was the judge's verdict.

If all this was being made into a Buena Vista-style documentary, now would be the time the director skipped through

the rest of the morning with a cleverly cut humorous montage of shots showing student and teacher running the gamut
of first-lesson emotions. There'd be Neill repeatedly trying to
achieve the balanced playing position, Neill failing repeatedly,
Neill nearly losing his head on Pastor's Pastor-height ceiling
fan, Pastor with head in hands, Pastor chewing bottom lip,
Pastor desperately looking for more fags, and Neill doing very
silly finger movements while he was in another room looking
for them. Finally, it would end with a weary student returning
his bricks to the roof and – thanks to the wrong choice of
door – coming face to face with a hideous four-legged bald
creature tethered to a chain.

The roof beast looked at me with what was either a lopsided friendly grin or a pre-lunge maniacal sneer and, preferring emotional ambiguity to grievous injury, I carefully backed
away, muttering 'Nice doggy' until I was safely out of the chain's
reach.

'What the hell is that up there?' I asked Pastor when I arrived
back downstairs.

'It's a Dobermann,' he replied, sweeping the remnants of
brick dust into a neat pile.

'Yes, but what happened to it?'

I should point out that the hound formally known as a
Dobermann was almost completely hairless, its skin looked dis-
coloured and scabrous, and the faraway look in its eyes hinted
at some terrible encounter in the recent past. 'I fed her some
cakes about a month ago and all her hair fell out,' came the
slightly embarrassed reply.

This should have been a good enough warning to treat all
consumable offerings in the Panes household with the utmost
suspicion and, when Pastor offered me an end-of-first-lesson
drink I did try to back out honourably. Honest. But courtesy
prevailed over common sense. 'What is it?' I asked as an
unmarked bottle of clear liquid was brought out of the kitchen.
'Something strong,' came the reply, followed by a suggestion

(well, more a command actually) to add some water. 'Jesus, Pastor,' I spluttered after swallowing what I imagine Siberian truck drivers lubricated their engines with, 'what is that?' The back of my throat felt like it was melting. 'Neat alcohol,' came the equally hoarse response.

Placing your faith in a man who feeds cakes to animals – a man whose very name worryingly suggests both shepherding and baking skills – might be considered a bit of a gamble. But when you also know he keeps a Christmas tree up all year, feels perfectly comfortable wearing women's watches, uses a carving knife as a teaching accessory, and drinks antifreeze to relax, you've got to have really lost grip of your senses. I cycled home distracted by thoughts of basses on bricks, thumbs in jars, and Pastor at home rummaging around in his wife's wardrobe, but happy in the knowledge that music lessons were not going to be boring.

7. Finger Boot Camp

It took less than a week with Pastor before I was cursing Jeff and his stupid 'forgiving instrument' comment. From very early on it was clear that brawn rather than brain was the key to taming the beast and that only someone with a gift for irony could put the motto 'merciful and mild' on their double bass case.

Fingers. Suddenly, fingers became the most important part of my body. Physically under-prepared after years of lounging around, my soft-tipped digits understandably reacted strongly to the new challenges they were being set. The left-hand note-selecting set had the worst deal. Required to perform a sort of circus low-wire act, employing muscles that had been wasting away for years, they illustrated their grievance with sore red tips (at best) and weeping blisters (at worst). The little finger in particular − a non-essential protrusion in normal life but an indispensable workhorse in bass playing − took a hell of a beating in the first few days, its motor-neurones sending a constant stream of 'Ow!' messages to the brain, which in turn sent back apologetic missives saying, 'Sorry, but the guy in the black cap says you've got to keep going.' On the right hand, meanwhile, the response to my 'friction not traction' antics was equally livid.

Informed by Pastor that wearing plasters was not an option, I hurriedly sought advice from all quarters on how the tough-ening-up process could be accelerated. Rubbing the fingers with walnuts (fine, but there were no walnuts around), soaking them in a mixture of neat alcohol and lime juice, and scrubbing them with coconut husks were three of the more believable remedies. Bathing them in my own urine, suggested by a bassist whose hand I no longer wished to shake, was one I chose to ignore. In the end, I went for the most widely recommended suggestion and sat down every evening with my fingertips submerged in a bowl of vinegar. Well, all except the two with open wounds – I'm not that hard. If they had needed any further convincing that their new lodger was not quite of the normal sunbathing and salsa mould, young Tanita and Liana now had all the evidence required for a full playground announcement.

On the second week of my daily visits to the White House (Pastor beamed with pride at my references to Crackling's Casa Blanca) I made two new discoveries. One was Rosalina, the watchless, painfully shy wife, who emerged unannounced from the bedroom one afternoon.

Rosalina worked as the catering coordinator at one of the main hospitals and when not organizing goat stew and plantains for 200, she was flat out on her bed watching soap operas, or *telenovelas* as they are called. I soon learned that Cubans are avid soap opera fans – even Fidel would not dare to interrupt a *telenovela* for politics – and to feed the insatiable demand, a black-market rental system was on hand to supplement the offerings on Cuban TV with cassettes of recorded Latin American soaps. Rosalina habitually did six episodes in a sitting and, apart from meal stops, would probably only press the stop button for life-threatening distractions like a burning house or an approaching hurricane. She was so hooked that Pastor was forced to maintain a precautionary stockpile of tapes just in case supply got cut off. A *telenovela* junkie going cold turkey was, he informed me, not a pretty sight.

The second discovery was that building work had started on the west wing (the main bedroom), and it didn't take great powers of deduction to connect the arrival of cement and gravel with the recent matriculation of a new bass student. I wasn't just learning to play double bass, I realized, now I was also the main financial backer for the new White House extension. Privy to Pastor's plans to increase the size of the sleeping quarters, add a new dining area and sort out a roof for a chicken pen upstairs, I didn't know whether to be aghast at his presumptuousness or full of admiration for his level of ambition. Initially I settled for a bit of both, but the more I got to know the man – from his dedication to his instrument to his indestructible glass–half–full approach to life – the more my respect and affection outweighed any nagging donor discomfort. While Pastor's house was a relatively new addition to Calle 3 ('between 2 and 4', said his helpful instruction on my scribbled map), my teacher's entire forty-two years had been spent living on the site where it stood. He was a Crackling man through and through. After his mother had abandoned the family at an early age he'd grown up with his four brothers and three sisters, all of them raised by a variety of aunts, cousins and grandparents. In all there were twenty of them living under one roof. Pastor followed his father into the army, becoming an engineer with specialist knowledge in the running and repair of WW2 Russian tanks (a definite trump card in the 'What did you do before bass?' game) and occasionally breaking from his studies to play electric bass with a military band. One year of his active service was spent in charge of the maintenance of a tank division outside Guantanamo Naval Base, a posting, he claimed, that provided him with little action but plenty of time to practise scales. It wasn't until his early thirties, though, that he decided to become a full-time musician. Fed up with his post-army job in one of the Santiago bus terminals, he said goodbye to oil-stained fingers and Eastern European hunks of metal and hello to calloused fingers and Eastern European hunks of wood. He put in hours of practice, got a job in a traditional *son*-playing *septeto*, and like all Cuban musicians, supplemented his meagre monthly state salary (410 pesos = 17 dollars) selling CDs, giving lessons, and generally *luchando*. In Cuba, the term '*luchando*' ('struggling') seemed to be used as much to describe the state you were in as the extra-curricular activities required to maintain it.

Pastor's big financial break – the one that funded the White House – was a six-month tour to Europe with a band called Mi Son. Each band member was on a contract of 40 dollars a day, and unlike some of his travel companions, the double bass player had switched off from all the retail temptations around him and set about raising his house-building target. Holed up in various apartments, eating cheap kebabs and playing computer games, he only ventured out for gigs and late-night sorties to retrieve discarded electrical goods from skips. 'I mended six TVs and three videos during our time in Paris,' claimed a proud Pastor. When I asked him what had impressed him most about Europe – the architecture, the culture, the beautiful landscapes? – he thought about it for a few seconds and then his eyes lit up as his favourite highlight sprang to mind. 'The motorway signs,' he replied with a gaze of dreamy reminiscence. 'In Cuba you can drive from Havana to Santiago and hardly find a single sign, but in Europe you have so much information. Distances, speed limits, fuel stops, traffic reports – it was amazing.' Given his other eccentricities, this admission wasn't really so bizarre.

If I still had any doubts about Pastor's commitment to my cause, they disappeared the afternoon when, in yet another unexpected deviation from the *How to Teach Double Bass* manual, he insisted I watched a martial arts film with him. 'This is one of the greatest kung-fu films ever made,' he declared, giving the top of the TV its necessary activation thump. Faced with a choice of suffering torture or watching torture, you can probably understand why I temporarily stashed away my normally lukewarm reaction to badly dubbed kick-fests and eagerly pulled up a rocking chair to watch *The Thirty-six Chambers of Shaolin*. The film was all about a young student having to pass a series of physical and mental challenges before he could rightly claim to be a real fighting monk. Each task had to be completed before the novice could pass on to the next figurative chamber. To get across a water pool, for example, he had to master the art of stepping from one floating log to another. To improve his strength, he was ordered to carry buckets of water with arms outstretched and knives attached to his elbows. If the arms dropped, he punctured himself on both sides. Swap the words fighting monk with double bassist, and replace knives attached to arms with knives held by teacher, and you can see that reality was blurring ominously with TV entertainment. Obviously, the wise old monk character in the film didn't chain-smoke or keep a hairless Dobermann in the attic, but he did have an uncannily similar habit of chuckling when his student screwed up. Corny as it was – both the film and its use by Pastor as a parable for musical advancement – there were a lot of uncomfortable similarities between the mind-numbingly repetitive exercises the kung-fu student was being asked to perform and the equally soul-destroying, utterly tedious assignments handed out by Pastor. Finger-strengthening and note-learning were my chambers one and two, and as my mentor conjured up yet another finger-pressing routine – up and down and across the four strings in a bewildering choreography of painful moves – I couldn't help but remember a scene from another famous martial arts movie. 'Left hand polish on, right hand polish off,' will be a familiar piece of dialogue to all those who have endured one too many viewings of *The Karate Kid*, and although I hadn't yet been asked to clean the White House floors, I was definitely at that same grim-faced 'What's this all in aid of?' stage of learning.

In conjunction with my involuntary enrolment at finger-boot camp, I was also signed on to the next stage of the Panes programme for perfect hand and finger positioning – the first stage being the knife-enforced thumb rule. I'm afraid a little music theory is required at this point but I promise to make it brief.

Imagine you're sitting in front of the keyboard of a piano and (assuming it isn't a Cuban one and therefore missing keys) you should be able to identify a line of white notes interspersed with groups of two and three black notes. The black notes take their names from the white notes adjacent to them. If a black note sits to the right of the white note it is a sharp version of the white note, and if to the left it is a flat version. So if the white note you chose was C, the black note to its right would be called C sharp or D flat. The distance in pitch between any note and its nearest neighbour (black or white) is called a semitone. And if that all sounds complete gobbledegook you should try taking it all on board in Spanish – Cuban Spanish.

Okay, so now try to imagine you want to play a note on the piano and then go up the scale another two semitones. Assuming the note you wanted to start with was somewhere on the left-hand side of the keyboard, you'd probably play the first note with your little finger, and with no effort or change in facial expression, use the next two fingers along to play the next two notes. Even someone with hands as small as Mini-Me would be able to make a stab at it.

Now let's go and try playing across three semitones on a double bass, starting with, say, G sharp (the top note on the G-string), followed by A and B flat. Pressing down your index finger of the left hand on G sharp, you would then need to stretch out your fingers – and I'm talking a rope-assisted Pilates-style stretch here – so that your middle finger can reach A and your little finger B flat. Unlike the piano, spanning a three-semitone divide on the double bass requires big hands, a pre-attempt warm-up, and a tension-building drum roll before executing the leap of faith. And then, assuming you've managed to get your hand into this ridiculous position – the thin membrane of skin between your fingers webbed out to its tightest limit – you've got to press down hard enough to get a clear note. Try doing this for an hour and you'll soon understand why there aren't many child prodigies in the double bass club. Or, for that matter, many prodigies, full stop.

'Good left-hand technique is everything,' said Pastor earnestly after showing how his small hand managed to achieve what my large hand couldn't. 'The day you play on stage, the first thing any musicians in the audience will look at is your left hand. They'll be able to tell just from the position of that hand how well you've been taught and how much work you've put in.' Well, that was a comforting thought. At least there were two reputations on the line, not just one.

Frankly, as it stood right now, I would have happily swapped striking the right pose just for an ability to strike the right notes. I looked at the fingerboard — neck craned round in a position that threatened to add a new type of player injury to an already long list of possibilities — with all the familiarity of an unmarked stretch of Cuba's main motorway. Somewhere along that scary expanse of track, there were notes to be found. Or perhaps, more accurately, there were lots of nearly-notes to be stumbled upon.

Bloated from years of wine trivia, my memory took to the note-retrieval challenge with all the sharpness of a wet sponge. There were four strings tuned in fourths (G-D-A-E) and from the top of the fingerboard down to — well, in theory down to where it stops, but in my case down to as far as Pastor thought was realistic, you could draw imaginary perpendicular dividing lines to show where the notes lay. Or you could forget imagination and just shove on the same little pieces of marker tape that Jennifer had resorted to. Okay, so you've got your embarrassing cheat's ladder — the distance between the rungs getting smaller as you descend the strings — and you know, because Pastor has told you, that at each level down the fingerboard you go up a semi-tone. That means, from the top rung to the twelfth rung of your ladder, you've got twelve possible notes you can play (thirteen if you include the open string). Bring in the other three strings — sadly necessary — and you've got forty-eight possible notes (fifty-two with the open strings). You could descend another twelve tightly spaced rungs (another forty-eight notes) and add endless harmonic possibilities to take you well over 100 notes, but then you could also become really depressed and saw off half the fingerboard and use it to beat up your teacher.

Fifty-two notes. One for every week of the year – hey, this wasn't looking so bad, was it?

'Play me *Sol sostenido*,' said Pastor, on our first day of note testing.

'*Qué?*' I responded, employing a tone and gormless grin that Basil Fawlty would have recognized.

'*Sol sostenido*, it's the note that sits between *Sol* and *La*,' he directed, revealing far more patience than the famous hotel manager. Oh dear, oh dear. What little of Mr Freeman's hard work had survived the twenty-odd years in the musical broom cupboard, none of it contained any mention of *Sol* or *La*. I, like most Englishmen who grew up to the sound of Julie Andrews yodelling across Alpine pastures, knew perfectly well that *Do* was a deer (a female deer) and that *Re* was a drop of golden sun. But ask me how *Do*, *Re*, *Mi*, *Fa*, *Sol*, *La*, *Ti* matched up to A, B, C, D, E, F, G and the hills were alive with the sound of silence.

Agreeing, more for his sanity than mine, to stick temporarily to the familiar, Pastor laboriously went through each of the notes going up the fingerboard (confusingly, 'up' referred to the musical not physical direction you were heading, which of course was down – more silent muttering) and then back down (or rather up) again. He then divulged a few tricks or '*picardias*', as he called them, that he said would help me steer through the minefield. *Picardia* number one. If you knew one note, you could quickly work out its adjacent partner on the next string along thanks to the fact the bass was tuned in fourths. If you were heading from Damned across to God (Jennifer's G-string – if you get my drift), for example, the adjacent note would be three letters up (so next to G on the D-string was C on the G-string) and if you were heading the other way (from Damned towards African) then it would be three letters down. Are you still with me?

His other tips were a little easier to grasp. If you had one note and wanted to find the same note an octave above, you just went down two semitones and across two strings. If you went down five semitones and across a string in the other direction, you would also find the same note. Even scales could be remembered by the recurring pattern of note positions. I then got into the spirit of Pastor's wily methodology by adding my own *picardias*. If I slid my fingers down to the square piece of wood that Peter Tyler had pegged into the fingerboard I knew I would find a line of notes that spelt out BEAD. Such tactics would doubtless have been frowned upon in any music school but in my position – a mature student with a keenness to move quickly – I was more than happy to bypass the Queensberry Rules and scrap it out with whatever stratagem brought results. Armed with these various route-finders and tested every day by Pastor – him shouting out a number between one and twelve, me attempting to give him the notes at that position in less than five seconds – the once blank fingerboard slowly became filled in with sharp Fs, flat Es, natural Bs and a motley collection of strange, memory-triggering phrases like Does God Clean Fingernails (tenth position) and Gallic Cows Fart Ballistically (third position). I was on my way, perhaps unconventionally, but on the way none the less, towards Chamber Three.

If Pastor was my font of knowledge and daily motivation and Ernesto my source of youthful stimulus, then it was an old double bassist called Roberto Napoli who provided the all-important inspiration and will to keep going. Whenever I got really hacked off with my sluggish progress (about as often as I got an electric tingle in the shower), and whenever I needed a reminder that thirty-five wasn't really that old to start learning a musical instrument, all I had to do was go and watch Napoli play and the grumbles were forced to recede. I first saw him at the Casa de los Dos Abuelos (The House of the Two Grandfathers), a small music venue on my favourite square in the city, the Plaza de Marte. Like the Casa de la Trova, its discriminatory dollar-only door policy (a form of financial apartheid that meant ordinary Cubans had nowhere to go and listen to their own music) left it feeling like a musical zoo for tourists. The Cubans on stage ploughed out their usual medley of hits, the foreigners listened politely, and outside in the Plaza de Marte, bored young Cubans filled in yet another evening doing nothing.

Napoli played in a band called Estudiantina Invasora, and while the current line-up might have stretched the definition of student invasion to its most post-post-grad level of maturity, they still prodded backside, or whatever the oldies' equivalent of kick-arse was. By now I had begun to suffer from what I assumed must be an early sign of Carpal Tunnel Syndrome, one of the musical injuries I'd read about on Bob Gollihur's site. Whenever I went to watch a band, I entered into a sort of bass-locked trance, zooming in on the only instrument I was interested in and completely blanking out the other players and indeed anyone unlucky enough to have joined me for the evening. On this particular occasion, my tip-seeking eye had honed in on a man with some notable qualities. For a start, he looked at least a couple of decades beyond the normal retirement age, second, he had the most bizarre right-hand action I had ever seen, and third – and most impressive of all – he was playing with only three strings.

This wasn't the first time I had seen someone a string short of a full fingerboard. In fact, the three-stringed bass became a common sight in Santiago. When people said Cuban musicians were great improvisers, they weren't just talking about the way they played, but also what they played on. In a letter published in Santiago's *El Noticioso* on 11 January 1824, Eusebio Serrano, a mulatto double bassist of great renown, complained bitterly about the lack of strings in Cuba and how he often had to resort to making his own from goatskin, horse intestines, or a vegetable fibre called *canamo*. As Serrano rightly insisted, how could you do justice to a piece of Dragonetti if you were bowing across a stretched length of old nag's guts?

In 2001, the situation had improved very little. A new set of double bass strings (if you could find some) cost about 60 dollars in Santiago, the equivalent of over four months' musicians' wages. Most bass players relied on foreign donations – my spare set had already been passed on to Pastor who had two of his snap in one night – and if those didn't materialize, they simply resorted to playing a smaller number of notes. Normally, it was the tighter, more heavily used G-string that went first, and if he couldn't get hold of some nylon fishing line (no joke) to act as a substitute, the bassist would simply shift all the strings along one and do without the low E-string. Which is exactly what Napoli had done on this particular occasion and – to my untrained ear – it didn't seem to be doing his playing any harm.

'Do you know how old the bass player is?' I asked the barman as he handed me another Mojito. Two dollars got you a plastic cup half-filled with rum, garnished with a sprig of limp mint, and topped up with a squeeze of lime and some lemonade. It wasn't a textbook version of this classic Cuban cocktail but it invariably did the job.

'*Noventa y pico?*' came the uncertain reply.

He didn't look ninety and a bit. Admittedly, he sat down between songs and his lack of bodily movement made it hard to tell who was propping up whom, but there were no signs of anxious family members in the wings and his timing and rhythm gave nothing away. He was dressed neatly in well-pressed trousers and a temperature-defying, long-sleeved shirt with the top button done up Nelson Mandela style. A pair of giant-framed, ill-fitting spectacles – safety cord dangling from each arm – a big smile with a chipped front tooth and a handkerchief mysteriously tied around the very top of the bass created an endearing image. I found myself forcing back the urge to run up and hug him. His playing technique encouragingly paid scant regard to textbook orders. The left hand gripped the neck as if it were a javelin and simply shifted up and down without bothering about tiresome aesthetics like finger separation. The thumb's visible presence, meanwhile, proved without doubt that Napoli had not been for a top-up class with Pastor, or maybe he had and Pastor had a no-knife policy for the over-nineties. It was poking around the side in blatant defiance of the 'You shouldn't be able to see it' rule. At the other end of the finger-board, the right hand was behaving equally belligerently. Bent into a claw-like hook, it pecked at the strings with all four fingers glued together as one. Rather than the accepted tech-nique of trying to oscillate the strings from side to side, it was almost as if Napoli was trying to hook his fingers under the string and pull it out perpendicular to the bass. The result was a distinctive double-edged sound. You could hear the note being played but at the same time you also got a percussive sound of the string snapping back against the fingerboard. It was neither friction nor traction but the effect was impressive.

At the end of their set, I went up to say hello and check what drugs he was on. '*Gracias, amigo,*' he whispered, as I helped him slide an old sackcloth bag over his bass. If he was trying to get me to go all dewy-eyed he was doing a good job. The sack was far too big for the bass and once he'd tied the oblig-atory chain around its sagging neck and clicked the padlock shut, it looked more like some sort of badly set up escapolo-gist trick than a well-protected instrument.

'Are you sure it's safe?' I asked as he leaned it against a wall and headed off to the bar.

'Of course,' chuckled Napoli. 'Who is going to steal a three-stringed bass?'

He had a point.

I asked if we could sit down and talk for a few minutes, and apologizing that he was tired from playing, he proposed I came round to his house the following day. Neither one of us had pen and paper but he insisted it was an easy house to find.

'Walk down San Pedro until you find the pink-coloured house on the right – if you get lost just ask for Napoli.'

Having neglected to organize a meeting time – and having

no phone number to do so – I headed off the following morning at a respectfully late hour. In the end, out of curiosity more
than need, I did try the 'Do you know where Napoli lives?'
test, and even though I was a few blocks off, the old woman
I asked guided me to the house as if it were her own neighbour I was coming to visit. The door was ajar, as all Cuban
front doors seemed to be, and I could see Napoli sitting in a
chair not doing anything.

Hearing the tap on the door he looked straight at me and
asked, 'Who is it?'

Either he had very bad eyesight or more likely, in a country
with a chronic shortage of glasses, his prescription hadn't been
changed for a decade.

'It's the Englishman you met last night,' I replied.

'Come in, come in. So you found the house okay?'

I admitted to using a little assistance and he laughed and
said, 'You see what a small place you are living in – in Santiago
we are all neighbours.'

Shuffling off to make some coffee, he left me to nose around.
It didn't take long. The house was old but probably not much
older than the man living in it. There was a minimal amount
of furniture and no sign of the usual Cuban collection of kitsch
– plastic flower arrangements, ceramic animals, and the ubiquitous lurid wall tapestry of cuddly kittens and puppies were all
notable by their absence. There was no TV, no stereo, and only
a small cabinet of books offered signs of domestic entertainment. On one wall a plastic clock had stopped at 7 p.m. while
nearby a poster of Chepin Choven – one of the great Santiago
orchestras of all time – was peeling at one corner. On the other
side of the room, a small montage of Napoli memorabilia took
pride of place. There were lots of good-worker certificates from
various official state organizations, an old black and white
photograph taken in the 1930s with a serious-looking Roberto
dressed to kill in a well-cut suit, and a recent 'Happy 90th birthday' note from the Casa de la Música.

'I looked good back then, didn't I?' came Napoli's voice behind me, and I straightened up and guiltily took the small cup of coffee he was offering.

'I still try and look smart when I play but no one wears a suit these days.'

We sat down and there was silence as both of us sipped our sweet, lukewarm coffee. He spoke first, asking me how London was in the way someone might ask about an old relative they'd heard wasn't very well. I briefly considered a moan about pollution, house prices, and the fact that none of our neighbours ever talked to each other, but in the end, not wanting to tarnish an old man's picture (whatever it might have been), settled instead for telling him it was doing just fine. Suddenly, Napoli's eyes widened as if he'd forgotten to switch something off.

'Did you meet my wife?'

'No,' I answered, wondering how I could have missed her on the way in.

He got up and showed me to the doorway of a bedroom off to one side of the main room and there, sitting on the bed, silently staring out of the window, was a frail old woman dressed in a thin, greying nightie. Looking at her hunched figure – she can't have been that much older than her husband – suddenly put Napoli's physical and mental acuity into perspective. By rights, he should have been on the other side of the bed doing a similar act of geriatric gazing. '*Buenos dias,*' I called out, and without moving at all she returned the greeting as if I was standing outside the window. 'She hasn't been well,' said Napoli, leaving her to eavesdrop on a heated conversation in the street.

'So what made you choose double bass?' he asked as we returned to our seats. I quickly gave him the shortened version of my now finely tuned spiel, deliberately missing out the forgiving instrument bit and playing up the whole rhythmic challenge thing. 'And you've come to learn Cuban bass?'

'I hope so.'

'Who is teaching you?'

'Pastor Panes?'

The nervous inflection on the ending suggested full faith in the lover of motorway signs had yet to be established.

'Ah Pastor, he's good.' responded Napoli with an approving nod of the head. 'I wish I still had his energy.' I told him I thought his energy levels were just fine.

'And you – how did you start?' I asked.

The big toothy grin returned. 'Well, I never meant to be a double bassist. It just happened by accident.'

After a long pause, as if waiting for the biographical tape to rewind, he took me back to 29 April 1911, the day he was born in nearby Calle Fermín. His parents, he told me, came from Baracoa, the idyllic palm-fringed town in the far eastern tip of Guantanamo province, and being the smallest member of the family, he became known as Baracoita. His first contact with music came through an aunt who ran and performed in a *tumba francesa* – a percussion-led dance with Haitian origins. The young Baracoita started with a drum called a *bocu* and by the age of ten he was playing in a children's group called Los Niños Divertidos – The Funny Kids.

Napoli spoke clearly and with great detail but he had a habit of jumping from anecdote to anecdote – often totally uncon-nected – as if he had pre-selected the highlights he thought I'd like to hear the most. With a sudden skip of the tape we were at New Year's Eve, 1923 with a twelve-year-old Napoli leaving the house to meet friends, and assuring his mother he would be back by his 10 p.m. curfew. On his way across town, he passed a group whose percussionist had walked out on them, and with no one else around to fill the gap, 'a confident little black kid', as he put it, was soon playing timbales in front of a cheering crowd. By the time he finished singing 'Tres Lindas Cubanas', a beautiful piece of *son* written by the leader of the band, Sexteto Habanero, there were coins scattered all over the floor in front of him and, less encouragingly, it was 11 p.m. and an hour past his curfew. 'I felt enormous that night,' remembered Napoli, 'but I was also very scared of my mother's reaction.'

A member of the band said he would take him home and explain to his mother what had happened. The man duly showed her the money they had collected but Napoli's mum – still fuming over her son's disobedience – refused to take it. The man held his ground. 'But this isn't my money, *señora* – they were throwing it at your son.' Napoli's memory is a bit fuzzy about what happened next, but either the money, the charm or the armistice of New Year's Eve must have soothed his mum because he does remember going out again that night and eventually found himself playing in the house of one Facundo Bacardi.

'Facundo Bacardi?' I spluttered.

'Yes, the son of Facundo Senior,' confirmed a beaming Napoli, 'and a few months later he broke my guitar.'

Without needing any prompting he continued the story. 'Sometime around my thirteenth birthday, I bought a guitar and helped form a group called the Sexteto Tropical. We called it that because the local brewery was called Tropical and I had this idea that we could be their sponsored band. I went and had a meeting with the brewery representative and he just laughed and said, "God, you are an ugly little Negro." But we got the suits and the job. One day, we were playing down at this beach resort and we had to stop because I broke a string on my guitar. Facundo was in the audience and he told us to keep playing. I went up and explained about the broken string and he just exploded and threw the guitar on to the beach. The next day we came back again and Facundo apologized and gave me fifty pesos, a lot more than I needed to buy a new guitar.'

Napoli made this story sound so matter of fact you almost forgot the significance of the person he was talking about. There can't have been many people left in this city who could claim to have met the son of the founder of the world's biggest rum empire, let alone had their instruments destroyed by him.

I asked him if he could remember the first time he played the double bass. '*Como no!*' came the immediate response. 'It was 1932. I was playing guitar with Bernardo Choven and Electo Rosell, the two men who went on to set up Chepin Choven. One night we were doing a concert in Santa Clara and I just picked up the bass for a laugh and started playing around. Choven liked what he heard and asked me to play double bass in his new band. When I started I didn't know anything. Choven would be doing foxtrots and pasodobles and I would be completely lost. He had to start teaching me *solfeo*.'

'*Solfeo?*' I asked.

'Music theory.'

'So you've never been to a musical school?'

'Never. Bernardo was my school.'

In 1985, Napoli had an operation that he described as '*bastante grave*' ('fairly serious'). The operation was a success but his doctor advised him that after so many years of playing, his mental health would suffer if he didn't keep on going. At the age of seventy-four, he knew it wasn't going to be easy to find work, but by chance a position came up in Estudiantina Invasora, the group he'd started playing with in 1927. 'I went down to the Centro de Música and the woman behind the desk told me, "This position is for a guitarist but you are down as a singer." So I went home and dug up my musician's carnet from 1938, the one that said "bassist, singer and guitarist", and I went back to the office and showed it to her. There wasn't much she could say and I got the job.'

I asked him how long he believed he could still keep performing and for the first time since I'd met him, a sad expression appeared on his face and he sighed as if the question had reminded him of something he'd rather not think of. 'I'll do it for as long as I'm enjoying it and for as long as the rest of the band want me. But it does tire me out much more than it used to.'

Conscious of the fact that my quick visit had extended to

nearly two hours, I thanked him for talking to me for so long and made my excuses to leave. Just as I got to the door, I remembered something important I'd wanted to ask him. If anyone could help me out in my search for the elusive *bomba*, this was surely the man to ask.

'Roberto. Pastor says I'm going to have to find *la bomba* but I'm not entirely sure what *la bomba* is.'

'*La bomba?*' He grinned, poking his giant glasses back up his nose. '*La bomba* is how we Cubans put our own stamp on our music. You can't look for it, it's either there or it isn't.'

'But can a non-Cuban have *la bomba?*'

'I don't know. I don't see why not.'

And with that, the wise old master went back to whatever he wasn't doing before his visitor arrived, and young Luke Skywalker – no nearer the truth about finding the force within him – trundled home to put in some more light-sabre practice. Well, all right, a few scales then.

8. Following Frank

Like those of all the other foreigners seeking to stay in Cuba for a long period of time – sex tourists, journalists waiting for an interview with Fidel, professional musicians trying to add Cuban rhythms to their repertoire – my long-term plans rested on finding a way around the standard thirty-day tourist visa.

One option was simply to extend said visa for the permitted extra thirty days (already done), then buy a return ticket to somewhere close to Cuba and keep repeating the process every sixty days. Given that the cheapest international flight out of Santiago was to neighbouring Haiti – a 300-dollar round trip that required a week's stay – this looked expensive and time-consuming. Nor did it appeal to my cowardly sensibilities. An attempted coup had recently been foiled in Port-au-Prince, making it a great place to escape the hordes but not somewhere you'd want to go without checking your life insurance.

A second possibility was less dangerous but required a rather drastic change in lifestyle. I could simply marry my way around the visa problem. Finding a willing partner wasn't a problem and ironically, despite the Government's apparent determination to keep tourists and Cubans apart, the knot-tying procedure was relatively hassle-free. 'Quality and efficiency guarantee our services,' said the marriage brochure I picked up from the *notaría especial* in Santiago. Inside there was a list of prices and a checklist of requirements.

Compared to the 40 pesos it costs for two Cubans to marry – 100 pesos to divorce – a foreigner had to stump up a rather larger wedge of pre-nuptial cash. First there was a basic fee of 525 dollars. Then there was an extra 100 dollars if you wanted to have the wedding outside the register office, another 100 dollars for something referred to as '*protocolización*', 140 dollars for an '*invitación*', 75 dollars for '*inmediatez*' (presumably the Cuban equivalent of Fast Track), and a token 100 pesos for the official stamps. In all, I worked out it would cost about the equivalent of three trips to Haiti, but then I could discount from that the future savings on rent, assuming of course that my new bride's family didn't mind taking in a large piece of wood as well as me. Unfortunately, down in the small print, it mentioned that I would need to get my birth certificate and proof of single status 'authenticated' by the Cuban Consulate in London. A shotgun wedding was, therefore, out of contention.

The last, and without doubt the most attractive route to getting past this little immigration hurdle, was to enrol myself at the Universidad de Oriente. A friendly woman at the university's Department of International Relations informed me that to sign up for the Spanish course for foreigners I would just need to bring in three passport photos and a 10-dollar stamp from the bank. Matriculation cost 25 dollars, tuition fees were 5 dollars an hour, and the minimum studying time was eight hours a week. It looked a perfect solution. For 160 dollars a month I could avoid having to leave the country, improve my Spanish, and get my hands on a nice green student carnet that would get me into baseball matches for just 1 peso.

Despite what the Habaneros liked to tell you, Santiago was a city with a fine academic reputation. It was here in 1722 that the country's first seat of higher education, the Seminario San Basilio el Magno, began accepting its first students. It never received the title of University but at one point the Pope did grant it the right to issue graduate degrees in theology and canonical law. In later years the Seminario became a regular educational centre and its ex-alumni even included the teenage Fidel Castro Ruz and his brother Raul.

The city didn't get a proper university until 1947, and had

the authorities known what clandestine activities would go on within its walls, they'd probably never have let it open at all. It was here during the mid-1950s that a young student called Frank País began organizing an underground movement to support Fidel's revolutionary struggle. País didn't look like your average insurgent. The son of the founder of the Baptist Temple in Santiago, he played the accordion, loved painting, and directed the choir in his father's church. But the quiet young man had become a determined political activist following Batista's coup in 1952, helping to organize protest marches and regularly writing articles highlighting the injustices of the regime. His religious connections provided a good cover and he even used names from the Baptist scriptures as code words in secret correspondence between himself and Fidel.

While at the university studying pedagogy, Frank and Pepito Tey, the President of the Student Association, set up an opposition group called the Acción Revolucionario Oriental and began collecting arms and supplies – stealing the former from the Santiago Hunting Club – and training young soldiers to fight for Fidel's army in the Sierra Maestra. Amazingly, none of the university staff got suspicious about the odd defence formations in Frank's basketball team nor did they question his regular attendance at the firing range. With help from other students, the ARO had already managed to set up a revolutionary newsletter and, with the purchase of a multilith printer, they started publishing a clandestine newspaper called *Ultimas Noticias* (*The Latest News*). The paper was printed in one of the neighbourhood churches and distributed using a milk van called El Dandy. Secret letters were written on the colourful paper that lovers used for romantic correspondence, and important documents were transported around the city under women's skirts. It was a highly organized underground campaign and thanks to the messages it sent out, the disruption it caused and the supply lines it established, Fidel's more glamorous campaign in the mountains was able to survive and eventually succeed.

On 30 June 1957, Batista's government staged a large political rally to show there was no revolutionary activity in Santiago. Frank and his brother Josué had planted a bomb to go off during the event and prove exactly the opposite, but it failed to detonate. In his attempt to re-activate the device, Josué was captured and assassinated. Then, exactly a month after his brother was killed, Frank was stopped in the street while trying to move from one safe house to another. The police took him to a quiet side street behind the Iglesia San Francisco, shot him over twenty times, then sat down and had something to eat beside his body. He was just twenty-two years old.

One afternoon, a few weeks after I arrived in Santiago, there was a massive gathering of people outside the Town Hall. A storm was brewing up but the threat of a good soaking hadn't dissuaded the crowd who continued to stream into Parque Cespedes until it became so full the queues backed up along the connecting streets. When I asked what was happening, a young man told me it was the anniversary of Frank País's death. Every year, on 30 July, thousands marched from the centre of the city all the way to the cemetery to pay their respects. The young student's sacrifice had not been forgotten.

País's old home was now a museum, his face stared out from numerous political billboards around the city, and giant 3-metre-high letters spelt out his name on the roof of the Frank País School of Pedagogy overlooking the bay. Unfortunately the 'P' had fallen down at some stage so the bold name on the horizon was now Frank Aís.

The university where País studied, or rather pretended to study, hadn't changed much since he was there. The campus was spread over a hill near to the Revolution Square. To get there required a twenty-minute cycle ride along the waterfront, back past the railway station and distillery, up the Paseo de Martí – home of the famous Los Hoyos congo – across Los Olmos with its wafts of charcoal smoke and rumba, past the little park where pensioners were practising early morning t'ai chi, along the potholed Avenida Lumumba and then a final climb up the university approach road where a large billboard of Fidel and Che announced triumphantly, '42 Januarys of Victory!' It was on 2 January 1959 that Castro's army had taken over Santiago.

Opposite the entrance, a group of students were huddled around a stall selling *batidos*, Cuban milkshakes made with a local fruit called *zapoti*, milk powder, ice and water. Having arrived far too early for my first day of classes and lost a couple of litres of fluid to get here, I joined the queue for one. The glass of viscous pink liquid went down in three greedy gulps, causing a stab of pain from the cold. I was just about to ask for a top-up when I caught sight of the dirty block of melting ice being used to make the drinks. My stomach immediately began to release a series of ominous gurgling sounds. The first day of classes and I had just made what could turn out to be a fatal error of judgement. If a Cuban restaurant toilet was a no-go zone, then a Cuban university toilet probably had police crime tape across the door.

The main university building was an ugly triumph of function over aesthetics, decorated with a vast abstract mural that doubtless held some message about opening minds and striving for common goals but on fourth glance still looked an incomprehensible mess. People were milling around near the central stairway where a board listed a variety of activities available that month. A quick scan noted a Saturday night disco, a sculpture exhibition, various sports trials and a screening and discussion of the Cuban Missile Crisis film, *Thirteen Days*. Along one wall, a revolutionary slogan reminded the casually-dressed crowd that 'Revolution is to struggle with audaciousness, intelligence and realism.' Like the rest of the city, the campus was littered with these '*Revolución es* . . .' catchphrases – they were like the socialist equivalent of advertising slogans. Instead of 'Coke – It's the Real Thing' or 'Omo – Cleans Whiter than White' you got 'Revolution is equality and absolute liberty' or 'Revolution is the feeling of a historic moment.' The problem was that unlike in the advertising world, there was no attempt to capture the readers with a little humour. You were desperate to turn a corner one day and find that someone had replaced the usual worthy message with something like, 'Revolution is a shaggy beard and a love of green fatigues.' It was the sort of thing a student would do, indeed should be doing, but sadly there was no sign of late-night drunken graffiti at this seat of learning.

After two or three requests for directions, I managed to locate the bike compound, a fenced-off shelter manned by a young woman with a baby in an improvised cot by her side. It felt a bit embarrassing putting my fancy, multi-geared Italian mountain bike next to the motley crew of patched-up Chinese wrecks, and even though the attendant told me a padlock wouldn't be necessary, I still attached mine to the front wheel before handing over the 2-peso fee.

Alongside the bike shed was an all-weather sports court where two teams of baggy-shorted beanstalks were playing volleyball to a soundtrack of competitive verbal jockeying. Further down, another group was playing basketball using the only hoop that still had a rebound board. One lot attacked while the other defended. And right down the far end, attracting the biggest group of cheering onlookers, was some sort of cross between football and baseball. Instead of throwing a small hard ball, the pitcher was rolling a football along the ground and the person at the plate had to kick it as hard as possible and then run to first base. At no British university would you have found so much activity at 8.30 in the morning.

From my chats with Antonio and Carlos, I'd learnt that Cuban students generally had a far harder time than their British counterparts. Having managed to get through the tough pre-selection tests at high school followed by the exams to get into university, they were then tested regularly throughout their degree courses and failure could mean immediate ejection. On top of that, they were expected to do regular voluntary work in rural areas – try asking a British student to go potato picking

– and then after their five-year degree, they had to do a mandatory two years of social services. Given the tiny minority that actually ended up in the vocation for which they had studied, the cynic might question why so many bothered putting themselves through it all in the first place. 'Preventing boredom' would doubtless be high up in the list of answers.

Returning towards the reception area, I found myself doing a double take as a bright yellow bus went past. It was one of those classic American high school buses you see in the movies, and just to add an even more surreal twist, there was a French warning sign on its back window that said '*Arrêtez aux Signeaux Clignotants*'. This wasn't the strangest donation I'd seen in Santiago. That prize went to the South Yorkshire double-decker bus seen parked outside one of the hospitals, still displaying its 'Meadowhall' destination sign as if the driver had taken a wrong turning coming out of Pond Street bus depot and ended up travelling through some magical portal straight from one socialist city to another. Confused passengers were, I imagined, still walking around trying to find the number 38 home.

Daydreaming about Don Valley bus disappearances while trying to work out what a *Clignotant* was, I was snapped back into more focused thinking by the abrupt ignition of the Campus Radio. A woman began reading out the day's events in the cheery, over-enthusiastic style of a holiday camp announcer, and my suspicion that the microphone might have been hijacked was reinforced when the first bit of music came on. Instead of an inspiring piece of *trova* we were given Take That and a pre-lecture mantra of 'I want you back, I want you back, I want you back for good.' It was a confused man that finally walked into the Humanities Faculty.

The dilapidated state of the building suggested that a search for the university maintenance department would prove fruitless. There were missing slats in many of the wooden window shutters, doors coming off hinges, one lone dripping air-conditioning unit with a bucket underneath it, and a pervading stench that seemed to confirm the worst about the toilets. Students were milling around in the corridors and stairs. It could have been a pre-lecture scene in any university around the world except for the fact that everyone was here on time and nobody was holding a mobile phone. On the way up the stairs, I walked past a variety of noticeboards filled with time-tables and various patriotic posters. On one there was a montage of 'heroes of the homeland' alongside information on Cuba's national symbols. Outside one of the first-floor class-rooms was a student-designed display on Aids with a message about safe sex illustrated by a large cartoon condom. Nosing further along the corridor, I came across some sort of survey on drug use in Santiago. For a country with supposedly little or no drug culture, it was somewhat surprising to find that Santiago had three different rehab centres. They could, of course, have been full of ex-Argentine football stars but the other facts and figures in the survey suggested a few Cuban patients. Alcohol was listed as the main drug of choice – my own daily rum consumption confirmed its addictiveness – followed, in descending order of use, by cannabis, benzop (whatever that was), barbiturates, crack and cocaine. Two figures stood out in the various tables of results: 32 per cent of all drug addicts in Santiago were students and an incredible 55 per cent were in secondary school.

The Spanish courses were held on the top floor. They were divided into three levels of proficiency, but since there weren't enough people for an intermediary level, I'd been put into an advanced class that had started a few weeks before. The room was minute, which was fine because there were only four of us. A young German called Timo seemed to be the most confident. He said he was here doing some sort of research on *jineteras* (a cunning excuse), and although he claimed to have got some good interviews done, it wasn't made clear whether he'd had to pump the information out of them or whether this was a cash–for–questions scenario.

Then there was Philippe, a very shy Belgian who was trying to sort out the paperwork to allow his long-term Cuban girl-friend to visit him in Europe, and a strange little Italian man called Giovanni who, oblivious to the heat, wore a black builder's beanie hat pulled down to his eyebrows. Our young teacher, Maria Victoria, had a kind smile and, as was revealed in the first half-hour, plenty of patience.

Asked to talk about our experiences over the weekend, Timo and Philippe gave fluent accounts of their respective weekends in Baracoa and Manzanillo, two towns at opposite coastal extremes of the Oriente, and then Giovanni stood up and let loose on what a miserable weekend he had had with his Cuban wife. 'Everywhere we go, she must show her carnet,' moaned the Italian in heavily accented Spanish. 'We go to the swim-ming pool and they don't let her in because they think she is a prostitute. We walk down the street and people look at her like she is a prostitute. They have no respect here, she is my wife, we are married.'

Part of me felt sympathy for him. I knew, for example, that Tania felt uncomfortable just walking to the market with me because she said people would assume she was '*jineteando*', the word Cubans used for prostituting. It was sad that a foreigner walking with a Cuban of the opposite sex was automatically assumed to be having sex with them: sad but understandable. Santiago was full of tourists looking to put another bottom on the back seat of their moped. And the Italians formed the biggest group. I knew of one Italian renting a room on the same street as me, who commuted between Milan and Santiago, bringing in suitcases full of women's clothes and bartering them for sex. And what did Giovanni really expect? What were people meant to think when they saw a stunning nineteen-year-old Cuban walking down the street with an old man who wore a woolly hat in the hottest place in the Caribbean? Maria Victoria just nodded sagely while all this went on and then as soon as Giovanni had run out of steam, she grabbed the opportunity (and the chalk) and said, 'Right, let's get back to the past sub-junctive, shall we?'

She had a tough task on her hands. For eight hours a week she had to try to fine-tune our Spanish, knowing full well that as soon as we left the grounds of the university we'd be listening to (and inevitably copying) a language that at times bore absolutely no relation to that being taught in the language course. As with their cars, Cubans had taken the basic structure of an imported language, then ripped out those bits deemed superfluous to their needs (the endings to most words, for example). Santiagueros were often accused of being the worst offenders on the language bastardization front but, in their defence – this was my adopted home after all – they did have mitigating geographical circumstances. In a place where hills and humidity contrived to leave you breathless most of the time, the vernacular had simply been snipped of its cumbersome edges and pared down to a model that guzzled the least amount of energy. Then they'd added their own lighter spare parts of varying origins, and customized the whole thing with a form of verbal delivery that, to my ears, often sounded like someone trying to speak through burnt lips while sucking a large gobstopper. And just to make their reconditioned communications van even more unrecognizable, they had then spray-painted the whole thing with a colourful coat of slang that allowed them to hold conversations that even fluent Spanish-speaking visitors couldn't unscramble.

Years of slavery had obviously left a strong African imprint on Santiago's language but there were also reminders of the city's other immigrants. For example, there had once been a huge French presence here – most arrived after fleeing the revolution in nearby Haiti – and although the pâtisseries had sadly disappeared, there were still signs of that Gallic occupation. The ubiquitous rocking chair was called a *balance* – from the French *balançoire* – and a unit of agricultural land in the Oriente was often referred to as a *caro*, an adaptation of *carreau*.

Even the baseball team held a little French flair – the crowd favourite was a home-run legend called Gabriel Pierre. Then there were the Anglicisms. Santiagueros often talked about going for a *drinqui*, wearing pairs of *chor* (shorts) and paying visits to the dollar supermarket known as *el shopping* (pronounced 'chopping' by Cubans). Someone who bought a lot of things in the dollar outlets was considered to be *'muy shoppeano'*.

But what probably worried Maria Victoria most was our obvious attraction to the more colourful aspects of the street code, and in this respect, Pastor was not a good influence. One of the first things he gave me was a 300-page dictionary called *Popular Cuban Language of Today*, and even after the briefest of reads it was hard not to admire the effort Cubans had put into finding new words for male and female genitalia. The former far outweighed the latter and provided ample proof of a some- what over-inflated male pride. *El fenómeno* (the phenomenon) was by far the funniest of the penis pseudonyms.

Apart from using the university classes to try to moderate the Cuban in my Spanish, I was also hoping to use the cam- pus facilities to get some much-needed exercise. During the half-time break one day I asked whether there was any way I could join one of the student baseball teams. After she even- tually stopped sniggering, Maria Victoria told me there was a Faculty meeting outside the building after the lesson and that I should go and speak to some of the other students about it.

Sure enough, at midday, a big group of people was milling around under the shade of some nearby flame trees. Eventually, one of the men called for quiet and after a few introductory announcements, started lecturing the crowd about the poor sporting reputation of the Humanities Faculty. I hovered at the back and tried to keep up with what was being said. In among the mostly unintelligible slur of chewed-up words, I did hear the repeated demands for *'más participación'* and the need for *'acción colectiva'*. Unfortunately I didn't catch the end-of-speech instructions about lining up according to departments, hence my rather isolated position, not to mention gormless expression, as everyone suddenly reshuffled into ordered lines. 'What are you studying?' said a young guy with a crew-cut and an old Megadeth T-shirt. 'Spanish,' I answered. 'Then you need to be over there with the Languages group.'

Organized into little squadrons of students, it looked suspiciously as though we were about to have some sort of parade-ground inspection. 'What are we doing?' I whispered to the stern-faced woman to my left. 'Marching practice,' she replied without turning her head. Take That in the morning, square bashing at midday; in any other country that would be a recipe for an ugly student demonstration.

A volunteer went out to the front and to much stifled giggling in the ranks, went through the various moves that some of us might have forgotten or had never bothered to remember. Quarter turns, half turns, slow march, rest position, full speed ahead – horrifying memories of Thursday afternoon school cadet training came flooding back. I was never much of a trainee soldier. My beret refused to assume the right shape and position – meaning I always looked more like Frank Spencer than a lean fighting machine – and after a term of failing to tie up puttees correctly, I was eventually persuaded that my talents might lie elsewhere.

Mind you, for years I'd secretly nurtured an unfulfilled desire to do some synchronized goose-stepping with fifty other people and it's not often you get the opportunity. Here was my chance at last. Perhaps it was the lack of stirring music, the heat and the fact that we were attempting to march across an uneven lattice of badly laid slabs, but there was nothing remotely goose-like or, indeed, synchronized about our movements. Looking at this shambolic display of discipline and co-ordination, it wasn't hard to see why the Humanities Faculty hadn't delivered any sports trophies in a while. Failure to listen to instructions, inability to turn 180 degrees without losing balance, and a healthy disrespect for taking things seriously –

these are not the qualities of great athletes. For half an hour, we high-heeled it up and down, until the third-year student-cum-camp comandante finally decided he'd seen enough and told us we were dismissed.

I found out what the drill practice was for later that week while waiting in the queue to pay my first month's student fees. The student in front of me was a Jamaican in his first year of a four-year course in International Civil Law. He laughed so hard when I told him about my goose-stepping experience that he caused a head to poke out of the money-taking hatch and we were given a stare you would normally associate with an All Black Haka. 'It's for Fidel,' said Wesley, still giggling, 'he's coming to Santiago in a month's time for a big demo and all the Cuban students have to go.'

It was soon clear that Wesley wasn't entirely happy with his choice of university. He'd nearly gone to study in Britain but in the end decided the Cuban option would be cheaper and warmer. But after only two terms, he was rueing the decision. Fed up with being squeezed into a dirty dormitory with six others, he was about to move out and rent a cheap (and illegal) room with a family. He said most of the foreign students ended up doing this. He told me how hard it was to get hold of the necessary books, how his emails were being read and in some cases deleted before he had the chance to see them, and how the only way to survive the food was to bring back two suit-cases full of provisions every time he went home. Such was his craving for good bread that he was about to make a 400-kilometre weekend trip to Ciego de Avila just because he knew there was a decent bakery there. When I asked him how he got on with Cuban students, he shook his head and admitted he mostly hung out with other foreigners. 'The Cubans d'drainin all dat y'got man,' he responded, his exasperation seeming to strengthen the Jamaican accent. 'Day espectin' you to pee for evryting.'

My own attempts to mix with Cuban students weren't

proving to be very successful either. Word had quickly got out about an unfamiliar language student caught guffawing during the slow march and a few days later, Maria Victoria gently informed me that my participation would not be necessary again. Meanwhile, attempts to join a student baseball team were being met with so little enthusiasm that I started to think there might be a conspiracy against thirty-five-year-old Englishmen with a poor track record in rounders. A crazy paranoid hunch, I know, but five cancelled practice sessions did seem a little strange.

Then one day, an unexpected opportunity to mingle with Cuban students did present itself. As I walked out of class, a fierce-looking woman stopped me in the corridor and after confirming her suspicion that I was English, asked whether I would sit in on an English-speaking club she was trying to set up. 'They have so little chance to hear it spoken correctly,' she explained with her own heavy accent. Karin was from Leningrad. She had come to Cuba in the 1970s to teach Russian and now, with the disintegration of Cuban–Soviet ties and the increasing importance attached to tourism and computer literacy (both requiring a grasp of English), she found herself teaching her second language. All Cuban university students were now required to study English for two years. I agreed to come for the first session and in return received a flash of Russian dental work and a knuckle-cracking handshake. 'I've asked them to speak about the Beatles,' were her last words as I headed down the stairs.

Before coming to Cuba I would have said this was a strange choice of topic but two months in Santiago had taught me otherwise. Not only did Cubans adore the Beatles, very often the only English words they could speak were the lyrics to Beatles' songs. In part, Fidel had to be thanked for this situation. For a long period during the early years of the Revolution, the most famous band in the world was as good as banned in Cuba. Associated with the hippy movement and the sort of permissive behaviour deemed unacceptable in Fidel's new morally strict society, the Beatles were simply wiped off the official playlists. And following the adage that banning something inevitably makes it even more popular, Paul, Ringo, John and George all became even greater cult stars. The censorship was eventually removed, and during the unveiling of a John Lennon statue in Havana, Fidel admitted the banning had been an over-reaction. Today, it was common to hear Cuban bands doing Beatles covers. Santiago didn't have a Lennon statue but it did have a set of cutlery used by Paul McCartney. According to popular folklore – there were sadly no pictures to prove it – Macca had made a flying visit to Santiago a few months before my arrival. Apparently, he had been recognized sitting quietly at the back of the Casa de la Trova, and when someone approached him for an interview, he'd politely declined and said he was just here because he loved traditional Cuban *son*. He bought a bunch of tapes in the shop, stopped for lunch in the restaurant next to El Morro – the knife and fork he used were now framed on the wall – and then it was back to the private jet and off back to the Bahamas. He was on the island for less than a day but they were still talking about it six months later.

Karin's language class proved to be a fascinating insight into the depth of this musical obsession. After a group rendition of 'Imagine' – the words bizarrely projected up against a photo of an Icelandic Airways Jet – groups of four students went up to the front in turn and gave a prepared speech about some aspect of the Beatles' lives. The obvious enthusiasm for the subject matter was touching. Expecting an embarrassed series of 'I like Paul . . .'-style admissions, it was a bit of a shock to listen to the first bunch get up and start talking about the influence of Yoko Ono in John Lennon's music. They even had slides!

I think it was during the third presentation that the little light bulb came on and the horrible truth dawned. Quite clearly, there was no way I was going to be allowed to leave this class-room without demonstrating my own love for the Fab Four. I desperately prayed for a miracle, a fire alarm or the sudden arrival of the anti-dengue fumigators. I even considered faking a bad case of the runs. How do you explain to a group of fanatics like this that although you come from the same country as the Beatles, you have only ever owned one Beatles record (*Sergeant Pepper's Lonely Hearts' Club Band*), have never visited the Cavern Club, and have never bothered to learn the lyrics to any Beatles songs? Fortunately, in the end, the extent of my ignorance was never revealed. Unfortunately, the escape route involved something far worse. As the last group returned to their seats, Karin handed out sheets of paper containing the lyrics to 'Yesterday'. Then she asked, in a manner that left no room for refusal, whether I could stand up and sing it for the class. 'Richard is here studying music,' she announced, causing a spontaneous ripple of pre-performance applause and the sealing of all possible exits.

'Now, listen to how the words are pronounced,' said Karin to the sadly rather more attentive class. Thankfully, I am not a stranger to 'I'll just get my coat' levels of embarrassment. I am the man who once teed off in a foursome with Greg Norman's teenage son – at a press do for the launch of his dad's own-label wines – and in front of a packed crowd, video cameras, girlfriend and Greg Norman himself, took a big swing and watched my ball do a hop, skip and a jump all the way to just short of the ladies' tee. Singing 'Yesterday' to a bunch of Cuban students was way down on my humiliation scale. Or at least it would have been if I'd managed to sing 'all my troubles seem so far away' without missing the 'seem so far' summit by at least a couple of semitones.

The aftermath of this embarrassing episode should, by rights, have been much worse than it was. Mentally, I had been prepar-ing for sniggering in the corridors of the Humanities Faculty for weeks rather than days. But then out of the blue (as in blue

NewYork sky) came something that erased all memory of badly sung 'Yesterdays', something that removed all sniggering full stop.

'Someone's flown a plane into the World Trade Center,' were my friend Aquiles's first words on opening his door on the morning of Wednesday, 11 September 2001. Aquiles was a musician who lived a few doors down from 101 and as I often did, I was just dropping round to have a coffee and a chat. From the moment I walked into his kitchen to find a crowd of friends and neighbours huddled around the TV, it was clear that coffee and chat were off the agenda. In an unprecedented move, Fidel had allowed the broadcasting of live CNN pictures on national Cuban television, and like the rest of the world, we sat down with mouths agape watching jet airliners repeatedly fly into the World Trade Center.

In the Cubavision news centre, the two presenters tried in vain to keep up with events – bits of paper being passed to them every few seconds by fleetingly glimpsed hands – but eventually the director obviously decided it was too much for their technologically challenged team to cope with and abruptly switched from the event of the century to something easier to present and slightly less traumatic to watch – the opening of a new Salvador Allende school in Havana. It was like breaking off from the Moon landings to show the highlights of the indoor bowling championships.

Desperate to get my voyeuristic fix of apocalyptic action, I grabbed my bike and pedalled off in search of a television with CNN. Either there were a lot of people who still didn't know what was going on or maybe they did and just didn't care, because the streets of Santiago were alive with the normal pedestrian bustle. Unlike the President of the United States, I took the bold decision to go straight to the White House. I knew from experience that Pastor was not favourable to cancelled lessons but these were mitigating circumstances. Terrorist attacks were more important than trying to distinguish a tonic from a dominant. Cycling over in record time, I found he too was cursing the head of programme scheduling – they had now moved on to a story about the visit of the President of Mali to Cuba – while desperately trying to find news on his radio. After filling me in on all the details I had missed out on earlier, he suggested I went to the Hotel Santiago. Access to satellite television stations in Cuba, apart from the illegal dishes you found in some Havana homes, could only be found in the big hotels. Not only did the staff in these tourist enclaves enjoy the luxury of dollar tips (tips that could push their salaries well above those of surgeons and university professors), but they enjoyed a nice little side business copying movies off the HBO channel and renting them out to entertainment-starved Cubans. More Blockadebuster than Blockbuster.

The woman behind the reception desk wasn't at all happy at letting a non-guest, a very sweaty non-guest, use the facilities, but after I insisted I had friends in New York (true), she eventually relented and allowed me to go and watch the TV in the poolside gym. So, with kids screaming and splashing about in the background and – unbelievably – a couple of men still pounding away on running machines, I sat and watched the most mesmerizing television show in history, perched on the saddle of a cycling machine. If I was expecting to see evidence of a little *Schadenfreude* among my Cuban friends, it never revealed itself. All were as stunned as the holidaying foreigners. Even Fidel was moved to divert briefly from his usual school-opening speech that evening, sending condolences to a country he was not accustomed to sympathizing with. 'Today is a tragic day for America,' he began, 'and you know well that here the seeds of hate have never been sown against the American people.' He continued in the same vein, keen to point out that despite the continuing friction between the two countries, there was an important distinction between Cuba's relationship with ordinary Americans and its battle with a powerful minority in Florida. 'We haven't forgotten that over 80 per cent of the American people supported the return of Elian to our country,' he added. He was referring to Elian Gonzalez, the five-year-old boy who became a political pawn when picked up by US coastguards in 2000. Suddenly, it looked as though Cuban–American relations might actually improve as a result of the tragic events in New York. In the immediate aftermath of the attacks, the Cuban Government offered whatever medical assistance was required, the Cuban delegation at the Latin Grammies symbolically donated blood for the injured, and the tone in the Cuban media was one of respect and sympathy.

But it didn't last long. As soon as Bush started up his war-against-terrorism rhetoric, rallying the world into action with cries of 'You're either with us or against us,' so the Cuban position shifted to a harder line. It didn't help that Cuba, amazingly, was still on the CIA list of countries harbouring terrorists. With the United States sticking up Wanted posters for Bin Laden and gearing up to start an economy-boosting offensive against Afghanistan, Randy Alonso and his select panel of journalists on the nightly *Mesa Redonda* TV discussion decided it was time to point out the real reason why the Cuban people felt such empathy for the citizens of New York. 'Cuba has been one of the greatest victims of terrorism in the last forty-two years,' Randy noted a week after the attacks. The studio decoration had now been modified to include a backdrop that showed the faces of the five Cubans in jail in the United States on spying charges. And as he reminded his audience that there had been over 600 attempts on their leader's life, you couldn't help but agree with his accusation that this new war on terror stank of double standards. You also couldn't help but be a little pessimistic about the US chances of hunting down the world's most ruthless terrorist. If they had struggled to eliminate a tall bearded target parading visibly on their doorstep for the last four decades, how on earth did they expect to track down a tall bearded target hidden away in an inhospitable mountain chain thousands of miles away?

Out on the streets of Santiago, it wasn't long before a new political catchphrase had joined the ubiquitous '*Revolución es . . .*' slogans. Following Fidel's announcement that Cuba was against terrorism and against war, almost overnight the state's graffitists had plastered the city with '*Contra terrorismo, contra la guerra*' notices. On our street, someone had put a slightly different spin on it with the message '*Abajo el Bloqueo, Abajo el Terrorismo, Abajo La Guerra*' – 'Under the Blockade, Under Terrorism, Under War' – written out in big white letters across the road.

But apart from that, life quickly returned to normal in the Hero City. Spared the sort of media saturation that was keeping the 9/11 show rolling around the world, and faced with the more pressing concern of their own day-to-day struggle, Cubans' conversations in Santiago bars quickly reverted to type. The heat, the price of a bottle of cooking oil, and Cuba's performance in the upcoming baseball World Cup in Taipei were deemed to be of far greater concern than the removal of the Taliban and the hunt for Bin Laden.

9. Washing Machine in C Major

Life in Santiago might have felt totally disconnected from the events unfolding on the other side of the world but it soon became clear that Cuba was not immune to the global impact of 9/11 and the subsequent war in Afghanistan. Tourist numbers had quickly dropped off to the extent that I soon felt as if I was almost the only *pepe* left in town, and as the flow of incoming dollars started to slow, so the dollar–peso exchange rate began to deteriorate. In the space of a month, the peso dropped in value from 22 to 27 to the dollar, leaving all Cubans (whose salaries obviously hadn't changed) struggling to pay for the essential items only available in dollar stores. The rooftop bar at the Casa Grande hotel closed due to lack of business, the Casa de la Trova rarely had a half-full house, and *jinetera* numbers thinned out to levels where you could even walk across Parque Cespedes without getting hissed at.

At the White House, the mood remained surprisingly buoyant, although I believe this had as much to do with Pastor's surprise appearance on national TV as with his resilience to economic difficulties. As part of the celebrations to mark the Cuban Day of Culture, various concerts were performed around the country, and Pastor was asked to join a Santiago all-stars *son* group due to play at the Hotel Santiago. Knowing there was a good chance it would be televised, the man from Crackling had made sure he dressed up for the occasion, and I nearly choked on my beer when the moment arrived and the Cubavision cameras panned across the various members of the band. Sporting some sort of kaftan-style outfit with a ridiculous white Tommy Cooperish fez on his head, it was clear my knife-wielding mentor had taken the extreme outfit route to securing maximum TV attention. Regrettably, he'd forgotten that the bass player is always placed at the back of the stage and, not being a man of great stature, most of his fifteen minutes of fame was lost behind two tall trombone players. For most of the short set, a bobbing white fez was the only evidence of Mr Panes.

By now, any semblance of a formal teacher–student relationship had long since withered away. I was eating lunch with him almost every day and our beer sessions in La Cocinita had become so regular we practically had our own table. Having spent so much time with the man, it wasn't hard to spot a change in mood and one morning, as I went through my normal pre-class routine (park bicycle, pat the now partially haired roof beast, fetch bricks, pour a coffee), I noticed things were far more subdued than normal. Pastor was seated at the dinner table with a pen and paper. There was a calculator at his side and he appeared to be trying to solve what looked like a tricky mathematical conundrum. I knew it must be serious because he'd rented out the neighbourhood PlayStation for a couple of days – he particularly loved the James Bond game – and remarkably, it was switched off. That and the fact that he'd been chewing his bottom lip so hard there was a line of teeth marks under his mouth. Remembering his early advice that 'Music is maths, Richard – when you have a problem just break it down mathematically,' I thought perhaps this was another cunning 'Chambers of Shaolin'-style teaching moment. Master pretends he has problem to show student the way forward, that sort of thing.

Playing the game, I pulled up a chair and asked him why he wasn't firing at a bunch of heavily armed computer-generated thugs. He said he'd discovered a bar of music in my *True Cuban Bass* book that wasn't, as he put it, 'mathematically correct'.

'You see these four notes?' he asked, pointing to some crotchety things with double dots next to them. 'Well, it's

¾ time, so it should add up to three beats, but I've tried it and it doesn't.' I looked at the four notes, glanced at Pastor's pad with its various scribbled sums, stared back at the notes again, and then after a short contemplative silence, confidently told him I hadn't a clue what he was on about.

'You have done some music theory, haven't you?' he frowned, quickly fumbling for a crisis-meeting cigarette. And that, without going over old Mr Freeman anecdotes (which of course I did), was how I ended up signing on at the music school.

The main seat of musical learning in Santiago, the Conservatorio Estaban Salas, was named after a man whom many regarded as Cuba's first great composer. Estaban Salas was born in December 1725, in Havana. From an early age, he saw the light and it definitely wasn't one of the flickering variety you found down in the local tavern. It was the light of the Lord and it left him blinded to all other earthly distractions. He studied philosophy and theology at Havana University, played the organ, always dressed in black, and in between books and prayer, observed a life of absolute chastity. When the Church leaders started looking for a suitable candidate for musical director of Santiago's cathedral, one man stood at the top of the list.

In 1764, a year short of his fortieth birthday, Salas took up his new post in the Eastern city and immediately asked for a 1,450-peso annual budget to help him set up a decent choir and a small orchestra. Although the Church leaders regarded him as a bit of an emotionless loner, none of them questioned the man's commitment to putting Santiago on the musical map nor the strength of his religious devotion. After a big earthquake shook the city in 1766, damaging the cathedral and destroying the chapel of Nuestra Señora del Carmen, Salas was found grief-stricken among the ruins. To raise funds for restoration, he immediately cancelled all his social engagements (what few there were) and sat down to write music. Psalms, hymns, carols, masses; there was nothing in the religious music shop that Salas couldn't master. For speedy composition, he put the pro into prolific.

The next twenty years were good times for the visionary music director. Aside from his writing and teaching, he managed to scrounge more funds out of the Church to expand the choir, a choir whose fame had not just boosted Santiago's image within the music world, but had put religious music on the map, too. In 1789, Bishop Antonio Feliu visited the city and in recognition for services rendered, ordained Salas. Overjoyed, our man went home a little earlier than normal, and after loosening the top button of his robes, treated himself to an evening of undisturbed Bible reading. For Salas, this was the pinnacle of his career, the reward for years of hard slog and religious devotion. Nothing, he probably mused to himself while re-reading his favourite parable that night, would ever be as good as this.

And he was right. It all went downhill from there. When the Supreme Court of Indias − the power brokers and dosh providers to Spain's colonies − demanded back its loan given for cathedral repairs, the canons in Santiago poked around in their kitty bag and found nothing but a few measly offerings from the previous Sunday's collection. With no way of repaying it, they looked for someone to blame and decided Salas was the man to take the fall.

Furious at being set up as a scapegoat, Salas sent off a letter to the King of Spain explaining his innocence and asking for his name to be cleared. Unfortunately, the postal service at the time was even more unreliable than it is today, and by the time the King's apology came back, seven years had passed and anxiety and stress had left Salas a broken man. He died three years later.

If his ghost were roaming the streets of Santiago today, it would be dismayed at the state of the rebuilt cathedral, its base now a not-so-divine ring of tourist outlets, its attendance figures at their lowest ever, and its choir and orchestra both slim shadows of their former selves. And a visit to the Conservatorio named after him would be equally spirit-sapping. The building itself

wasn't so bad. It was a solid if rather neglected colonial structure with a central courtyard surrounded by sparsely furnished
classrooms and tiny practice cubicles. Fortunately, learning to
play music does not require beautiful furniture and fine art on
the walls. It does, however, rely on having something to play
on and something to play, and in both these departments the
Conservatorio was struggling. Instruments were the biggest
problem. The pianos were in a terrible state of disrepair; some
with missing keys, others so out of tune it wasn't worth asking what key a piece of music should be played in. But at least
the pianists had something to play on. Violinists, cellists and
double bassists were faced with a practice regime based around
a system of instrument sharing so stretched it made my under-
use of HP seem criminal. Sheet music was also in short supply
and I soon understood why Pastor had marvelled at my
Fundamentals of Double Bass Playing book like a Cuban boy
handling a new baseball glove. Apart from the Russian music
theory books, teaching material was as hard to find as a Cuban
bookshop without a politics section. Perhaps this was why the
path to musical perfection was, for a Cuban, such a long one.

The duration of study depended on the instrument you were
learning. For saxophone, trumpet, guitar and double bass it was
the short path of four years' elementary and four years' intermediary. For piano, violin and cello, the study time was extended
to seven years' elementary and four years' intermediary. Then,
assuming you had passed all your exams you could go and apply
to do another four to five years of 'superior' level at the Institute
of Superior Arts in Havana. To reach the pinnacle of musical
achievement involved a tortuous journey of mind-numbing
dedication and personal sacrifice. It made my attempts to achieve
something tangible in a single year look like total folly in
comparison.

Being over eighteen, I wasn't eligible to join classes at the
Conservatorio, but on the other side of the road was the Centro
de Superación del Arte y Cultura, otherwise known as the

Centre for Instrument-playing Adults, who thought a tonic was something you mixed with gin and a double flat a reason for kicking your wheel hubs. This was the school where Santiago's untrained musicians – the majority of the city's working *soneros* and *trovadores* – came to learn to read music, and although I didn't strictly fall into this group (I did ask Pastor when one could legitimately call oneself a musician and his answer was a succinct 'Not yet!'), we managed to find a teacher willing to give me lessons.

Yamira was a big-boned, soft-voiced angel with a smile that could soften a Cuban bread roll. The minute Pastor introduced me to her I knew I'd found the yin to balance my knife-wielding yang. She taught music to young children at the Lauro Fuente music school, gave classes to adults at the Centro de Superación, and to release the stress built up by those two, also sang in the Santiago Choral group. She came from one of those families that suggested musical ability did have a genetic component. Her grandfather had run a famous orchestra in Bayamo and her father, Roberto Gonzalez Pantoja, was almost as much of a teaching legend as Salas. It was Roberto who had founded the Centro de Superación in Santiago, in response to the huge numbers of working musicians who had never had the chance to learn music theory.

Like the Conservatorio across the road, the school was in desperate need of renovation. The whole building sagged like a rain-soaked sweater. According to Yamira, it had been a guest-house for wealthy tourists before the Revolution, and during the years of Frank País's underground struggle, secret meetings were held in one of its upstairs rooms. Just in case any of the students failed to remember why their music classes were free, an enormous black and white photograph of the boat used to bring the revolutionaries from Mexico to Cuba filled one of the walls facing the central courtyard. Some months later I would find out from another music teacher that officially, even in the music schools, ten minutes of political discussion were meant to be included in each session. It must have made for some interesting mid-class segues. 'Right, that's enough syncopation for today, now who can give me five reasons why capitalism is not a morally or ethically sound model for development?'

The classroom Yamira had chosen looked even more neglected than the ones at the university. Its door was swinging drunkenly off one hinge, a ceiling fan revolved with such lethargy you could stop it with your hand, and the desks looked as though they'd put up little struggle if a student decided to take home some extra firewood. Visually, there wasn't a single distraction to the task in hand. No pictures, no books, not even a scribble on the blackboard. In fact, there wasn't any chalk. But at least there was a piano, and it still had all its keys.

My first assignment was to try to decode a page of music. This required the dredging up of twenty-three-year-old memories of crotchets and quavers, and once salvaged, the attachment of new Spanish names to them. For example, the familiar five lines on which the music was written ('a stave', I excitedly announced to Yamira) would from now on have to be referred to as a *pentagrama*. At the left-hand edge of the *pentagrama*, the little squiggly sign was the thing that would tell me what clef (or rather, *clave*) I was working in, and the two numbers next to it indicated how many beats there were per bar and what the value of each beat was. In truth, that last bit took far longer to understand than I just made it sound. For the benefit of fluidity, I've skipped out the half-hour on Time Signatures for four-year-olds that enabled me to distinguish the difference between the nice friendly 2/4 time, the not-so-friendly 6/8 time and the avoid-at-all-costs 9/8 time. Then there were the notes. A semibreve (the round circle with no stem) was now a *redonda*, a minim a *blanca*, a crotchet a *negra*, and a quaver a *corchea*. And with the help of Yamira's child-teaching trick of starting with a whole apple and cutting it up into bits, I somehow found a way of remembering how many beats were attached to each. And so it went on until eventually the page that had previously looked about as familiar as an off-road rally map across Uzbekistan slowly began to transform into a decipherable route with starting point, finishing line, and a series of instructions for gear changes and steering commands. Mind you, just as the piece of paper that Colin McCrae's co-driver has on his lap becomes a rather more challenging proposition when the car's going at 80 m.p.h., I knew that reading this piece of music in peace and quiet was one thing, actually doing something with it was something totally different.

For the first couple of sessions, Yamira's theory classes seemed no more painful than Pastor's practice. Very soon I was racing through her little note-spotting tests in the speed of a hemidemisemiquaver (that's a sixty-fourth note, by the way) and she even inspired me to start reading my *AB Guide to Music Theory*, a very useful introductory book I had brought with me to Cuba but as yet failed to open. I learned about major and minor scales and something called the circle of fifths, a theory for working out the number of flats and sharps in a scale best taken on board after a generous helping of five-year-old rum. I noted (but chose to ignore) the section on simple and compound time, sorted out my tonics from my dominants, and decided that whoever allowed the Italians to define musical speed limits needed their head examining. You could play something Allegro (quick), Allegretto (fairly quick but not as quick as Allegro), Andantino (slightly faster than Andante), Largo (stately), Tosto (swift), Presto (fast), Volante (flying), or my personal favourite, Tempo Comodo (at a comfortable speed). It was a recipe for a musical pile-up.

One day, perhaps sensing the need to remove the slight edge of cockiness creeping into her new student's demeanour, Yamira went and spoilt it all by asking me to sing. To be precise, she told me to go up and down a scale in C major with my only reference being the middle C played on the stand-up piano in the corner. And unlike Pastor, she insisted on me giving the

Spanish names for the notes, a little extra humiliation to add to the already sizeable embarrassment of singing in front of someone without the benefit of bathroom acoustics. On Cuban television they had a programme that taught pre-primary school kids to recognize different musical notes and Yamira proudly informed me (totally unnecessarily) that her two-year-old daughter could now sing Do, Re, Mi in perfect tune. I think I was listening to the confusing whistles and bleeps of the Clangers when I was two.

In a quiet room, I might have made a reasonable stab at hitting clean notes but with a nearby trumpet player and drummer playing havoc with my already overworked auto-tuner, the result was a messy ascent, a face-pulling, voice-wobbling moment at the summit, followed by a tortuously slow trudge back down caused by my inability to sing Do, Re, Mi backwards. 'Don't slide into the notes,' said Yamira, a comment that three months ago would have warranted a poke in the eye with a sharp tuning fork. Now it was water off a duck's back, rain off a banana leaf, rum off an ice cube. Neill was developing a tougher skin.

Or at least he thought he was until the next challenge was set. The tonal torture in question involved being given a note on the piano and then a second note either higher or lower, the goal being to work out what the second one was as quickly as possible. Suffice to say, my team was in no hurry to put hands on buzzers. First I had to try to memorize the second note before mentally going up or down the scale (concentrating like a child trying to recite his multiplication tables) until I hit a note that vaguely matched the one in the memory bank. For some reason, the notes that were closer together proved harder than the ones further apart and it wasn't uncommon for me to get it wrong when the two notes were adjacent to each other. According to Yamira, this ability to maintain a cerebral record of notes was an essential requisite for musical progression. Armed with his skill, I would instinctively know if my bass was out of tune and learn to recognize notes played by other instruments. The evidence suggested I had yet to be armed.

While I was thrilled to be finally waking up the long-dormant musical side of my brain, I was less grateful for a couple of infuriating habits that accompanied the activation process. The first side effect was potentially the most psychologically damaging, for the occupants of 101 as much as for me. At first I didn't even notice I was doing it until one day I overheard Liana telling Tania she'd heard me singing the titles music to the TV news in the shower. Inadvertently, I had taken on parrot-like powers of theme tune repetition and my repertoire soon included the maddeningly catchy melody that came with the appearance of the Cubavision logo, the challenging, slightly Dr Who-ish music from a daily history slot called *In This Day* and, most irritating of all, the opening jingle from the girls' favourite show – an Argentine sitcom about a family who live with a cartoon character called Dibu. This wasn't, I should hasten to add, the result of some new television addiction but rather the unavoidable consequence of living in a nation of telly addicts. A combination of having only two channels, an open door (and window) policy and the Cuban habit of turning the volume way up, meant that aural avoidance of television was impossible.

There is probably a technical name for my other musical affliction but I came to know it simply as toneitis. It was a bit like tinnitus only the sounds buzzing in my ears kept changing tone. I suddenly felt duty-bound to work out the notes for any sound I heard in the house, on the street, or even while lying in bed. It was during the early stages of this new state of heightened tonal sensitivity that I discovered HP was emitting an odd noise. At first I thought I was imagining it, but after bringing in various members of the family to verify the claim, it was unanimously declared that HP had developed a rattle. Closer investigation revealed it was coming from just below the left-hand shoulder, perilously close to where Peter had said he'd done an internal patch-up job, and although it only happened when I played certain notes (and made little difference to the quality of what was being played) its presence clearly couldn't be tolerated long term.

Truth be told, this wasn't a good time for HP to be showing signs of weakness. Despite the obvious bond forged from our shared travel experiences (not to mention shared bedroom), our relationship had undeniably drifted into a bit of a rocky patch. Attempting to trace the origins of this slight but perceptible rift, I couldn't deny it wasn't connected to regular visits to the White House. Okay, so Pastor's bass didn't have an end pin, its tuning keys were far too loose and its pale varnished looks were nothing special, but for some reason his sturdy piece of Russian pine seemed easier to play and there was no doubt it made a far more impressive noise.

At first this new allegiance provoked some strange feelings (was I two-timing on my partner?) and the more I played away from home, the more I wondered whether bringing HP had been a big mistake. To use a wine analogy, I felt as though I had turned up at a dinner party with an elegant German Riesling and found roast beef was on the menu. In a country where *pizzicato* (plucking with the fingers rather than using a bow) was the norm and where a bass's depth of sound was revered more than its precision of tone, those chunky bits of Russian craftsmanship, shipped across from Moscow in the 1970s, looked far more at home than a slim, curvy model more used to orchestra pits than crowded Caribbean bars. Put simply, and I'd be the first to stand up and rubbish the culture of machismo, I didn't think HP was butch enough for the job. She was short on muscle, lacked oomph. And now she had a rattle.

The next time Pastor came around to the house, I showed him the offending vibration and, demonstrating a gentleness that belied his normal brusque approach to bass handling, he carefully tapped around the shoulder searching for the problem.

'There it is,' he announced, suddenly ditching the softly-softly approach and pushing his thumb so hard into the tender area that HP let out an audible splinter of protest. 'I know where it is,' I responded with mild agitation, gently rubbing the now visible crack before propping HP up against her corner slot. 'What I need is someone to fix it.'

Mending a double bass was, I already knew, no DIY affair. During my extensive Internet research before leaving for Cuba, I'd read that the repair of string instruments was a delicate operation that could and should only be undertaken by a trained luthier. The opening up (and glueing back together) of a double bass carried the risk of irreversibly altering the sound it made, which is why the world's top musicians were willing to pay top money to get the best hands working on their treasured possessions. And we were talking top money.

I remember Tony at the Contrabasse Shoppe showing me pictures of an old double bass that a luthier in Greenwich had restored. Months of painstakingly detailed work had gone into cleaning and reinforcing the entire structure, so that eventually a long-neglected piece of wood was brought back to life. The final bill ran into thousands of pounds.

'Would forty dollars be okay?' asked Felito, propping HP up against his workbench one hot afternoon a week later.

'And you've opened up an old bass like this before?' I pressed nervously.

'Look, I promise you won't recognize your bass when I've finished with it.' He must have realized that didn't sound as reassuring as it should have done because he quickly added, 'It'll be a much better bass.'

I found Felito through Pastor, who had recently recruited Felito's wife, Vivian, as a new singer. Felito himself was the bass player for a local *son* band, a band whose fame I didn't truly appreciate until I saw them at the Casa de la Trova a few nights after dropping HP off. As I slowly realized who Felito was, I desperately racked my brain to try to remember what hideous faux pas I must have uttered during our first conversation. Had I said something tragically ignorant about *son*? The odds were very high. Straight after the gig I rushed home and pulled out my *Rough Guide to Cuban Music* and, sure enough, there on page 52 was a photograph of the Valera Miranda family, described by the guide as 'a living repository of the history of *son* in one family group', with Felito standing almost out of focus in the spot always occupied by the double bass player – the background.

The Familia Valera Miranda, headed by Felito's parents, Felix and Carmen, was one of the Oriente's great musical treasures. In the tradition of *son*, the group had got their musical genes from both Africa and Spain. One side of the family was of Andalusian descent, while the other side had Bantu origins. Their current repertoire was based on music passed from one generation of their extended family to another by aural tradition – big family get-togethers were the favoured form of musical education – and allegedly it was not unusual to hear them sing songs about life under Spanish colonial rule or even old Afro-French melodies brought across from Haiti. Known throughout Cuba, the family had achieved overseas exposure with the release of two foreign-produced CDs, the second and most recent one involving the collaboration of Antoine Chau, brother of the hugely popular Manu Chau. The measure of their international success could be seen in the size of Felito's magnificent television, a monster that he insisted on switching on to show me the quality of both the picture and the sound. TV pride was everything in Cuba. Regrettably, being the member of a famous *son* band, the proud owner of a self-made baby-basse, a smaller, slim-line electrical version of a double bass, and an all-round nice guy, still did not make Felito a luthier. In other circumstances, I would have demanded slightly better bass-dismantling credentials, but compared to the next-best option – a carpenter friend of Pastor's who didn't even know where the end pin was – Felito seemed more than qualified to do the job. Besides, after the effort of bringing the patient to the doctor, I didn't fancy lugging her home again with rattle unremoved. The bass transportation from 101 to Felito's house, next to the old ice-making factory, had involved Pastor riding on the back of a motorbike with HP tucked under one arm. He could only get a decent grip if the cover was off, so the stunt scene had to be performed without any protection. I observed all this while frantically trying to keep up on my bike.

A week later, I cycled back over to Felito's house to hear the results of the first medical assessment. The news was not heartening. HP's troubles apparently went far further than just a little rattle and as I listened to the list of problems, I sensed that Peter Tyler's words, 'It's not exactly an investment buy,' were about to come back to haunt me. According to Felito, the connection where the base of the neck joined the body of the bass was very fragile and if it wasn't sorted soon the whole thing could snap apart. Next, the fingerboard had a big hollow in it, which was why I was having so much trouble getting clear notes in the central section – at last a legitimate excuse for poor playing. And the reason for the lack of power in HP's voice, the oomph I had envied in Pastor's bass, was because the sound post and the bridge were not in the correct positions and the metal end pin was directing all the sound into the tiled floors. The sound-post repositioning was easy to fix, and the simple insertion of a new plastic tip would sort out the end-pin situation. But the other work was trickier. The rattle could only be removed by opening up the bass and pegging a support structure on the inside of the crack, and to fill in the dip under the strings, the whole fingerboard would have to be taken off and then sanded down to a smooth playing surface.

'Is that all?' I asked, trying to squeeze some humour out of the situation.

'Yes, that's all.'

'How long will it take?'

'You'll have to leave it with me for a couple of weeks.'

It turned out that Felito was about to buy a car — a major status symbol in Santiago — but since the vehicle in question could only be bought in Havana, he was facing a 1,600-kilometre round-trip journey to pick it up and bring it home. This was going to delay the start of the rebuilding process by at least five days.

'Do you want to see the bass I've been working on?' he asked suddenly.

Until now, I hadn't got past his living room, and as I followed him out on to the back patio, I wondered whether seeing a work in progress was such a good idea. What if I didn't like what I saw? Taking HP away now would probably cause huge offence and the news that I'd refused the help of a member of the Valera Miranda family would probably get around the city in a matter of hours. I would become a persona non grata in the City of Heroes.

Ducking my head to get through the low entrance to his small, makeshift repair shed, I found myself in a badly lit room with a long wooden work table, various jars of unrecognizable liquid and a few old tools lying around. On the floor lay a very old bass opened up into its two halves. I noticed a Russian manufacturer's sticker on the inside of the main body and what looked like a ball of hair in one of the corners. 'I just finished opening it up this morning,' said Felito, hastily picking out the worst of the detritus and putting it in a nearby bin. 'It took me ages to get it apart — the Russians use very strong stuff to seal their basses.'

Split apart and lying flat on the ground, the huge piece of Soviet wood looked surprisingly flimsy. This was the first time I had seen the inside of a double bass and it looked a sad and rather pathetic sight with its rough, anaemic inner skin, its criss-cross pattern of supportive pegs no longer hidden away, and its messy dribbles of glue clearly visible around the edges. 'It doesn't look pretty but it's a good bass,' assured the man with the job of making it playable again.

When the time came, I returned to witness the start of repairs. Just opening up HP was a painstakingly slow process involving the use of hot water, a thin screwdriver and various wedging devices. Watching Felito work away at the seam between the main body and the top of the bass, I was amazed at his delicacy, ingenuity and patience. Inch by inch, he eased it open, repeating the same three-part procedure over and over again. First, he gently dabbed the join with hot water to soften the glue, then he gently levered apart the two sections of wood with a large flat screwdriver, and finally he tapped in little wooden wedges to hold it open. I didn't actually see HP in two halves, and it was a deliberate decision. It sounds stupid, but although I had no problem looking at an anonymous Russian instrument with all its innards showing, I felt far less keen to see the state of HP's interior. We'd slept together for four months now. If there was a ball of unwanted hair rolling around her belly, I didn't want to know about it.

So I stopped making visits and waited for the news that HP was back together again. When the phone call came I could hardly hide my excitement. I grabbed my bicycle and pedalled over to Felito's home in record time. The bass I found propped up in the corner of the living room looked, on the outside, exactly the same as the bass I had dropped off a month earlier. My initial reaction was one of disappointment. I think part of me had expected to see some physical evidence of a post-op HP.

'Try it out,' said Felito, hovering quietly behind me.

Far more gently than normal, I moved HP into the playing position and, ignoring my embarrassment at not being able to tune her in (I'd left my tuner at home), I started to play a few notes at random. After five or six I stopped abruptly. It was amazing. HP did not sound like HP any more. There was a depth and resonance to her voice that was almost unrecogniz-able. The weedy German has-been with an arthritic rattle had disappeared and in her place there was now a rejuvenated German with – well, there was no other word for it – oomph. Hearing this new improved sound, I felt a twinge of guilt at my previous lack of faith in HP. I didn't like to admit it, but when the rattle had first come to light I had even considered the possibility of donating her to the music school and buying a Russian bass that Pastor had found. Now, fickle man that I was, all possibility of donating my partner had disappeared. Thanks to Felito, we were a team again. Battle could recommence.

10. Hit Me with Your Rhythm Stick

'Who are the Gobateens, Richard?'

'It's the Go Betweens, they're an Australian band.'

'They play salsa?'

'Not exactly.'

Pastor was nosily flicking through the sleeves of CDs I had brought with me from London and reading the names out loud as if checking attendance for a detention.

'David Gray, Bruce Springsteen, Randy Crawford, Loo . . . Loodon . . .'

'Loudon Wainwright III,' I prompted.

'*Quién es?*'

'He's an American singer–songwriter.'

I slotted the disc into the machine and pressed play. It didn't take long for Pastor to react. After just a minute of the opening track, he grabbed a pen and paper from my desk, scribbled something down, and held it up for me to read. It said 'RITMO!!!' in bold capitals, the triple exclamation mark emphasizing the importance of the message. He didn't look at all happy.

'Rhythm?' I proffered nervously.

I hadn't a clue where this was going, but the deep frown now ruffling up the front of Pastor's black cap indicated the destination was approaching fast.

'Richard, how can I try and teach you Cuban rhythm if you are listening to people like these, these Gobateens and this London man? You don't have a single bit of Cuban music in this room!'

A little aggrieved at the accusation (I did have one Maraca Valle CD and an old Los Van Van tape), I none the less had to reluctantly agree he was in the right. For all his merits, David Gray had yet to experiment with Cuban bass lines, and the chances of me finding *la bomba* down Thunder Road were as slim as Bruce breaking into a salsa routine with Steve Van Zandt.

'Tomorrow we go and buy some Cuban music,' informed a suddenly happier-looking Pastor, clearly relishing another opportunity to spend my money. '*Algo con ritmo!* Something with rhythm!'

Up until this point, the dreaded R word had not been mentioned in any classes. That's not to say my confrontation with it hadn't been lingering in the back of my mind ever since I arrived in Cuba. In fact, the first beads of worry began even before I left London. During my research on Cuban music I had come across the following doom-laden piece of information in the *Rough Guide to World Music*. 'The thread that links the earlier Cuban styles of danzon and charanga to son and salsa is what music writer Peter Manuel has called the "anticipated bass" – a bass line pattern in which the final note of a bar anticipates the harmony of the following bar.' And just in case the reader (as in me) might have been foolish enough to consider this anticipation lark to be of minor significance in the grand scheme of things, the author had cruelly thrown cold water in my face with the neat summary: 'It is this Cuban rhythm pattern that underpins the whole basis of Latin music.'

The idea of me underpinning anything might have been deeply disturbing had it not been too ludicrous a thought even to warrant attention. I had asked Jennifer what the 'anticipated bass' was all about and, correctly sensing the truth would cause her student to come out in an anticipatory rash, she'd told me to worry about the basics first. 'Hon, leave the rhythm stuff until you get to Cuba,' was her succinct advice on the matter. Which, of course, made me even more convinced of its hostile nature.

Now here I was in Cuba, and with no idea of the rules of engagement, the first skirmishes were imminent. Apart from knowing it was impossible to spell it without a spell checker, my knowledge of rhythm was slim. I knew an orchestra had a rhythm section but I couldn't tell you which instruments were in it. And I'd heard the expression, 'The game fell into a rhythm' but wasn't sure whether this meant some football matches had a sense of rhythm and others didn't.

'One way to understand it is to think of a familiar tune,' said my trusty *AB Guide*, 'although the tune itself could not be played on a table, its rhythm could be tapped out on one'. Fair enough. But in all honesty, I needed more than just definitions. How about detailed coordinates of where I could find it (the Cuban version specifically), and then some simple instructions on how to hold on to the little bastard once I'd tracked it down? Experts on the subject would probably suggest it was a lost cause. The common belief is that rhythm is a natural gift. You either have a sense of it or you don't, and if you don't, there isn't a hidden formula. 'Hit me with your rhythm stick,' sang Ian Dury in his biggest hit, but we all know there's no such thing as a rhythm stick, just as we know it probably isn't fun to be a lunatic. Except in the movies of course. Turning uncoordinated stiff-hipped plodders into dance-floor sensations has always been a favourite Hollywood trick. Remember Kevin Bacon teaching the country bumpkin how to dance in *Footloose*? And what about Patrick Swayze's young partner in *Dirty Dancing*? One minute she's moving with all the sensuality of an Aeroflot air hostess, the next she can samba like a Brazilian on carnival night. Cruelly, I had no such magical wand at my disposal. I had Pastor, a hastily purchased collection of cassettes – post-yoga wind-down was now accompanied by Trio Matamoros, Los Compadres and Candido Fabre – and a growing belief that it was time to be making some sizeable offerings to the *santeria* deity in charge of musical matters.

At least I took some solace in the fact that the rhythm problem was not exclusive to me. Santiago received a regular influx of foreign musicians keen to add some Cuban experience to their CVs, and almost all, regardless of talent, appeared to struggle with the local rhythms. One of my foreign friends in Santiago was a Scottish flute player who, like me, was here on a musical mission. Unlike me, Jo knew how to play her instrument. I first spotted her jamming with a band in a house just off Parque Cespedes. Lured to the open window by the quality of the music and the crowd of people huddled on the pavement, I was surprised to discover the flute player was a pale-skinned, blonde-haired woman with a large tattoo on her ankle. I was very impressed. Here was a non-Cuban who not only danced like a Cuban, but to my ears, played like a Cuban too.

'It's just lots of practice and lots of playing with Cubans,' answered Jo when I asked her afterwards how she had got over the rhythmic hurdle. 'If you do it enough, eventually it soaks in.'

One afternoon, she came to a jam session with Sones de Oriente and I sat and watched in envy as she confidently raised the flute to her lips and began playing. After about a minute of what sounded to me like perfect playing, Pastor called everyone to a halt and with no concern for the use of tact, turned to Jo and said, '*Es demasiado Inglés!* – It's too English!' Telling a Scot she's playing 'too English' was the sort of comment that, in other circumstances, might have caused ceramic elephants to be hurled at fake Christmas trees, but to her credit Jo just lowered her instrument and calmly asked Pastor what he meant. 'It doesn't sound Cuban enough,' came the answer, followed by an impressive aural impression of the difference between Jo's solo and one with the appropriate Cubano in its blood. I admit I felt a tiny flush of guilty pleasure at hearing another *pepe* being put in their place but it was quickly erased by the recognition that if Jo, with years of playing behind her, was having difficulty, my chances of success were slim.

Edging nervously into the uncharted depths of Chamber Four – the Rhythm Room as it was to be known – I allowed my mentor to introduce the challenge at hand. They were called *tumbaos*, looping bass lines that formed the repetitive rhythmic heartbeat to traditional Cuban *son*. Most were based on a very simple combination of tonics (the first and most important note in a scale) and their harmonious partners in crime, the dominants (the fifth note in a scale). Around this structure, the bassist would then add his own improvisations. 'Con comida – with food,' was how Pastor described the more elaborate bass lines.

Sensibly we stuck to the low-calorie option, and in isolated laboratory conditions with no aural interference, it was hard to see what all the fuss was about. Sure, my fingers started grumbling after less than a minute of repeating the same few notes over and over again, but stories of talented non-Cuban bassists being felled by a few Cuban *tumbaos* seemed utter exaggeration. An urban myth designed to scare off would-be foreign interlopers. Or at least it looked that way until Pastor started tapping two bits of wood together at the same time as I played the *tumbao*. Then the legend became a sobering reality. Yes, a little instrument called the *clave* was the pin that burst my rhythmic bubble, deflating my steadily rising confidence with a humiliating whoopee-cushion exhalation of air and causing moderate levels of panic in the White House operations room.

The *clave* looked innocuous enough. Thought to have originated in Havana's shipyards in colonial times – ship-building pegs were known as *claves* – it was just two pieces of hard wood (one hollowed out, the other solid) that were tapped together to create a distinctive, woodpecker-sharp sound. If the bass was the engine driving everything forward in Cuban music, the *clave* was the anchor making sure the whole instrumental bandwagon stuck together as one. In theory, the two instruments were workmates striving for a common rhythmic goal. In practice, or at least in my practice, the *clave* was a distracting nuisance, an annoying tic whose clear intention was to trip me out of my stride and leave my neatly revolving *tumbao* resembling some potter's wheel disaster.

The problem was easily identified. The *clave* and bass were like two motors running slightly out of synch with each other. They did join up at the beginning and middle of each loop, but a couple of coinciding notes were not enough to prevent cerebral confusion. I was like an inexperienced news anchor trying to concentrate on reading news item A off the autocue while an editor was feeding instructions about news item B into his earpiece. The result was the musician's version of a vacant stare and a verbal stumble.

Frantically, I grabbed my *True Cuban Bass* book and was relieved to find assistance at hand. The whole of Chapter Two was dedicated to 'the Clave and its relation to the bass'. Scanning down the few paragraphs of text, I immediately fell upon the following stern instruction: 'Any of the rhythmic patterns of the Cuban bass lines, without melody or harmony, are always correct with the *clave*.' And close by, neatly answering the obvious follow-up query from the man with the sticky tape on his fingerboard, it offered in somewhat nonchalant fashion, 'the musician should know – or better yet, feel – where the *clave* lies correctly.' By rights, this announcement should have caused mild concern, but secure in the knowledge that there would be other rhythmic distractions to contend with as well (bongos, maracas, guitar and *tres* had yet to appear) I was forced to take unprecedented action. A mid-class shot of Pastor's moonshine was immediately called for.

If he was worried about my inability to do the musical equivalent of rubbing your stomach while simultaneously patting your head, Pastor concealed it well. Calmly knocking back his own medicinal shot of sinus-clearer, he told me to put the bass to one side for a minute and then asked me to perform a simple test of polyrhythmic ability using nothing but my feet and hands. All I had to do was step down with my left foot, then do a left-right-left slap of the thighs with my hands, step down with the right leg, left-right-left on thighs, left foot down, etc. and keep repeating the exercise until hands and legs were moving as fast as possible. It was like watching a scuba diver with a bad dose of nitrogen narcosis. As soon as I tried to increase the velocity a fraction above slow motion, the multi-functional department of the brain shut down and I became tangled up in step 'n' slap knots.

Test Two involved a set of spoons. With my left-hand spoon I had to tap out one beat, with the right-hand spoon another, and just to spice it up a bit, Pastor struck a steady rhythm with his own set of cutlery. Needless to say, the noise we produced – or rather, the noise *I* produced – was polyrhythmic in only the very loosest sense of the word. 'Your problem is *la síncopa*,' smiled Pastor, his relief at having pinned down the root of the problem briefly masking his fear of how he was going to dig it out. 'We need to buy some drumsticks,' he declared confidently. Knives, kung-fu movies, spoons, drumsticks; he could be accused of a lot of things, but teaching bass by the book was not one of them. *La síncopa*. Syncopation. It sounded like something you got from sitting on cold concrete. Again I resorted to the textbooks and found a clear but not exactly comforting definition. 'Syncopated rhythms are felt to go against a regular pattern of strong and weak beats,' it said before illustrating said patterns with an incomprehensible digression into gospel music. Pastor tried a different tack. 'It's like this, Richard. With your Bruce Springsteen and your Gobateens the bass lines go with the main percussive beat but with Cuban music the bass lines are *"contratiempo"*, against the beat.' Oh good. Not only had I discovered that my forgiving instrument was actually very unforgiving but now I was discovering that the music system I was trying to plug into worked on a totally different wiring to everywhere else.

I had already accumulated a bizarre armoury of German, Russian and Cuban music books from Pastor's collection, and it was now joined by *Progressive Steps to Syncopation for the Modern Drummer* by Ted Reed, acclaimed author, I noted with some disquiet, of *Famous Drum Solos and Fills*. It only took a couple of days of Ted's exercises – drumsticks bashed against my bed to muffle the sound – for me to retract all the derogatory quips I've ever aimed at drummers. I'll have it put on record that you are a highly talented bunch of individuals who deserve far more recognition.

While seeking the mattress-battering route to rhythm acquisition, I also turned to Yamira for some theory-based assistance. Viewed from a distance, a page of *son* or salsa looked no different to any other piece of sheet music you might pick up. But up close you noticed something *was* different. Just as Cubans have laced their language with 'Cubanismos', so too have they taken the standard musical ingredients – a few crotchets, a sprinkle of quavers, half a pound of minims – and garnished them with three dish-altering condiments.

The first two seasonings were ties and dots. Cubans loved nothing better than tying two or more notes together with a little loop or extending individual notes by placing an innocuous little dot to the right-hand side of its head. The effect, in both cases, was to lengthen notes, in the same way as a pianist draws out a note by pressing down on one of the pedals. And the third and far more devious form of rhythmic displacement was the sneaky insertion of spaces, or rests, as they should correctly be named. 'Music is not just about sounds,' informed Yamira, 'the silences are music, too.' She told me Cubans called it '*el aire* – the air' and that an ability to grasp Cuban rhythm was about understanding (and dealing with) these liberally scattered bits of air. In essence, she was telling me that to feel the flavour of Cuban music I wouldn't just have to mind the gaps, I'd have to learn to love them too.

Yamira's formula for mastering these three syncopating snags was simple. She just wrote out line after line of complicated rhythms in a variety of different time signatures and my job was to mark out the beat like a conductor. I've often wondered why those men with batons get paid so much money, particularly when no one in the orchestra ever appears to be looking at what they are doing. Well, to Sir Simon Rattle, respect (of the Ali G variety) where it is due. Never has a man been so humbled by the four points on the compass as I was. Taught to make different noises to distinguish the different length notes, I spent hour after painful hour waving my right hand from north to south to west to east and back to north while doing a good vocal impression of a constipated sheep. Yamira threw everything at me: semiquavers divided into triplets, crotchets with dots, dotted quavers tied to two crotchets with a sneaky little space in the middle. Like a champion boxer preparing for a fight, I learned to deal with every trick in the book, every syncopated shuffle and rapid-fire combo of notes. Unlike a champion boxer, my performance in the ring sadly bore little resemblance to the quality of my sparring in the gym.

Every time I went into proper battle − in the red corner Neill and his bass, in the blue corner Panes and his *clave* − I'd invariably end up on the canvas before the end of the first round. No matter how much I understood the theory of Cuban rhythm, I just couldn't translate my newly acquired conducting skills into actual playing ability. I could talk the talk but I couldn't walk the walk.

'Can you dance salsa?' asked Pastor after yet another messy confrontation with his deadly sticks.

'Sort of,' I replied.

'What do you mean, sort of?'

'Well, I danced a bit when I was in Chile and I took some lessons in London.'

'How many lessons?'

'Four?'

'I think you should take some more now. If you can dance salsa, you'll have a much better feel for Cuban rhythm.'

Los Van Van gigs excluded, I've always been a bit of a reluctant dancer. When it comes to moving about rhythmically with a member of the opposite sex, I believe the world splits neatly into two camps. There are those who see the dance floor as a place associated with enjoyment, flirtation and creative expression, a place to release the exhibitionist within. And there are those who find the dance floor an intimidating space where any self-consciousness and lack of coordination can be cruelly exposed. To those of us in the latter camp, dancing is the human equivalent of the pre-mating prancing routines found in the animal kingdom. And like the gazelle that prefers to nibble on some grass rather than settle a shagging dispute with a pumped-up dominant male, I'd much rather sip a drink at the bar than humiliate myself out in the open.

'I can make you roar like a lion,' assured my new dance instructor, Rafael, after laughing at my wildlife analogy. Rafael taught salsa and he was convinced the rhythm problem could be sorted out with an intensive course of lessons. Looking at my steadily depleting finances, I reckoned my lion might have to settle for a gentle purr rather than a full-throated roar.

In a city where just about every young adult male claimed dance-teacher status, finding a good one was a lottery. I had chosen Rafael because, quite simply, he seemed to be the hottest thing on the dance floor. I'd watched him regularly at the Casa de la Trova, a big Cheshire cat grin stretching across his face as he deftly manoeuvred unresponsive foreign imports around the tiny space. He reminded me of a skilled forklift operator pirouetting cumbersome loads out of tight corners. As well as being a great dancer, he was a *santero*, the first stage to becoming a *santeria* priest (called a *babalao*), and as was the custom for new recruits he wore white from cap to shoes. The only other colour on show was the bright yellow and green beaded bracelet of his chosen protecting saint. With his sweat-mopping flannel poking out from the back of his neatly pressed white slacks, he looked like a cross between a very sexy hospital orderly and a bowls player in need of a ball to polish.

Santiago was a city of *santeros*. Its long history of slavery had made it the heartland of the *santeria* cult, which was supposed to be a fusion between Catholicism and African ancestor worship. Although it was a religion associated predominantly with black Cubans, in Santiago you regularly saw whites with the distinctive coloured amulets on their wrists. Becoming a *santero* wasn't a cheap exercise. Rafael said he'd spent about 5,000 pesos (just under £200) on the initiation rituals. First there were the 1,500 pesos that had to be paid to a *padrino* who organized everything. Then there was a list of costs that included the new all-white wardrobe, payment for the *babalao* who conducted the ceremony, animals for sacrifice (cocks and doves), someone to do the sacrificing, another person to do the cleaning up, and of course plenty of rum to lubricate the whole event. Then once you'd become a *santero*, the bills didn't stop. Your chosen *santo* (or *orisha*) would need regular gifts, *santeria* parties would need to be organized and paid for, new pairs of white shoes bought. To sustain their religious habits, *santeros* were forced to hunt vital dollars – in Rafael's case via salsa classes – which is why you saw so many men in white hanging around with tourists.

I arranged to visit Rafael at his home in Asunción, a neighbouring *barrio* to Chicharrones. As instructed, I knocked on the door marked '*Presidente*' – his sister was the president of the local neighbourhood committee – but no one came to the door. A woman pulling a bucket of water out of a hole in the ground nearby shouted that he was on his way. Sure enough, Rafael pitched up a few minutes later, almost unrecognizable in coloured civvies and with no cap on. 'Nappies,' he explained after rocking his moped on to its stand and apologizing for being late. He'd been buying nappies for his two-month-old baby son and since nappies could only be bought with dollars he'd had to travel across the city to a dollar store to get them. He opened the door and on the way in rapped his knuckles three times against a small wooden cabinet just inside the entrance. I asked what it was for and he told me the box held the three *orishas* – *Eleggua*, *Oggun* and *Ochosi* – that protected the house and those that lived in it. 'You must always pay respects to them when coming in or going out.'

The three weren't alone. On some shelves in Rafael's room

— a tiny, neatly arranged space with a bed at one end, cooking area at the other and clothes and personal possessions in the middle — were five jars with a variety of beads and ornaments draped around their necks. Each represented a little shrine — one for his chosen *orisha*, one for his wife's, one for the baby's, and the other two for other family members — and each contained little gifts for the respective deities. Spiritually, Rafael had all the bases covered.

There were thirteen people living in the house, yet what served as a living room, entrance hall and dance classroom was barely big enough to fit four. A couple of rocking chairs and a table were the only furniture. On the wall was an old black and white photograph of Rafael's beautiful half-mulatto, half-Japanese grandmother next to a certificate demonstrating his acceptance into the order of Freemasons. In the passport-style photo attached to the certificate, he was sporting a thick moustache and looked very serious. 'There are many Masons here,' he replied when I asked how strong the organization was in Cuba. 'When things are very bad we help each other out.'

As we moved the chairs to one side, an old woman appeared at the back of the room and after asking about his latest salsa student, shuffled her way along the wall until she found a chair to sit on. 'Cataracts,' Rafael whispered to me after carefully placing a glass of water in her hands. I felt a combination of pity and relief. No one likes to watch an old woman incapacitated by such an easily treatable disease but at the same time no one likes to have observers at their first dance class.

'Okay, just try and follow what I do,' said Rafael, now shirtless. We started off without music, standing side-by-side facing the wall. 'Ready, one, two, three and one, two, three.' Staring at my teacher's feet, I tried to copy exactly what he was doing. 'And again! One, two, three and one, two, three! Head up! Don't look at your feet, move your hips! Don't stick your bum out so much!' Even his mum was smiling and she couldn't see what was happening.

We tried it again really slowly. 'One. Left foot back, front knee bent and heel off the ground. Bend your hips! Look up! Two. Heel back down and straighten the front leg. Three. Left foot to the front again. And hold it! And one, two, three!'

As the lesson progressed, my audience grew, each new arrival tapping the box as they came in. First there was Rafael's wife, Amber, cradling little two-month-old Miguelito, then came Rafael's older brother whose alcoholic status was confirmed by the fug of rum fumes that preceded him and the fact that he introduced himself as Peter Pan, followed by his sister, *el presidente*, and his body-building younger brother. Finally, just as I was perfecting my dance-alone routine, a beautiful young girl walked in wearing a skin-tight one-piece outfit that left nothing to the imagination. She didn't bother telling the *santeros* she'd arrived. 'This is Yordanka – she will be dancing with you,' said Rafael, introducing me to the tall teenager. Yordanka looked about as enthusiastic as any person who knows their toes are about to be trodden on repeatedly. We paired up and my partner stared at somewhere past my shoulder and chewed her gum with determined boredom. She was supposedly a professional dancer but it was hard to see it in the way she moved. Admittedly my signals ('You're the boss – you have to let her know what you want to do,' ordered Rafael) possibly weren't the clearest, but dancing with Yordanka I was reminded of a stubborn horse that knows exactly what you are asking for but still refuses to budge. And just as the same stubborn nag gallops off to the paddock as soon as the saddle is off, so Yordanka practically bolted for the door when our time was up.

Rafael looked mightily embarrassed about the attitude of his business partner and perhaps as some sort of recompense – or an incentive to keep me interested – he invited me to join him for a *santeria* party that he was going to that evening. Curious to learn more about this world of strange rituals, animal sacrifices, chanting and trances, I accepted. With the luxury of hindsight, I now know that curiosity is a temptress best ignored and that ignorance, while not always bliss, does at least prevent you from being cleansed by a pigeon.

'Who is the party for?' I asked as we approached the distinctive pulse of *bata* drums later that night.

'It's a celebration for *Oya* – the *orisha* of the cemetery,' he replied.

'Oh good,' I murmured to myself. My first *santeria* party and I get the most ghoulish celebration of the lot. Before getting to the house, Rafael gave me strict instructions to follow what he did in front of the shrine and not to shake hands with any of the *santeros* – protocol in such gatherings was a lowering of the head with arms to the sides. The *santero* would do the embracing, I was told. 'Oh, and I should warn you that there will be lots of *maricones* in there,' he added with a laugh. *Maricón* was a widely used expression (among heterosexual men at least) for Cuban homosexuals.

Looking at the big crowd milling around outside the front door, I contemplated the stupidity of the situation. I was about to gatecrash a ceremony for the patron saint of the deceased on a badly lit street in a neighbourhood I had been warned not to visit at night. And all because Pastor reckoned some dance moves might help me tackle syncopated beats. Before I had time to pull out we were squeezing our way past the outdoor spectators into a room chock-full of moving bodies. I could feel myself being watched on all sides – never mind no other white faces, there weren't even any mulatto faces.

Everyone was swaying to the hypnotic overlapping beat struck by the three drummers seated in the corner. A man in what looked like old army fatigues was leading some sort of call-and-response dialogue with the rest of the crowd. After each of his impassioned announcements, delivered with the theatrical panache of one of those TV evangelists, the room would sing a reply in unison. Rafael shouted to me that the words were a Cubanized version of Yoruba. We went straight to a shrine at the far end of the room. There was a large doll-like female figure – presumably *Oya* – surrounded by plates of chicken, two large cakes, fruit, candles, various bowls of an unidentifiable liquid, and a glass jar with some coins and peso notes stuffed in it. Rafael lay down on the floor in front of it, forehead on the ground and arms to the side of his body, and someone came forward and swept a horse's tail down his body. This completed, he stuffed a note into the jar and then picked up a long dried seedpod and shook it vigorously while muttering something unintelligible. When he'd finished, he motioned me forward and just as he'd told me, I copied the whole procedure. Apart from the unintelligible muttering. Annoyingly, a last-minute attempt to extract a suitable dona-tion left me pulling out 10 dollars rather than 10 pesos and the smile on the face of the horse-whip man suggested *Oya* would not be the beneficiary of my generosity. I got up and quickly retreated to one wall, doing my best impression of a tall, pale-coloured lampshade while Rafael disappeared into the throng. Even the most cynical observer would have to admit there was a strange energy in the room. The rhythm of the *bata* drums seemed to be getting faster and faster and although no one was drinking, the dancers didn't look at all sober. Dominating the scene was a group of very effeminate, overweight men wear-ing brightly coloured satin outfits with tasselled epaulettes. On their heads were what looked like deflated chefs' hats. The men gave the impression of being in a trance but it can only have been a semi-trance because when people came up to them, they'd break from flouncing around and give them a big bear-hug followed by a bizarre rub-down.

After I'd spent about ten minutes observing this, one of the dancing chef types spotted me and started heading in my direc-tion. In a panic, I hurriedly scanned the room for Rafael, but he'd blended into the tangle of swaying limbs. The next second, my hand had been grabbed, and unable to decide what to do, I allowed myself to be led down a corridor by a man who looked like Ainsley Harriot dressed up as Aladdin. He took me to the kitchen where, unlike a party anywhere else in the world, there was no one present. He sat on a chair and tapping his thigh said something I couldn't understand. Fortunately, Rafael appeared just as I'd made up my mind to run for it, and after a rapid exchange he insisted I must do what the man instructed. 'He's had some visions about you and now he will tell you what he has seen,' explained Rafael discouragingly, looking the most serious I'd ever seen him. 'You must sit on his knee while he talks.' Feeling utterly ridiculous, I gently lowered my bum on to Ainsley's generously proportioned thigh and steadied myself by placing one hand on one of his gold epaulettes. Odd people kept coming in and out of the kitchen and unbeliev- ably none of them blinked twice at the sight of a six-foot-three male sitting on another man's knee.

After about ten minutes of very fast talking – with Rafael writing everything down on a piece of paper – I was allowed to get up. 'You must pay him something,' said Rafael. I handed over the 10-peso note I had intended for the jar and without waiting for a translation, informed Rafael it was time to go. Safely outside, I asked him what the man had been talking about.

'He said he saw you in an accident in the streets,' said Rafael, 'and he said you must be cleansed to clear away the bad spirits – we will do it before tomorrow's class.' As if to assure me this was no joking matter, Rafael insisted on holding my arm every time we needed to cross the road, even when there was not a vehicle in sight. And he walked me all the way home. I decided it would be best not to tell anyone at 101 where I had just been and what had just happened there. A picture of Jesus rather than a cabinet full of *orishas* was the first thing you saw when you walked in the door and I was sure that any mention of encounters with strange men wearing make-up would only raise Tania's blood pressure an extra unnecessary notch.

The price of the cleansing ceremony was 50 pesos plus the cost of one pigeon, a jar of honey and two coconuts. It took place the following day in the same room where I danced. Rafael brought out the jar representing *Oya* and placed it on the floor in one corner. Candles were lit and I was instructed to take off my glasses. First, he opened the box with the three house protectors and started to have a conversation in the same half-Spanish, half-Yoruba I had heard at the party, shaking a long black seedpod as he spoke. Then he came over and, holding the pigeon by its feet, told me to turn around in clockwise circles while the flapping bird was moved up and down my body. It wasn't as unpleasant as I expected. The process was repeated in anti-clockwise circles and, after doing the same to himself, Rafael released the bird out the door. Next, pieces of coconut were rubbed in honey and pressed into my palms. The second coconut was smashed on the floor and the pieces picked up and repeatedly thrown on the ground. It looked as though Rafael was trying to conduct some sort of conversation with the broken bits of husk. Every time he threw them on the floor, he'd look at the pattern and say either '*Sí*' or '*No*'. This went on for a long time but eventually he picked them up, blew out the candles and told me it was all done.

'I'm clean now?'

'Very clean,' he laughed back, 'but you must still be careful with the traffic.'

While washing the honey off my hands, a totally ridiculous idea crept into my head.

'Rafael?'

'*Sí?*'

'Is it possible to cleanse objects as well as people?'

'You can't really cleanse something but you can bless it — make it carry good luck.'

'And you could do this with, say, a musical instrument?'

'Of course.'

The idea of blessing a bass might be seen as a sign of desperation but I knew that months down the track, when the moment of bass-playing truth dawned, I'd be needing all the assistance (spiritual or otherwise) I could get my hands on. As soon as I got back home that afternoon I opened my diary, and flicking ahead a couple of months, wrote the reminder, 'TAKE HP TO RAFAEL!' in bold letters on a random page.

Looking at my most recent November entry, I was reminded that I had now been in Santiago for over four months. There had been no falling leaves or smell of bonfires to remind me winter was almost here but the tropical weather had certainly cooled off considerably in the last few weeks. In place of the milky heat haze and exploding cumulus clouds of summer, we now had deep blue skies and stunning displays of feathery, high-altitude cirrus. '*Hay mucho aire*' was the Santiaguero way of saying there was a nip in the air, as in 'There's lots of air', and suddenly everyone in the street was wrapping up in pullovers and jackets at night even though the temperatures rarely sank below the twenties.

The music progress report was a mix of 'promising signs' and 'could do betters'. The good news was that my fingers had toughened up to the extent that if I drummed the tips on a table it made a satisfyingly calloused sound. I had even developed some sort of skin-flaking condition on my hands – a reaction to the metal strings, so Pastor informed me – and rather than hiding them with embarrassment, I proudly showed off my moulting digits whenever the opportunity arose. The habit of craning my neck to look at the fingerboard hadn't disappeared yet, but at least I was starting to hit the right notes instinctively and, thanks to my dance lessons with Rafael, the Latin rhythm was slowly beginning to seep into my bones. Pastor was sufficiently pleased with my efforts to agree to my ludicrously optimistic idea of recording a mini-CD with his band sometime in the New Year. As well as providing the all-important proof to sceptical friends back home, this would be an important marker to see if I was on the right track towards D-Day at the Casa de la Trova in just over six months. By the time summer came around again I would have to be ready to put on my blue suit, peel away the sticky tape markers from my fingerboard, and stand with HP on one of the most famous stages in Cuba. Operation Beat-Those-Dutchmen had nearly reached the halfway stage.

11. Neighbourhood Watch

My continuing search for some humour in the city's political propaganda was finally rewarded by the discovery of a brightly coloured wall mural outside the regional headquarters of the Comités para la Defensa de la Revolución (Committees for the Defence of the Revolution), or CDRs as they were called.

Established in 1960 as a response to the CIA's attempts to foster opposition groups within Cuba, the CDRs became Fidel's eyes and ears in the battle against counter-revolutionary forces. Having managed to overthrow Batista's regime, thanks to the activities of a clandestine urban movement, the shrewd leader was hell-bent on making sure the same would never happen to him. By the end of 1961, there were over 100,000 CDRs set up across the country – every block in every city had one – each with its president reporting directly to the MININT (Ministry of the Interior). It was like a giant political version of Neighbourhood Watch.

The cartoon-style drawing I found outside the Santiago office depicted a variety of confrontations between a criminal and a vigilant woman on CDR duty. In one scene, the man in black and white stripes and an eye mask was shown trying to sell some black market goods, and the next image in the sequence had the woman bashing him over the head and saying, 'I'm sorry, but I don't buy illegal things.' Two things made me smile. First, the fact that the artist – without doubt a male artist – had drawn the woman with an enormous over-inflated bottom (in Cuba women are more likely to say, 'Does my bum look too small in this?'), and second, the knowledge that residents would never act in such a way.

The whole country functioned on the existence of a black

market and virtually no Cuban could say they hadn't come into contact with black-market goods at some time. Ubiquity protected the system. In some areas it had even become semi-official business. Trucks of black-market bricks, for example, could be bought without risk because the State – lacking the resources to distribute bricks itself – allowed the sale of building materials to middlemen. Other examples hinted at police pay-offs. In my search for cheese one week, I came across a man selling cassettes outside one of the dollar stores down on Calle Alameda. 'I have cheese,' he said, disappearing into the men's public toilet and returning a few seconds later with a sack of goodies. As well as an ominously solid sausage of Cuban mozzarella, he offered French mustard, HP Worcestershire Sauce, and Heinz Ketchup. 'Where did you get these?' I asked incredulously. 'The hotels,' he replied. 'The staff sell them to me.' Unbelievably, he showed not the slightest bit of concern about the policeman standing barely 20 yards away.

The Cuban economy seemed to function rather like the two halves of a synchronized swimmer. There was the calm bit above water – on show for the judges to see – and then there was the unofficial messy bit under the surface where all the hard graft went on. In our local CDR I had already witnessed plenty of the underwater activity and at no point had a woman with a large bottom come out and beaten the sales person in question. In fact, he or she was far more likely to be welcomed in and offered the hospitality of the house. Almost every week, I bumped into a man bringing illegal squid and prawns from the fishing port of Manzanillo (there was no official fishing industry in the Port of Santiago) and only a fear of severe food poisoning prevented me from buying them. Then there was the man who offered a shopping list of medicines in short supply for Cubans (pain relievers and asthma inhaler refills being in highest demand), the optometrist who sold black-market spectacles, the occasional illicit coffee-bean drop-off (almost all the coffee grown in the Sierra Maestra went for export), a thriving video rental business run by three innocent-looking old ladies, gas canisters for cooking, and illicitly siphoned kerosene-stretched petrol. More often than not it was the Government employees who controlled the system, so if you wanted to find black market fuel the best place to go was the nearest Cuped gas station.

But while a blind eye was turned to '*la bolsa*', as locals called the hidden market, other CDR duties were adhered to strictly. Every Sunday morning, members of each CDR – membership was voluntary and cost 3 pesos per year – came out and cleaned their section of the street. Every night, on a rotating system, someone would sit on guard duty looking out for robberies and other crime, and at the regular CDR meetings to discuss neighbourhood issues, the high turnout defied rumours that the organization didn't have the support of old.

A couple of weeks after the New York attacks, Santiago's residents had celebrated the forty-first anniversary of the creation of the CDR movement. In my CDR, homemade decorations (flattened beer cans turned into bunting) were strung up, plants were placed along the street, and a chipped bust of José Martí – Cuba's most revered hero from the struggle for Independence – appeared on a table along with a thick volume of his poems.

On the night before the big day, a party was held on the street and I was invited along as an honorary resident. My only obligation was to bring extra rum. Tables were set up with homemade pasta dishes, cakes, rum and beer, and a giant cauldron of *caldoso* – a traditional Cuban broth cooked at all outdoor fiestas – was left to boil away on a blazing fire in the middle of the road. They say Cubans will find any excuse to have a party, but there did seem some irony in a bunch of people celebrating an organization that encouraged them to sneak on one another.

At 10.30 p.m., Salvador, the Presidente of the CDR, called for quiet and said a few words. He talked earnestly about the continuing importance of the CDR system, gave a detailed rundown on what had been spent on the party (to the last peso), thanked one resident for donating blood four times in the previous year, and then asked everyone to sing the national anthem. It ended with a passionate collective cry of '*Viva Fidel!* (Long live Fidel!) *Viva Socialismo!* (Long live socialism!) *Patria o Muerte!* (The homeland or death!) *Venceremos!* (We will win!)' This was followed by various groups of children giving small performances. Some sang, some read pieces of José Martí poetry, and others just danced to their favourite salsa hit. Then the party proper began.

You don't have to live in a Cuban *barrio* for long to discover how strong (and transparent) its community life is. In London, a stranger can move into a street and sometimes even his neighbours might not know for weeks. In Cuba, they know you've moved in even before you've arrived. It is like living in a social colander. Open doors, thin walls, communal living, plenty of free time and little entertainment; all these things combine to make keeping a secret almost as hard as finding solitude. Cubans live and thrive off conversation and gossip – even without a CDR watchdog in place it would be almost impossible to start an underground organization – and only the most introverted person can walk along a Cuban street and not end up shaking someone's hand or stopping for an impromptu chat.

Once, when I was standing in the queue at Cadeca – the official dollar–peso exchange – a security van pulled up and, while two heavily armed men went inside to pick up bags of cash, another stayed by the vehicle with a shotgun. During the wait for the return of his comrades, a friend of his strode up to say hello and the two embraced and chatted as if the gun wasn't there. It was obvious a Cuban could never rob a bank. They'd never be able to get in and out quickly enough without stopping for a chinwag with one of the cashiers they knew.

There were two main focal points of communal activity in our street and one of them was right outside our front door.

The doorstep of the neighbouring house was unofficially the social centre of the block. Partly, this was because of the large quantity of people living there. At least fourteen (at a guesti-mate) lived in a house that was similar to 101 in only size and age. A glance inside was a stark reminder of the difference between the dollar-earning haves and the peso-earning have-nots. At 101, access to tourist dollars had helped buy a washing machine, a video and a new TV. Tania and Braulio cooked off gas, slept on decent beds, had showers, and earned enough to make sure the two girls ate well and had some decent clothes. Next door they had a wonky black and white TV, cooked off kerosene, washed out of a bucket and slept on dirty mattresses in cramped conditions. The three small boys ran around in dirty, torn underwear. I never found out half the names of the resi-dents but collectively I called them the 'Damelos' because the most regular shout I heard through the window of my bed-room was '*Damelo!* Give it to me!', inevitably delivered with a sharp '*cojones!!*' added for emphasis. I don't think Tania approved of me mixing with the Damelos — she hardly ever let the girls out on the street, arguing that she didn't want them picking up bad language – but she was always interested in hearing any gossip I had picked up while shooting the breeze with the neighbours.

Between the Damelos' house and the *bodega* on the oppo-site side of the road (the *bodega* was where rations of rice, beans, sugar and gloopy soya yoghurt were doled out each day) sat the *barrio* sports field. If you want an explanation for why Cuban sportsmen and women perform so well despite poor equip-ment and archaic facilities, the answer lies in the competitive-ness and ingenuity of their street games. Take baseball, for instance. Day after day, I watched young kids practising with a sawn-off broom handle as an improvised bat and metal bottle tops – spun by the pitcher like miniature Frisbees – as balls. If you could hit a tiny flying piece of metal with an inch-wide stick, imagine what you could do when someone gave you a proper bat and ball. For games, a rubber ball was used and a diamond of bases was formed using the corners of two build-ings and a lamp-post. To make it fairer for the fielding team – the outfield hazards were numerous – batters were only allowed to do a fast walk between bases. With no referees, the regular close calls had to be decided by furious group arguments and games were often delayed by lengthy verbal exchanges.

When not playing their beloved *pelota*, the local group of teenagers would string a rope between two houses and play netball or place two crudely welded metal goals on the road for a four-a-side football (barefoot, of course) competition. Less energetic members of the community sat down for a game of table football using a wooden board dotted with strategically placed pins. Each player would take it in turns to flick a 2-peso coin until it finally managed to thread its way though the metal maze and a goal was scored. For adrenaline sports, on the other hand, you had to go to the top end of Calle Santa Lucia, where a calf-straining gradient offered a perfect starting ramp for bicycle luge. Two boys would race side by side down the hill – heads tucked below handlebars to reduce friction – with the winner being the one that reached the *bodega* at the bottom first. No braking or pedalling was allowed but shout-ing was permitted if pedestrians strayed on to the track. Another equally dangerous hill sport involved strapping flattened plastic bottles to your feet and skiing down the slope.

But for real spectator entertainment nothing could beat a competitive game of dominoes. Every afternoon on the famous Padre Pico steps, the other major focal point of the *barrio*, two tables and eight chairs were ceremoniously brought out on to the steps. The steep incline between Calles Santa Lucia and Santa Rita used to be known as Corvacho Hill until Emilio Bacardi had a staircase built at the start of his tenure of mayor and the once hazardous slope became one of the city's great landmarks. In terms of political significance, Padre Pico held a powerful place in Santiagueros' hearts. It was at the top of Corvacho Hill that Spanish forces had first exhibited the dead body of Carlos Manuel de Cespedes in 1873, and eighty-three years later, on almost exactly the same spot, three young revolutionaries were killed while trying to attack the nearby police station. Every year, the brave attack was re-enacted in front of an audience of military bigwigs and ex-revolutionaries, and anyone lucky enough to have a house on the steps had their façade repainted for the event.

There were many reasons why I loved Padre Pico. The view from the top at sunset for one, and then there was the daily tide of locals heading to and from the market, and the friendly woman in the house at the bottom with the two strange-looking dogs called *perros chinos*. But most of all I loved it for the dominoes. The players split up into a quieter top table for oldies and a noisier bottom table for the younger crew. The games went on for hours at a time and the winning and losing were clearly only a small part of the exercise. The two key requirements for gaining entry on to the bottom table were artistic flair (everyone had a distinct style of slapping, slamming or sliding the dominoes into place) and an ability to deliver plenty of verbal abuse at those who either cheated, played badly, or simply deserved abuse. I learned all my best Cuban swear-words from dominoes.

One of my favourite Padre Pico characters was an old man called Roberto. Every morning, he'd set out a variety of objects on the shaded side of the steps. There were hinges, various springs of undetermined usage, old drill bits, funny bits of metal attached like keys along a piece of wire, various plumbing joints, and an array of other appliances whose origins were a complete mystery. Roberto must have been in his seventies, although he didn't look that old. He never wore a shirt, preferring instead to air what was clearly the prize stomach of the block. It looked as though he'd somehow managed to swallow a space hopper. He always wore bright blue trousers and threadbare boots whose backs had been worn down so much they now resembled builder's clogs. His voice sounded like Louis Armstrong's on a hangover and at times, I only caught 50 per cent of what he was saying.

We first spoke one morning as I headed off to the market. Walking past the steps, Roberto called me over and, placing a consoling hand on my shoulder, expressed his condolences and sympathy for '*los Británicos*'. It turned out Princess Margaret had died the previous day and although the news was never likely to ruin my day, I was still touched by this gentle giant's kind gesture. 'How did you hear?' I asked. '*El BBC!*' he proudly beamed back. Given that Roberto didn't speak a word of English and tuning into the World Service required the dial-tweaking skills of a safe-cracker, this seemed highly implausible, but I didn't have the heart to refute his claim. '*El BBC de Londres?*' I asked. '*El BBC de Londres*,' confirmed Roberto with a proud grin.

Although clearly a wizard with a short-wave radio, Roberto was the least successful salesman I have ever encountered. Offering quality goods is always a good start but it also helps if you at least know what you are selling. One morning there was a fight between the *perros chinos* and a stray mutt that led to a dog-separating scuffle and the trampling of one of Roberto's bits of merchandise. 'What was it?' I queried as he picked up the bits of broken plastic. 'I have no idea,' he replied.

The truth was, as I discovered over the weeks of seeing Roberto in action, his pick 'n' mystery hardware store was actually just an ingenious cover for his far more important position as the local king of *piropos*. *Piropos* were an integral part of Cuban street language – they were a bit like a more poetic and polite version of the builder's wolf whistle – and Roberto had one for every woman who swung her hips past his perch. Even the most overweight, ugly passer-by was told her eyes were like stars in the sky and her bottom a wondrous gift from the buttock gods. He had absolutely no shame.

By putting in the hours on Padre Pico I soon got to know

some of the rest of the cast in the street and there seemed to be at least two soap operas-worth of characters. There was Francisco, who worked for an Italian roofing company that had started a joint venture with the Cuban Government. He had a mobile phone, a car, Internet access in his office, and a sister in Italy who sent back money. He was the yuppie of the neighbourhood and his mum, who spent all day surveying the scene from her doorway, was the neighbourhood gossip.

There was Victor, a forty-five-year-old ex-chef who now guarded bicycles down at the market. He worked one day on, one day off, and the off was always spent with a hangover. Victor's drinking partner was Rafael, an ex-inmate from the much-feared Boniato prison. He'd done fifteen years for trying to get into Guantanamo Bay on a raft and claimed he would never be able to get a job again. Rafael was one of the skinniest men on the block, a position he shared with Chino, the local handyman and alcoholic. If there was a dirty job to be done and you could grab him in a relatively sober moment, Chino was your man. Then there was Alexi, the gay nurse, prone to bouts of deep depression, Angel, the shoe repairman, whose pile of work (badly made Cuban shoes that fell apart within a week of being bought) never diminished, Bigoti 'the Moustache' who drove off every morning in his Russian Kama truck to some unknown destination and job, and Rene the wounded soldier.

In a country not short of sad tales, Rene's tale was particularly poignant. A talented electronics engineer, he had studied in Bulgaria and then fought in Angola for three years. A parachute accident had left him with a hip that would never get through an airport X-ray and a spine so munched up he walked with a permanent stoop and could only move his head about 45 degrees from side to side. He was thirty-six years old and his army pension was 100 pesos (£4) a month. To survive he repaired hi-fis. He and his ex-wife, Sandra (it was complicated), and son, Frank, lived in a tiny two-room apartment with Rene's beloved Russian motorbike squeezed in against one wall and the rest of the living room cluttered with cassette players in various states of repair.

Our friendship began through my love of a local drink that Sandra made called *pru*, a non-alcoholic fermented brew made from roots and herbs found in the mountains. Sandra said it was good for your stomach and on the basis of my weekly consumption I reckoned I must have had the healthiest digestive tract in town. As a consequence of my almost daily *pru* pick-ups, I spent a lot of time round at Rene's either watching him operate on a dying patient – usually it was the speakers that had blown – or listening to him sing beautiful love songs with his battered guitar. It was Rene who invited me on my first *barrio* beach trip.

After sex, music and eating greasy food, going to the beach has to be the next most popular form of relaxation for Cubans, probably because it is a place guaranteed to provide all the first three. Sadly, the sand and surf options on the Santiago coast weren't great. When Teddy Roosevelt's rough riders disembarked on Playa Daiquiri's gritty brown stretch of shingle back in 1898 – the Americans had come to fight with the Cubans against the Spanish – they were probably a bit miffed it didn't look at all like the pictures in the 'liberate paradise' recruitment posters. The closest and most visited of Santiago's beaches is Playa Siboney, famous not for its turquoise waters and talcum-fine sand (like Daiquiri, it had neither of these) but for its place in revolutionary history. It was one kilometre from this beach, in a farmhouse called Granjita Siboney, that Fidel gathered his young recruits around him on 25 July 1953 and told them that actually the student carnival trip was going to be a little bit more hazardous than some of them might have thought. They were going to drive into town and attack a heavily fortified army barracks armed with a few shotguns and some wonky rifles. The road from Santiago to Siboney is lined with monuments to the brave men who died during the attack.

The destination for our Sunday outing was neither of these beaches. We were heading for Playa Juragua, described in my guidebook as nothing more than 'a beige-coloured beach popular with Cubans'. It sat just inside the western edge of the 32,400-hectare Baconao Biosphere Reserve, a protected wilderness area that stretches from Santiago's eastern suburbs to the border with Guantanamo province. Our mode of transport was a rented bus or *gua-gua* (pronounced wah-wah), as Cubans called them. Looking at the wheezing wreck reversing back up the street, I could only assume this nickname came from the sound of sobbing passengers when they broke down miles from the nearest settlement. The bus was of Eastern European origin and it was hard to tell whom it endangered most: the passengers who had to risk their lives in it, the pedestrians who had to breathe its noxious emissions, or the other road traffic.

More worryingly, the person responsible for matching number of seats to number of passengers appeared to have made a gross miscalculation, both of the size of the expedition party and the volume of gear being brought along. From my briefest of scans, I counted two giant inner tubes (inflated, of course), some sort of tarpaulin tent for shade provision, two guitars, a large beach ball, various bags of homemade food, a box of mangoes, and numerous bunches of *mamoncillos* – a popular green-skinned fruit about the size and shape of a lychee.

After much milling around, someone with a list shouted out names, and with children sat on knees and the central aisle a jumbled mass of human bodies, inner tube and bags, we pulled away from the kerb with a loud cheer, an ominous grind of gears and an impressive belch of black exhaust. It was close to 11a.m. by the time we reached Juragua – details of the terrain we passed through could only be guessed at since I was standing up and my head was wedged in the middle of the inner tube – and the curve of water lapping eroded matter (a beach would have been too generous a word) was already packed. Requisitioning a small piece of available territory, our team set about erecting the tent-like contraption, not an easy task given the number of missing pegs and the lack of firm purchase for the few that did exist. It didn't offer a lot of shade but that didn't matter much since I seemed to be the only one looking for it.

I don't know what the incidence of skin cancer is like in Cuba, but even taking into account the Cubans' darker complexions, it must be high. For a start, no one uses sun protector because no one can afford it, and second, the average Cuban treats a beach trip as an endurance test to see how long you can stay in the water. Even at the hottest part of the day – when you could probably cook a fish simply by putting it on some reflective foil – the sea was a mass of bobbing heads and wave-hopping torsos. Sitting under cover, slathered in factor 30 and reading a book (no Cuban ever takes a book to the beach), I felt a complete party pooper. The one time I did venture into the water I got caught up in a game of spin the rum bottle that – were it not for a masterly impression of a man with cramp – would have seen me having to snog some bucktoothed *jinetera* who had already shown a strong underwater interest in the strength of my swimming trunks.

On the way home, Rene started playing his guitar and it wasn't long before the whole bus was singing along to the sorts of songs they would be singing in the Casa de la Trova if they weren't always ploughing out 'Chan Chan' and 'Guantanamera'. It was a perfect evening. A huge ripe peach of a sun was melting into the horizon ahead of us and a soft warm Caribbean breeze blew through the open windows of the bus. And then Rene went and spoilt it all by strumming the first familiar chords of 'Hotel California'. Along with the Beatles, the Eagles held a special place in Cuban hearts and there was a time in the 1970s when 'Hotel California' was practically the national anthem. Telling a Cuban that you (an English-speaking you) didn't know all the words to 'Hotel California' was akin to admitting you'd never heard of Kid Chocolate. Mouths dropped, mothers calmed their children, and a noisy bus was reduced to shocked silence. I knew most of the words but most clearly wasn't good enough. Once again, I had failed my Cuban audience and, sinking into my seat with shame that afternoon, I vowed to make amends before my year was out. Honour would be restored somehow.

Although they were making a determined effort to make me feel part of the community, I could tell I was a source of some confusion to the residents of Calle Santa Lucia. I don't think they could quite get their heads around the fact that an Englishman had chosen to come and live in their street for a year, an Englishman who read books on the beach, didn't know how to play dominoes, claimed he once earned a living from tasting wine (for a Cuban that was a hard one to swallow), and who said he was heterosexual but hadn't shown any interest in the many single women on the street. My love life (or lack of it) had quickly become one of the major talking points. As a foreign visitor, specifically a single male foreign visitor, who had not yet succumbed to the pleasures of Santiago's abundant attractions, I was clearly seen as a bit of an anomaly, not to mention a source of some concern among the more macho dinosaurs. 'But you've got to keep the tubes clean,' replied one astonished musician when I revealed how long I had been celibate. This was the same musician who, a week earlier, had been playing on stage and turned white as a sheet on discovering that his wife, three current girlfriends and an ex were all in the audience at the same time.

Even Pastor, in rather more subtle fashion, felt obliged to check everything was all right. One afternoon, apropos of nothing, he casually mentioned that he knew a good '*espacio privado*' should I require a discreet little bolthole to release '*la presión*' as he called it. The Damelos were a little more blunt, demanding daily CNN updates on my *chica* progress. When the same '*nada*' (nothing) headline was delivered, they'd shake their heads as if hearing news that their neighbour was still bed-ridden with a strange illness. Even one of the Government housing inspectors joined in. When she caught sight of a female name signed into 101's official register (an innocent daytime visit of a university colleague) she apparently gave a sigh of relief and told Tania, 'At last Richard has a girlfriend!' You know things are bad when even Cuban immigration is cheering you on from the sidelines.

In the few months I had been in Cuba I had seen and heard every type of foreigner-with-Cuban relationship story and all were equally depressing. Take young Mattheus, for example. When I met this innocent nineteen-year-old German during the carnival, he was deeply in love (or more correctly, lust) with a young Cubana. Despite the presence of a small child and a brother who seemed to be around a lot more than most brothers, Mattheus ended up spending most of his holiday (and his money) convincing himself she was the one. Weeks after he left, I discovered that the so-called brother was, in fact, the husband, and the baby a sympathy-garnering prop lent by a relative who was also in on the act.

And it wasn't just men who fell victim to the classic Cuban love sting. On my way to the idyllic town of Baracoa one weekend, I stopped off in Guantanamo for the night and ended up having a drink with a devastatingly handsome young Cuban dressed up in expensive designer clothes and dripping in jewellery. Not only did he freely admit to being a gigolo, he even brought out a photo album of his previous female clients and told me how easy it was to pick up foreign women. He was about to marry a Japanese girl who, he announced with a cruel laugh, would be setting up a bank account for him and depositing a sizeable quantity of yen before the marriage took place. The night I met him, he was taking the train to Havana to meet a French girl he saw regularly.

Then there were Natalie and Ernesto. Natalie was a friend of a friend of Antonio's and she had come to stay in 101 for a couple of months while preparing for her marriage with Ernesto. Natalie was an overweight, heavy-smoking, fifty-something French Canadian divorcee. She told me she knew lots of Canadian women who had married Cuban men and that a group of them had set up a website with information and advice on how to get through the bureaucratic tangle. Ernesto was her twenty-three-year-old Cuban husband-to-be. I never got the chance to speak to him privately but he seemed happy enough with the brand-new running shoes, the gold watch and the expensive sunglasses, even though the smile wasn't so wide when he emerged from the bedroom every morning. Watching this sham of a romance it was hard to know who to feel more sorry for, but in the end the vote went in Ernesto's favour. Not only was he being forced to listen to Celine Dion on a regular basis but his wife-to-be insisted he took the same ten different vitamin and dietary supplements she took every morning. They married eventually but Ernesto was still waiting for his emigration clearance six months later.

Of course there were exceptions. Occasionally, you came across examples of true, uncorrupted love. Braulio's daughter from a previous marriage had married a young Spaniard she had met at the university. It had taken her eight months of waiting (and endless interviews at the Spanish embassy) before she could join her husband in Malaga, but watching her wedding video – we had weekly showings – even the most cynical observer would have to admit the mutual affection was genuine.

Like any other European male coming to Cuba, I had set off from Britain with an open mind, a bunch of condoms, and a motherly warning to be careful. *Unlike* most other European men, I had also come with the intention of avoiding the sort of eighteen-year-old leggy charmers that made Italian pensioners lose their beanie-covered heads. And as I soon discovered, once you removed the *jinetera* option from the language-exchange game-plan, the chances of a romantic dinner for two became as slim as the odds of finding a romantic restaurant to have it in. Most Cuban women were extremely wary of being seen with foreign men owing to an understandable fear that their family and friends (not to mention the police) would assume they had resorted to prostitution. A date with a *pepe* was more trouble than it was worth.

This was made abundantly clear on a date with Masleys, a beautiful, acorn-skinned mulatta who lived two doors down from the best cake shop in town. I blame my sweet tooth. Despite concerned mutterings from Tania ('Check who she is first, Richard') I decided to invite her to a concert being given by the hugely popular singer-songwriter Polo Montanez. In the wake of the Buena Vista phenomenon, a French record producer had discovered this humble but very talented *guajiro* (a simple country man) singing in a small hotel bar in Pinar del Rio. With his weathered face, straw hat and less than fluid dancing style, Montanez was certainly no pin-up material, but what he lacked in stage presence he made up for with an enviable song-writing talent and an ear for incredibly catchy melodies. 'Un Montón de Estrellas' ('A Mountain of Stars'), a song about how painful love can be, was the big music hit of the year and Cubans of all ages knew its lyrics by rote. His free gig inside the Moncada barracks was expected to be a sell-out (or whatever they call a full free concert) and I took the precaution of picking up Masleys with plenty of time in hand.

The decision proved prescient. Under normal circumstances, the uphill walk to Moncada would have taken us about twenty minutes but Masleys – clearly nervous about being spotted walking alone with a foreigner – insisted we take a detour around the main police points in the city and in the end our journey time was almost doubled. As we approached the line of police who were frisking everyone on their way in, my date suddenly turned to me and said, 'I'll see you inside,' before disappearing alone into the crowd. Normally, I get past the hour mark before they do a runner.

A disused army barracks was a fairly surreal location for a gig but that wasn't the only diversion from a typical concert back home. Here, there were no merchandizing stands or sponsors' logos, the giant arc lights illuminating the parade ground were not switched off even when the band came on, and instead of a Mexican wave, the Cuban audience entertained itself by inflating and releasing vast quantities of condoms into the brisk evening breeze. 'They're no good for anything else,' said the man next to me when I asked whether it was some sort of protest. 'They give us cheap Chinese condoms but we're not the same size as Chinese men.' Their protest was enhanced considerably by the fact that the wind was blowing directly towards the VIP area – equality may be preached in Cuba but it clearly isn't always practised – so the assorted army chiefs and Government officials spent the whole evening swatting away a constant bombardment of transparent Chinese balloons.

Polo gave a good show despite battling against a strong wind, a terrible sound system and the echoing effect of the Moncada walls. If you wanted proof that traditional Cuban music was alive and well, it was right here in this packed parade ground. Even the Rastas had turned up, although that might have had more to do with the lack of alternative entertainment and the group of foreign women they had latched on to. Masleys did eventually return but I could see she was not at all comfortable.

We hardly spoke on the way back to her house and, had I not been desperate to use a toilet, I would have declined her invitation to come inside for a drink. She lived with her mum and brother in the upstairs part of what was once a large colonial house. Like many Santiago homes, the old building had been divided into two with an outside metal staircase leading to the cramped top floor. Bending my head to enter the living room, I was reminded of that scene in *Being John Malkovich* when John Cusack's puppeteer arrives at the seventh and half floor and stoops to avoid smashing his head. Masleys' mother was watching a British film on a black and white TV that had clearly lost some vital component. The top and bottom of the picture were stretched so that everyone looked like they had Tefal heads and the bottom line of subtitles was missing. She offered me rum and, while she went to look for a glass, I asked Masleys if I could use the toilet.

Inside the little door she had pointed to it was pitch black and there didn't seem to be a light switch. Fumbling around, I managed to make out a rough target and with huge relief relaxed and prayed my aim was true. My prayers were sadly not answered. Instead of the sound of liquid on liquid, there was a terrifying shrill nasal scream and what I thought was the toilet suddenly got up and started to charge around my legs. At first I thought it was a giant rat and without even thinking to do up my flies, I screamed, opened the door, and ran out into the living room. The odds of a second date had already been slim but after pissing on the family livestock, I decided to leave Masleys (and the two pigs) in peace.

12. The Road Flatteners

Christmas arrived early at 101. Awoken by the excited screams of Liana and Tanita one afternoon in early December, I walked into the kitchen to find the entire family huddled around a newly purchased accessory. 'What is it?' I asked, secretly hoping it was a bread-maker with which we would be released from the daily disappointment of the Cuban bread roll. 'It's a rice cooker,' replied a proud-looking Tania, carefully extracting the shiny apparatus from its packaging. Rice was the cornerstone of Cuban cooking and a Cuban meal served without rice was simply not a meal. Even when I cooked a pasta dish for the family, Tania would still insist on dishing up the usual mountain of white grains despite my gentle protestations that rice and spaghetti didn't normally go together. Given the growing economic uncertainty, an electric rice-boiling machine seemed a totally unnecessary investment, but judging by the reaction of the two youngest members of the house, I had clearly misjudged the morale-boosting value of rice-associated accessories.

As someone who has generally found Christmas about as much fun as going to IKEA, I had to admit a sneaking admiration for Fidel's attempt to wipe it off the calendar. What a relief to be in a country with no pre-Christmas shopping frenzy, no drunken office parties, and no Slade on the radio. Despite the hasty erection of a Nativity scene above the entrance of the cathedral and the arrival of a few artificial Christmas trees in the dollar stores, there were still, five years after its return to official status, few signs of Yuletide activity. Back home, 25 December would be the usual overdose of calories and bad television. Here in Santiago I was told it would be a normal working day. The trolley traders would still rattle down the street, people would still be queuing outside the Cubana office for a slot on the waiting list, and the Peña Deportiva, the city's baseball fan club, would still congregate under the trees in Plaza de Marte to argue about Santiago's team for the upcoming season.

For all my lack of festive spirit, however, it was hard not to be moved by Tanita and Liana's excitement when 101's own small artificial tree was put in place and the flashing lights were switched on. Seeing the look on their faces made me determined to try to make this a Christmas they would remember. It was time for Santa Claus to go shopping. Calle Enremadas – the main shopping street in Santiago and scene of my struggle to find stocking fillers – was a shadow of its former retail glory. The redundant neon signs, shop names and crumbling colonial buildings gave hints of the lucrative trade once plied on this street, but now the busiest vendors were the mobile sandwich stands and the men mending and refilling cigarette lighters. Of the grand old shops of the Batista years, La Opera now sold tyres and spanners, El Louvre had become a third-hand clothes store, El Encanto's bare shelves offered tinned mackerel, matches and bottles of Ron Mulata, and La California had long ago been boarded up. There were a few signs of rejuvenation. The once beautiful Imperial Hotel was being renovated (well, at least the construction sign said so), the refurbished Fontana de Trevi restaurant was serving tomato-smeared floppy discs again, and the little park on Serrano where slaves used to be flogged was having a much-needed facelift. But generally, like the clocks on the wall at the Cubana office which all told the wrong time at destinations around the world, the signs were not encouraging.

I began my search for Christmas presents down at the bottom end of the street, near the infamous Cine Cuba. A new dollar store had recently been opened and, either as a laugh or an honest attempt to reflect the speed of service and range of goods, they'd called it El Siglo XX, The 20th Century. Looking in the window display, you had to side immediately with the joke option, because standing proudly on a raised plinth was an enormous, brand-new aluminium fridge with a price tag of $2,343.50. Assuming Tania had the luxury of saving her entire doctor's salary every month, I worked out it would take her 156 months (over thirteen years) to buy this fridge. It seemed like the ultimate retail tease and yet according to Pastor, they'd already sold three in six months.

For those without relatives in Miami, El Siglo XX had an upper floor offering a range of items for one dollar. There were toy gun caps (but no gun to use them on), a snorkel (but no mask), shaving foam (but no razor blades), and some packets of something called Geolimp that definitely didn't sound suitable for small girls. I bought a couple of coloured hair bands and moved on.

Up one block there was a small perfume shop. The girls hadn't really reached scent-using age yet but I went in to check the prices none the less. The most expensive was a brand called Alicia Alonso, named after Cuba's most famous prima ballerina and founder of the Ballet Nacional de Cuba. A tiny bottle cost 9 dollars. A variety of cheaper labels filled the locked glass case but their names didn't carry the required elegance and sophistication I was looking for. Superfizz, Immortal Love, Set Point and Eros XX were four of the less suggestive ones.

A couple of doors up, a giant outlet called Tienda Enramadas gave a true indication of the fragility of the peso economy. Its window display might have been funny had it not been so sad. A bunch of pencils had been stacked into a neat wigwam next to some industrial-sized containers of nail varnish, a few bicycle inner tubes and a lone aluminium bucket. Inside, the shop was split into two halves. Down one end was a variety of party accessories for rent. There were cowboy hats, swords, decorations and elaborate models of fairy-tale scenes. At the other end, lines of glass cabinets were filled (perhaps 'prevented from being empty' would be more accurate) with a range of goods that no seven-year-old girl could ever find a use for. There were machetes for 10 pesos each, huge gallon containers of white spirit for 25 pesos, two lonely-looking Betamax video cassettes, an assortment of plumbing joints (I even recognized something from Roberto's stock) and wine bottles filled with something called Kinsol. The skull and crossbones on the label suggested it wasn't drinkable.

In the end, I was forced to do most of my shopping in the Cubalse dollar store on Plaza de Marte. This was where Cubans came to buy soap, shampoo and detergent, while foreigners handed over $2.50 for tubes of out-of-date Pringles and up to 3 dollars for small blocks of rubbery cheese. As in all dollar stores in Cuba, anti-theft measures required that you hand in any bags before entering the premises and then have your shopping checked by a security guard on the way out. As well as finding a few things for the girls, I bought a set of wine glasses for Tania and Braulio, a bottle of Café de Paris champagne (at 8 dollars a bottle I suspected it wasn't champagne) to celebrate with the family, and some sweet Asturian cider as a backup for when they inevitably rejected the French stuff. I was tempted to buy one of the two turkeys sitting forlornly in the freezer, but then I remembered we didn't have a functioning oven at 101 and even after sawing off the legs it would have been a squeeze getting it into the pressure cooker. Besides, Braulio had said he was organizing the meat arrangements. After having my bags painstakingly checked in front of a queue of exiting Cubans – most were leaving with just a tube of toothpaste or a bar of soap – I quickly peeled off the price labels so Tania wouldn't know how much I'd spent and then decanted everything into my rucksack so I wouldn't look like Mr Gluttony on the way home.

A few days later, Braulio's meat arrangement was hauled kicking and screaming out of the boot of the Moskovich. At just over 70 lb she wasn't as big as I'd expected, but with all her resistance, it still required two adults to get the pig moved from the car to the patio at the back of the house. If there was a Christmas tradition in Cuba, then the *asado en pua* ('pig on a stick') was it. The animal was skewered from head to tail with a large pole − after being killed first, obviously − and then turned slowly over an open fire until the skin was crisp and the meat succulent and tender. According to Braulio, you could usually judge if it was ready to eat by the state of the bloke doing the turning. Still sober equalled undercooked, while fallen off the stool and giggling uncontrollably invariably meant your pork was overdone.

With the dinner set for the evening of the 24th, the killing of the pig was pencilled in for the afternoon before. This would allow the meat to hang overnight before being cooked. I'm not sure how I managed to secure the role of executioner but by the time Tanita and Liana had told the Damelos I was going to do it, I could see the backing-out option had gone. Part of me was genuinely interested in seeing whether I could go through with it. Like all meat eaters used to buying neatly packaged, carefully trimmed dead flesh I had become sanitized to the dirty work involved at the other end of the production line. At the age of thirty-five this would be the first time I had killed for my dinner.

For the three days that the pig was tied up in the back shed I avoided all contact. The last thing I needed was emotional attachment. This was not Babe the cute, intelligent, emotionally distressed piggie, this was a dumb, ugly, savage beast that had no idea it was on Death Row. Anyway, that's what I tried to convince myself. As the appointed hour drew close, Braulio set up the old metal operating table once used by the doctor who lived at 101, a fire was lit and a huge cauldron of water was put on to boil. Apparently, this was to help take all the hair off the dead animal. It took an hour for the water to boil and by the time it started bubbling and Braulio had handed me the sharpened kitchen knife, all my bravado had disappeared and the pig looked cuter and more innocent than ever. We decided (actually, I decided) that a shot of nerve-steadying rum would be appropriate and, opening a bottle of Corsario, I shook out the first few drops for the *santos* and then knocked back a large medicinal shot.

The screaming was the worst bit. Even with Braulio's hand clamped over its snout, the pig still managed to let out a continuous blood-curdling, pre-death shriek as we held it down on the wobbly operating table. There was no pretending this pig didn't know what was going on. The noise had brought a line of faces to the Damelos' kitchen window and, added to 101's audience, I reckon I had ten witnesses at the murder scene. It all happened very quickly. Braulio pointed to where I should stick in the knife and with adrenaline pumping and fear of a wimp-out scenario bubbling up fast, I took a deep breath and pushed the blade in hard. After the initial resistance at the skin, the metal slid in sickeningly easily and as the heart punctured, a spurt of warm blood flew out on to my arms and T-shirt. I felt sick. The screaming got even louder and even with Carlos helping us it was hard to keep control of the now writhing body. Braulio massaged the area around the heart and collected as much of the blood as he could in a tin. This, I discovered later, was to be used to make a Cuban version of black pudding. Eventually, after the sort of struggle that would make even the most ardent meat eater have second thoughts about the slab of flesh on his plate, the tin was full of thick beetroot-coloured liquid and the pig was dead. Some of the blood had dripped down on to the patio and Chiri was lapping it up like a cat at a bowl of milk. Tanita prodded the prone body nervously while Liana excitedly announced that there was *caga* coming out of the pig's anus. A round of applause came from the Damelos' window.

Without wasting time, we started pouring boiling water over the pig's flanks and scraped off its hair with a couple of knives. Very soon it was looking far more like the thing you'd find strung up in a butcher's shop than the grunting resident of the patio. With the hard bit done, I felt much less squeamish about running my hands over its body, holding its ears to remove the hair around them and picking off the hard exterior shell on its hooves. Even the act of giving it a final closer shave with a BIC disposable didn't seem or feel as strange as I expected.

The messy part of the procedure had to be done by Braulio since my knowledge of gutting animals could be written on a postage stamp. Bringing over a bucket, he slit open the pig's anus and after clearing away the last of the excrement, stuck his hand in and proceeded to give it a full internal body search. In a series of squelchy excavations he removed the intestines, the bladder, liver, stomach and heart. *Et voilà!* One hollow, ready-to-cook pig was hooked up by its nose next to the washing machine and out came the rum once more for a celebratory drink.

All that expenditure of nervous energy had helped generate a big appetite, and with wonderful cooking smells wafting around the house, I quickly took a shower and opened up a cold bottle of Hatuey. Under normal circumstances, I would have devoured the plate of fried liver that Tania put in front of me, but faced with the knowledge that I had looked into the dying eyes of its owner barely three hours earlier, I somehow couldn't bring myself to put fork to mouth. There were plenty of eager volunteers to eat what I couldn't but I felt a real prize *pepe* as I nibbled away at my salad.

Luckily, my appetite for dead pig was restored by the time we sat down for our Christmas Eve feast twenty-four hours later. Two friends of the family came round that afternoon to handle pig-turning duties and, four hours and a bottle of rum later, the pig was a beautiful dark bronzed colour and the two friends were far less coherent. I suppose there is no sophisticated way in which you can carve up such a dish but, even by Cuban standards, I was shocked by the manner in which the meat was freed from the bones. Having been carried like some sort of tribal offering into the kitchen, the roasted animal was literally ripped apart by four sets of hands. Marcela seemed to particularly relish the job, pulling, kneading and tearing at the rapidly disintegrating carcass with an enthusiasm that defied her normally gentle manner and calm kitchen presence. Hunks of artery-clogging crackling were placed on one plate and fistfuls of meat and fatty matter piled high on a tray. In addition there was rice and black beans (or *moros y cristianos* as they were called), sliced tomatoes and cucumber, and *mariquitas*, thin slices of fried plantain.

A couple of tables were set up end to end on the patio – Braulio surpassing all his many previous electrical feats by stringing up some improvised lights – and we all sat down for one of the best Christmas meals I've ever eaten. It was also one of the quickest. Cubans have to be among the fastest eaters in the world, and after hours of preparation, the actual consumption part of the event was over in less than twenty minutes.

Like all Christmas gatherings, the evening was not without its hiccups. An accident in the hospital kitchen meant that Rosalina and Pastor were delayed and by the time they arrived there was virtually nothing left. Then Tania announced that it was her eleventh wedding anniversary. The look of surprise on Braulio's face turned to undisguised discomfort as she presented him with a new watch and a small pocket radio. It was obvious he had completely forgotten – its coincidence with Christmas Eve left him with little excuse – and in an attempt to extract him from the mire, I jumped up and suggested this was an ideal time to open the champagne. Tanita and Liana couldn't retrieve the bottle from the fridge fast enough but after much twisting and grunting, the cork came out of the neck without even the faintest hint of a gassy release. Years waiting for a buyer in the warm environs of the Cubalse store had left our champagne in less than sparkling form.

Later that night, after I had accompanied Marcela to a packed midnight Mass in the cathedral, two bulging socks were quietly placed at the end of the girls' beds. And at six the following morning, the house got an early alarm call as a series of delighted screams announced the ripping open of presents. The little bottles of shampoo were a great success, as were the fluorescent marker pens, bracelets and hair clips, but there was some confusion over the presence of a couple of strange metal objects with loose wiring hanging out of their sides. Roberto hadn't been able to tell me exactly what they were but he'd insisted they'd be just what a ten-year-old girl would need when she grew up and had a house of her own.

The end of the year was celebrated at the White House and then, on the first weekend of January, the day the city had been waiting for finally arrived: the start of the baseball season. Like most of my fellow Brits, my knowledge of baseball was slim. However, having made the decision to spend a year in a *pelota*-mad environment, a place where the male baseball cynic was viewed with deep suspicion, I was forced to concede that giving baseball a go might be beneficial to general living conditions.

Being the reigning champions, Santiago had the honour of hosting the first game of the season against deadly rivals, Industriales, and like most of the city I was determined to go. But first, I required an immediate and intensive crash course in the rules of the game. After a brief consultation with Pastor, an afternoon was put aside for a session on his PlayStation, and a week after my inauspicious debut, the practice began to pay off.

Baseball was said to have started in Cuba in 1865 when Cuban students returning from US colleges began playing in Havana. The first officially recognized game was played on 27 December 1874 at Palmar del Junco in Matanzas Province between Havana BBC (Baseball Club) and Matanzas BBC. The Spanish opposed any activity thought to demonstrate and encourage Cuban identity, and in the years leading up to the first war of Independence, baseball games were judged to be nothing more than fund-raising events for the freedom fighters, and the sport was banned.

But it returned as soon as the Spanish left. The first baseball championship was held in Havana in 1905 and the Cuban National Amateur Baseball League was established in 1914. Although England surprised everyone by winning the first World Championship in 1938 (unbelievably, we beat the United States 4–1 in the final), Cuba won four of the next five annual events. Pre-Revolution, there were just four major teams in the national league (Cienfuegos, Almendades, Havana and Marianao) and each was allowed to hire five American players. Post-Revolution, Fidel – himself a huge *pelota* fan who once tried out as a pitcher for the Washington Senators – was determined to make it a truly national (not just Havana-based) sport, accessible to all players whatever their means, and 100 per cent Cuban. A national league was established, stadiums built in most of the big cities (entry to games was free), and a network of specialist sports academies established to nurture young talent.

Forty-two years after the triumph of the Revolution, the national league had grown into four regional groups with four teams in each. The season ran from October to May and all teams played each other home and away in two separate three-game series (the third game of the series was always played in a small town away from the provincial capital, giving fans in the *campo* a chance to watch their heroes in the flesh), with the top two teams in each group going through to the play-offs. The final itself was a seven-game series matching up the best of the East against the best of the West and inevitably it stirred up the Oriente *v.* Occidente rivalry to levels almost as dangerous as the TV-induced power surge on the national grid.

My first chance at practising the baseball patter came with the World Championships in Taipei. These took place a couple of weeks after Hurricane Michelle had ploughed through the centre of the island (Santiago, disappointingly, received nothing more than heavy rain) and a battered nation was forced to look to its baseball stars to deliver some much-needed good news. Within a week of the Taipei coverage starting, my PlayStation-induced bug had turned into full-blown baseball fever. Time differences between the Caribbean and Taipei meant that almost all the matches were being played at 4 a.m. Cuban time. I think Tania and Braulio really started to get concerned when they found me slumped in front of the television at five one morning engrossed in a very one-sided fixture between Cuba and the Philippines. Cuba won that one 17–0. They went on to beat Japan 3–1 in the semis, leaving everything teed up for the perfect final: Cuba versus the United States.

Of course, there were the inevitable comparisons between the US team, with its healthy smattering of professional players, and the 100 per cent amateur Cuban squad, but the sort of jingoistic fervour you might have expected from such an obvious David *v.* Goliath scenario never materialized. Only when Cuba came through victorious with a hard-fought 5–3 win did *Granma*'s editorial team let off steam with an undisguised dig at the non-amateur status of their rivals. Announcing the triumph of the 2001 World Champions, the headline read, 'You are not a rented product, you are a product of the Revolution!' Not the snappiest of headlines, but it made the point.

Delayed for two months by the World Cup, those same products of the Revolution prepared to start the national league in January. It might have been less glamorous than the Taipei event but to the real baseball aficionados, the domestic competition was the one that mattered most. Cuba beating the United States was a source of great pride, but Santiago winning the league was a three-month trial of nerves and stamina. With a full stadium guaranteed for the first game, I volunteered to cycle down early and buy tickets for me, Rene and a couple of the Padre Pico crowd. The match wasn't due to start until 2 p.m. but they were starting to sell tickets at 9 a.m. There were two prices: 2 pesos for a seat directly behind the plate, and 1 peso for anywhere else. Whatever the faults of the Revolution – and there were a few – you had to applaud a country that allowed you to watch the triple national champions for the princely sum of about two or three pence. The woman in the ticket booth wasn't impressed with my peso-paying intentions. Normally, foreigners were expected to pay in dollars. But with a long queue behind me starting to grumble, she begrudgingly slid back my student carnet along with five tiny paper stubs. I had to wipe the sweat off my hands first for fear the flimsy but extremely precious tickets would dissolve.

The Cuban baseball experience was a world away from the glitzy razzmatazz of the US equivalent. The stadium itself was an ugly old concrete affair overlooking a well-tended, though by American standards, uneven grass playing area with a giant electronic scoreboard that was almost impossible to read in the bright sunlight. There was a small press and players' family area down at ground level but those were the only proper seats in the place. Everyone else sat on concrete steps.

They say Cuba is one of the few places left where you can watch sport in its purest and most uncorrupted form. No performance-enhancing drugs, no playing times controlled by powerful advertisers, no sponsor's logos on shirts, and no teams made up of hired hands from all parts of the globe. Instead of revolving advertising hoardings you got Revolutionary slogans along the perimeter of the field. 'The Cuban Athlete – Example of Patriotism and Fighting Spirit' said one. 'Power of the Masses – Guarantee of Sporting Quality' extolled another. There were obviously no merchandise stands so there was no sea of replica shirts, no Santiago baseball caps, and no kids with Antonio Pacheco-signed gloves. The food came unbranded too. Instead of hotdogs and burger stands, you had hawkers walking up and down the steps peddling various snacks. There were little paper cones of peanuts, cardboard boxes of greasy chicken and rice, lurid green candies, sandwiches filled with pink sweating slabs of processed meat, and melting chocolate biscuits handed out from the box with clear disregard for food and safety regs. For refreshment, men with blocks of ice and a metal scraper offered cordial-flavoured ice shavings – a sort of poor man's slush puppy.

Consumption of alcohol was prohibited but despite the police checks at the gate, little bottles of smuggled-in rum were being passed around everywhere.

Experience of Santiago's baseball supporters' club suggested that the stadium would be at least 80 per cent male but surprisingly, women had turned up in equal numbers. Most were dressed as if ready for a post-match disco and as the late arrivals squeezed past, *piropos* rained down like complementary confetti. '*Oye Guapa!*', '*Mami, ven acá!*', '*Negrita!*' came the shouts from the stands, and the recipients acknowledged the attention by either slowing down or sometimes even stopping and pretending to look for someone.

For the first two innings, the crowd remained relatively restrained. With both teams looking rusty and no runs on the board, most of the attention was directed towards a small, overweight ball collector whose job it was to waddle around picking up the strays and handing them over to the umpire standing behind the plate. The little guy's name was Pipo and in big letters on his back it said '*Pipo el Sabroso* – Pipo the Tasty One'. Judging by the amount of friendly abuse that rained from the stands, he was an institution. 'How long has he been working here?' I asked Rene. 'Pipo? As long as I've been coming, Pipo's been picking up balls.' He had to shout the last bit of the answer because a huge roar of approval drowned out his voice. Santiago had come back in to bat for the third inning, but that wasn't the reason for the excitement. It was the movement of a group of men on a platform above the Santiago dug-out. Like a bugle call to battle stations, the shrill siren of a Chinese cornet cut through the vocal din and a few seconds later the stadium conga band (and the stadium itself) simultaneously exploded into life. The effect was instantaneous. Everyone rose to their feet and with arms raised in a praise-the-Lord sort of way, began shaking their tail feathers while doing the conga leg shuffle. To huge applause, a large woman in a one-piece black and white striped Lycra body glove climbed on to the flat roof above the Santiago players and began the most extraordinary bottom-gyrating, hip-grinding routine. In any other country she'd have been led away by the stewards and perhaps given a caution for indecent exposure or provocative bottom movement. Here in the Guillermón Moncada stadium, the police just smiled and let the show go on. The power of the conga was incredible. If the Industriales team had forgotten which part of the country they were in, they certainly knew now.

'Those are the guys you should be playing with,' said Rene, pointing to the dozen or so guys thrashing their instruments below us. Rene knew all about my interconnected rhythm-*bomba*-tempo problems but until now had not seen fit to divulge a suitable remedy.

'This is the most polyrhythmic music in Cuba. If you want to find *la bomba*, go play in the conga.'

Much as I welcomed any new advice on *bomba* discovery, Rene's suggestion did seem to be skirting around a couple of obvious points of concern. First, the conga was very much a black guy's turf, and even if I basted myself with baby oil for the next two weeks I was never going to pull off the brothers-in-arms trick. I had never seen a single pale-skinned Cuban playing in a conga band and this one was no exception. Second, they looked the meanest bunch of muvvers in town. I saw bandannas, gym-toned bodies, visible scarring, complicated hand-shaking ceremonies and at least two accidents with the peroxide bottle. All the signs of trouble in the hood were there. This was no place for a man who used a facial moisturizing cream and needed vinegar dip to toughen up his fingers.

The conversation soon spread to the rest of the group. 'A *pepe* in a conga band?' shrieked the youngest member of our entourage. 'You'd need to have very big *cojones*,' said another. '*Nunca!* – Never!' chipped in an eavesdropper behind us. Normally, I wouldn't have pandered to pathetic taunts like these but clearly I'd been in Cuba too long. Male pride was at stake. *Cojones* size was being questioned. The gauntlet had been thrown down and I knew that at some stage before the season was over I would have to attempt to pick it up.

Some two hours and much conga action later, an even bigger cheer went up when the giant Fausto Alvarez – at forty-two the oldest player in the Santiago team – struck one sweetly into the crowd for the first home run of the championship. *La Aplanadora* – 'the Road Flattener', as Santiago's awesome batting line-up was nicknamed, was already on a roll.

13. Temporary Twitcher

One afternoon, while alone in the White House waiting for Pastor to return from a cigarette-hunting expedition, I stumbled across a sobering reminder of the enormous difference (in aptitude and attitude) between the ex-tank engineer and the ex-wine writer. Over lunch, I'd asked Pastor whether he knew anyone with a video camera (I wanted to put down some visual proof to show my family), to which he'd pointed out the camera he was currently renting and told me he would be happy to do the video diary himself. With the house empty and the old camcorder connected up to the TV, I found myself unable to resist the temptation to take a quick peek at whatever he'd been filming. Quickly checking there was still no sign of him coming down the hill, I turned on the TV – a heavy thump was still required to bring the screen to life – and then pressed the play button on the camera.

The tape had been rewound to the beginning and after a few seconds of fuzzy nothingness, a black and white image appeared. I immediately recognized the familiar lurid wall drapes, the little Christmas tree and the elephant piggybanks. It was clear from the grainy 'Blair Witch'-style illumination and lack of background noise that the recording had been done very late at night and the stillness of the image suggested the camera had been set up on a tripod ready to record whatever was about to happen in this living room. Was I about to find yet more proof of my teacher's eccentricity? A midnight meeting of the Chicharrones Ouija Board club perhaps? A few seconds later, a bare-chested figure appeared in front of the camera (with bass in hand), and the purpose of the recording became clear. Rather disappointingly, it was nothing more exciting than a late-night practice session. After checking the instrument was in focus and centred in the middle of the viewfinder, Pastor took up the playing position and without saying a word launched into a lengthy bass solo that brought back memories of Cachaito Lopez's display at the Festival Hall. As I watched this rather eerie demonstration – if it was the middle of the night how come there were no annoyed shouts from the neighbours? – I realized with a depressing finality that I would never be as good as Pastor because I was never going to be as fanatical about the double bass as Pastor. Playing was everything to him. To me it was important but not that important. I certainly wouldn't get out of bed to do a midnight recital, and I definitely wouldn't record myself playing. Pastor couldn't wait to practise whereas I looked for any excuse not to. This was nature versus nurture. Pastor was a natural. I needed a lot of nurture.

It was now just over four months until I planned to stand up on stage with Sones de Oriente (unbelievably, none of the band members laughed when Pastor broke the news – they were too stunned to laugh) and bar a sudden leap in my progress rate or the rapid composition of some *son* that only required a single-note bass line, I knew I was facing humiliation of suit-wetting proportions. Depressed and not just a little scared by the thought of what was going to happen, I tried consoling myself with my musical achievements over the last six months.

At least I was now fingerboard friendly. I had cracked the 'name the note' tests to the extent that I was thinking about finally unpeeling the embarrassing little strips of marker tape. Just thinking, mind. Given a letter from A to G, I could go up and down the appropriate scale without thinking. I had reached the second CD of the *True Cuban Bass* book and I could play the bass line to 'Chan Chan' (as long as no one was playing the *clave* at the same time). And I now had fingers that were almost as ugly as Pastor's. For a man who, in Jennifer's flat, had taken over half an hour just to locate and play a note at the half position, it looked like I had come a long way.

But a long way wasn't far enough. I knew that to perform with a band I needed to be much further along the learning curve. I had yet to complete successfully a full song with the *clave*, let alone a full complement of other instruments, and just the idea of me jamming with a bunch of other musicians seemed utterly preposterous. My confidence was, in truth, as fragile as an old peso note, and as for my continuing search for *la bomba*, I had now resigned myself to the fact that perhaps my *bomba* (if it existed) didn't actually wish to be found.

'What do you think, *compay*?' interrupted Pastor, who had crept in without me noticing.

'The picture's a bit grainy,' I replied. 'And I was hoping to have something in colour.'

'The bass playing, *compay*, not the quality of the picture.'

'Oh, sorry, it was great – that bit with the harmonics was brilliant. What time did you film it?'

'It was three in the morning.'

'Three? Don't you ever sleep?'

'Sometimes I just wake up and feel I have to play.'

I was expecting him to be annoyed at my nosiness but the truth was I think he had deliberately left the camera connected to the TV. He'd wanted me to see what was on the tape. Here was another of those teacher–pupil moments, another jolt to remind me how becoming a musician required complete and utter dedication.

'Next week I want you to start coming to the group practice sessions,' declared Pastor, unplugging the camera and reconnecting the TV to the PlayStation machine. 'It's time you started getting used to playing with other instruments.'

'Could we make it the week after next?' I answered quietly, realizing the news I was about to deliver was going to cause a major upset.

'What's wrong with next week?'

'I'm . . . I'm going . . .'

Pastor had stopped flicking through his pack of copied computer games and was looking at me with an expression somewhere between frustration and resignation.

'I'm going to the mountains for a few days.'

'*Las montañas, compay?*'

'Yes, the Sierra Maestra. I'm going to climb Pico Turquino.'

From way back at the planning stage of my musical sabbatical, it had been one of my dreams to go trekking in the same mountains where Fidel's *barbudos* had waged their guerrilla warfare, and since arriving in Santiago, all my reading material had focused on that extraordinary two-year campaign in the Sierra Maestra. For foreign visitors the summit of Pico Turquino – Cuba's highest peak – was notoriously hard to reach. Not because the climb was particularly challenging or required extensive local knowledge – it was a well-marked track – but because it was very difficult to get permission to enter the park where the mountain sat. Paranoia over alleged CIA attempts to destroy the country's coffee crop by importing plant-killing diseases meant an enormous tract of wilderness had, on and off for years, been declared a tourist-free zone. Imagine my delight, then, when the Santiago branch of CITMA (Ciencias Tecnología y Medioambiente), the organization responsible for handing out permits, informed me that the restrictions had recently been relaxed and I would be allowed to follow in the footsteps of Che Guevara as long as I went with a guide. It was common knowledge that CITMA changed their policy on a regular basis, so I knew I had to take this opportunity, White House explosions or not.

I tried to put a positive spin on it. I told Pastor that this physical challenge would help me find the inspiration to climb other more metaphorical mountains in the months to come. Little Sindo Garay, one of Santiago's best-loved songwriters, had gained his spurs by swimming across Santiago's bay to deliver messages for the Mambi freedom fighters. Miguel

Matamoros had reached the depths of El Cobre's copper mines. Now it was time for Neill to reveal his inner toughness by hacking through the cloud forest.

Understandably, this image didn't seem to make any impact on my frowning friend, so I tried a different tack and put a musical spin on it. *Son* comes from the mountains, man seeks *son*, man goes to mountains, was the gist of my argument. Pastor was having none of it. Although I'd only left Santiago twice in six months, my announcement of a week-long trip to the *campo* had gone down like a power cut during a baseball final.

'You won't find *la bomba* in the mountains!' he shouted as I pushed the bike back up Crackling's steepest gradient half an hour and much arguing later. It wasn't often you heard Pastor shouting, and for the first time since I had started coming to Chicharrones, the two men cutting up plastic stopped what they were doing to listen.

'Do you really want to be a bassist?' came the aggrieved voice receding behind me. I knew it would be futile to respond so I kept going without looking back. 'We don't have time for mountains, *compay*!' was the last thing I heard before turning the corner.

Joining me on my trip to the Sierra Maestra was one of my friends on Calle Santa Lucia. Melian worked for the National Science Museum in Santiago. He was the most experienced and knowledgeable ornithologist in the east of Cuba and over the last three years had been undertaking research – funded by the Ornithology Society of Basel – on an extremely vulnerable endemic species of woodpecker called Carpinteros Churroso, or Fernandina's Flicker as it was more commonly known. On a budget that most European organizations would set aside for food expenses, Melian had spent months trekking across the Oriente tracking these rare birds. He was a walking donation – hiking boots, binoculars, rucksack, spectacles and bicycle were all gifts from tourists and foreign organizations. His favourite toy was a pocket Satellite Navigation device that could tell him the exact altitude and position where each bird sighting took place. Every time he turned it on, he would proudly announce how many satellites ('Six, Richard, we've got six!') he was picking up. Years of fighting against mosquitoes and bureaucrats had dampened neither his enthusiasm for his job nor his daft sense of humour. He once joked that he was one of the few Cubans who wanted to get into Guantanamo Bay but not leave the country.

'There are twenty-two wetland areas along this south-east coast and probably the most rich in terms of wildlife is inside Guantanamo Bay,' he told me. 'With all those mines, it has to be the most well-protected sanctuary in the country.' The irony tickled him enormously.

Melian was also a magician in the kitchen – no mean feat when you are still cooking off kerosene and your oven is a converted washing machine heated by burning wood. During the hungry years of the so-called Special Period, his kitchen had been converted into a laboratory as lack of ingredients forced him to invent his way through the crisis. Aubergines would be boiled and the water then left to cool until the small quantity of released vegetable oils could be strained and used for frying. Nothing would be wasted. Unused animal fat was turned into soap, the white pith peeled from oranges and mixed with water and sugar to make a dessert, the peel dried and used to make tea.

Today he was no less resourceful, and refused to allow his culinary ambition to be dampened when out on expeditions. His greatest boast was that he'd taken a group up Pico Turquino and on the first evening amazed them all by serving up meringues. Melian and I had come to a mutually convenient agreement. I would help him out by funding the expedition, allowing him to do some much-needed Fernandina Flicker research without digging into his already depleted resources. He would scratch my back by allowing me to become his research assistant for a week – a temporary twitcher, if you will

– thus allowing me the opportunity to get around the normal single-day tourist pass and extend my stay in the mountains to a more Pastor-baiting five nights.

'Just in case someone asks you a few questions about birds, you'd better have a look through this,' said Melian, handing me a doorstopper reference guide to Cuban birds one afternoon, 'but don't worry too much about the Latin names.'

Every day in the weeks running up to our departure I sat down and mugged up on bird life. Every evening Tanita and Liana would bring out the illustrated poster Melian had given me and test me on my bird-spotting skills. Revealing a worrying fascination for the minutiae of ornithological detail, I soon started to build a terrifying arsenal of bird trivia. I learnt that Bicknell's Thrush wintered in small numbers on the higher slopes of Pico Turquino, that the Cuban Solitaire was an extraordinarily gifted singer, and that the Cuban Toddy was very territorial and produced a peculiar whirring sound when it beat its wings. I was soon boring Antonio with monologues about the rare Cuban Pigmy Owl (nests in natural cavities, eats insects and lizards, tawny brown colouring, short legs – entirely feathered) and made Braulio nod off even faster than normal by informing him that hummingbird nests were made and tended exclusively by females.

Cuba, I quickly discovered, was a twitcher's paradise. The country boasted roughly 350 species of bird (about twenty-one of those endemic) including the minuscule Bee Hummingbird – at just over 6 centimetres long considered to be the world's smallest bird – and the beautiful national bird, the Cuban Trogan, whose vermilion belly, violet-blue crown and white throat and breast combined to form the colours of the island's flag. But it was a paradise being slowly eroded. A combination of habitat destruction, poaching and illegal smuggling had made a serious impact on bird numbers in the last fifty years and thirty species were now on the 'threatened' list. Poachers often used fine nets normally used for catching herring – whole flocks of Northern

Bobwhite were being cornered and captured using dogs – and smugglers earned thousands of pounds by taking exotic birds to the United States. A single Cuban Bullfinch, smuggled through Customs in a perforated cigar tube, was worth at least 300 dollars in Miami.

A few days before departure, a pre-trip pow-wow dispelled any illusions that we were going on a simple ramble through the countryside. Spreading out an old Ordnance Survey map on the table, Melian traced our route across contour lines that looked as tightly packed as fingerprints. The normal way up Turquino was a well-marked track that left the coastal settlement of Las Cuervas and climbed to Pico Cuba at 1,650 metres and then up the last 300 metres to the island's highest point. But Melian had his eye on the far more challenging West Face. Claiming there had been sightings of Fernandina's Flicker in a place ominously known as the Devil's Door, he suggested taking the harder route that shadowed the Palma Mocha River and followed a steeper and rarely used line to the summit. As well as guaranteeing an undisturbed ascent, this path would take us right past the scene of the 'Inferno of Palma Mocha', one of the first serious episodes of combat between Fidel's troops and Batista's army. Shaking off growing doubts about my physical readiness for such a challenge – half an hour of aerobics in the gym still left me in a position not dissimilar to Willem Dafoe's death scene in the film *Platoon* – I gave a thumbs-up signal to my team leader and took another swig of beer.

The plan was that we'd spend the first night at sea level with a friend of Melian's, climb up to Pico Cuba the following day and, after a night at 1,650 metres, strike out for the summit. After a few days of trekking and bird monitoring, we'd then descend back to the coast and try to find a bus home. Melian had prepared all the equipment we'd need for the six days away. Two sets of binoculars, a small tape recorder for logging birdsong, a video camera, two wafer-thin sleeping bags, water bottles, thermos, a couple of pots for cooking, cutlery – the man clearly knew what he was doing. And then came his food list, which clearly suggested that picking up local supplies was not an option. It included four tins of sardines, two packets of hot dogs, two tins of cooked ham, five packets of dried soup, five packets of spaghetti, a bag of rice, two bottles of tomato salsa (homemade), one bottle of what Melian called *condimento especial* (a home-made super-concentrated salsa), chocolate powder, powdered milk, a vast quantity of sugar, six packets of biscuits, three bags of boiled sweets, and three bottles of something worryingly labelled '*estimulante*'.

'*Estimulante?*' I queried.

'That's the secret ingredient to help us up the mountain.'

'So it's a difficult climb then?'

'Not too difficult, but you'll be glad of a boost.'

The boost in question turned out to be a very quaffable but lethal blend of sweet palm wine, rum and honey, which after being mixed and shaken was decanted into four cleaned-out Coca-Cola bottles. It probably contravened all mountaineering etiquette, not to mention the guidelines for successful bird-watching, but if it helped ease the pain that was good enough for me. The level of organization was staggering. The night before we left, I went round to expedition headquarters to divide all the food and equipment into our two rucksacks and found Melian hard at work at the ironing board. Not only had he broken down the rations into portions for every single meal and marked each bag with a felt-tip pen, he was now sealing each of the bags with a hot iron. As always, there was a perfectly good explanation for his eccentric actions.

'This way, the food stays dry and we don't eat everything in the first two days,' he explained.

I nodded in agreement, happy to let the professional take care of the culinary minutiae of our trip.

When the two rucksacks were put side by side, I felt ashamed at the state of my equipment. There was me with my sexy blue Kiwi-designed Macpac with its adjustable shoulder straps,

padded back and special Teflon-coated crampon compartment.
Spot the sucker for a sales pitch. And there was Melian with
an old canvas army rucksack that looked suspiciously like the
model being worn by Fidel in those Alex Korda black and
white snaps taken in the 1950s. It had two of the flimsiest
shoulder straps I have ever seen and the top flap was tied down
by a strap-and-buckle arrangement clearly poached from a
school satchel. No wonder the man had back pains.

After loading up all the food – my guilt ensuring most of
the heavy tins went into the Macpac – it was clear that we
were going to a) die of exhaustion just getting to the bus terminal and b) be very smelly when we got home. Even after ditching a few non-essential items from Melian's *smorgasbord* of
campfire goodies there was only sufficient room for one change
of clothes, a flannel and a small wash-bag. The sleeping bag had
to be wrapped in polythene and strapped to the outside.

Our journey to base camp was to be by bus to the town of
Chivirico, then a ride on a *camión* (the open-backed trucks used
as buses in most of rural Cuba) from Chivirico to Las Cuevas.
That was the plan, a plan that hadn't counted on petrol shortages and a complete meltdown of public transport along the
south coast. After sitting in the bus station for six hours, it was
evident we would have to employ the services of Mr Greenback
and switch to a less adventurous but slightly more efficient
mode of transport. Melian rang up a friend who rang up another
friend and after some haggling we managed to organize the
240-kilometre return trip to Las Cuevas in a nice air-
conditioned Peugeot for 60 dollars. Our taxi driver was a
mechanical engineer who had lost his job when the sugar mill
he was working in had closed down.

The road hugging this south-eastern corner of Cuba was
another triumph of the post-Revolution engineering programme. At the same time as workers were constructing *La
Farola* – the gear-crunching mountain hugger that finally connected Baracoa with the rest of Cuba – other road builders

were laying down concrete slabs along one of the most beautiful and isolated stretches of coastline in the country. According
to Melian, the many crosses seen by the side of the road marked
the graves of those who had died waiting for a passing boat to
take them to Santiago for medical attention during the nineteenth century. The bitter irony was that in 2001, the inhabi-
tants clinging to this rocky shore had a road but could still die
waiting for a bus to turn up.

Dipping in and out of heavily pot-holed sections, we passed
little traffic apart from the odd lone cyclist. A few scrawny cattle
and a dried-out, abandoned vineyard indicated this was not the
place to invest in a *finca*. Apart from the odd stony beach and
occasional pocket of mangroves, the only attractions on this
coast were the visible skeletons of Spanish ships destroyed by
the US fleet in the great naval battle of July 1898. These shallow
wrecks offered the few diving opportunities in what was
otherwise very deep and very dark water. Between here and
Jamaica lay the 7,500-metre deep Bartlet Pit.

The road got steadily worse, distorting our driver's Eighties
ballads collection to the extent that Bonnie Tyler sounded as
if she was singing 'Total Eclipse of the Heart' while gargling.
Just before Chivirico we passed Cayo Dama, a postcard-pretty
island barely 100 metres off the shore, where the Bacardi family
used to come for holidays. Their magnificent old wooden house
could still be seen under the shade of giant Royal palms. A
small fishing boat was tied up to the jetty but the island looked
totally deserted. Chivirico was a melancholic, one-street town
with a few stores, a crumbling cinema and a baseball stadium
with a mountain backdrop to steal bases for. There seemed to
be a lot of people loitering with no intent, and with its fishing
industry long finished, the town's only purpose was presumably as a hub for what little transport still existed.

Next up was El Uvero, an ex-lumbering community famous
for being the site of one of Fidel's most important military
victories. Many considered the battle of El Uvero to be the

turning point in the fight against Batista. On 28 May 1957, sixty revolutionaries successfully attacked and took over the well-protected military barracks – some of the insurgents didn't even have weapons – and the victory sent an important message not just to the dictator but also to the Cuban people who had heard nothing but Government propaganda since Fidel landed. A beautiful park lined with double rows of Royal palms had been built to honour those who died in the attack.

Some two and a half hours after leaving Santiago, we finally arrived at the tiny community of Las Cuervas, the entry point to the main Turquino trail. Darkening clouds were drifting down the flanks of the mountains rearing steeply above us and the smell of rain filled the air. Melian's opinion that my threadbare running shoes would be sufficient footwear now seemed extremely dubious. With the nearest telephone being 5 kilo- metres away at La Plata, there had been no way of contacting our hosts before arrival, but Alexis, the friend whose house was to be our base camp, seemed overjoyed to have visitors. Even out here, the CDR system was in place. On a pin-board on the veranda, a sign said CDR No. 3. Underneath there was a membership list (five names), a few community notices, and a handwritten two-page biography on Che. There can't have been more than twenty houses in Las Cuervas, yet like all Cuba's remote rural settlements, there was still a small school with a computer powered by solar panels.

During our car journey, Melian had told me about Alexis's father, Palomino, one of the most knowledgeable mountain guides in the area. He had retired and moved to Santiago for medical reasons and his protégé had now taken on the lead role. Photographic evidence suggested son was either just as good as father or just very well connected. Snooping around the living room, I found some snaps of him standing on the summit with Raul Castro and a bevy of bodyguards. You could tell they were bodyguards because they were the only ones refusing to say 'cheese'.

'That was last year,' said Alexis when I asked when the photo had been taken. He told me it had been a stressful job preparing for the visit.

'Before he came, I had to take photos of the entire route with all the potential danger spots for security and I had to make sure I could answer any question he had about the plants or wildlife.' Curiosity got the better of me and as tactfully as possible, I casually inquired how long it had taken the seventy-one-year-old to reach the summit. 'Oh, we took our time,' answered Alexis diplomatically, 'it took us about eight hours.'

We'd only been in the house twenty minutes when a knock on the door signalled the arrival of an official from the Flora y Fauna office up on the hill. He'd obviously spotted us struggling with our rucksacks and immediately twigged our intentions went beyond a quick day trip. From his deadpan reaction to Melian's first joke, it was clear the man had had a sense of humour bypass. Quickly realizing our appeal would depend on some academic spin doctoring, I casually dug out the bird book and began making notes with a suitably earnest expression.

The debate went on for nearly an hour. Melian showed him his Government-stamped letter allowing him access to all parks. I showed him my impressive student carnet that permitted me access to absolutely nothing. Melian talked about Fernandina's Flicker. I mentioned my postgraduate thesis on the importance of eastern Cuba as wintering ground for migrating Neartics. And somehow we managed to pull it off. Weighing up the odds of a bollocking from immigration against the odds of a shaking down from his bosses if Melian (and Fernandina's Flicker) were as important as claimed, the official reluctantly approved our request. Sadly, he wouldn't let us up the Palma Mocha route – something to do with Raul's holiday home being up there – but we were given a four-night pass provided Alexis joined us on the way up. Since we planned a pre-dawn start, he suggested we followed him up to the Flora y Fauna HQ to pay our 5-peso entry fee and sign our names in the book.

HQ was, perhaps, being a bit generous. His office contained just a table, two chairs, a two-way radio and an out-of-scale map of the park that looked as though it had been drawn by a six-year-old. I asked him what the temperature was like at the top and after a quick Broadsword-to-Danny-Boy call to the three men living at the refuge on Pico Cuba, a static-obscured voice came back with an answer of ten degrees and falling. Four bottles of *estimulante* was never going to be enough.

There should now follow a stirring account of our battle to ascend Cuba's highest peak – a tale of flash floods, daring leaps across yawning chasms, fraying ropes and gallant refusals to eat the last biscuit. But since I'm not much of a liar, here's what really happened. After eating rather too much of Alexis's excellent freerange duck that night and drinking enough rum to make me too comatose to notice the vast squadrons of tourist-starved mosquitoes, I awoke head-sore and bite-covered to find Alexis had saddled up a couple of sturdy mules.

'I decided you'd never get up there with those packs,' he smiled over a breakfast of sweet coffee and stale cake, and after I'd had a quick confab with Melian – in our hungover state, resistance was pitifully weak – we both quickly nodded in agreement. Yes, we'd use the mules and no, we wouldn't tell anyone back in Santiago. Half an hour later, I mounted my trusty steed and with much rein slapping and ankle nudging, rode off into a beautiful cloudless dawn with spurs attached somewhat ridiculously to my Nikes.

During our ascent, I did try to keep up with all the birds that Melian kept pointing out but it wasn't easy tracking un-familiar fast-moving objects while trying to ride a very stubborn mule and keep breakfast down at the same time. The path was well marked but at times so steep and overgrown that we were forced to lie flat against our chauffeurs' necks and take a blind leap of faith in their footwork and stamina. Below us, the Caribbean spread out like a dazzling blue carpet. Above, the first wisps of cloud drifted down to meet us, lacing misty fingers through the forest canopy as if the moisture was trying to blindly feel its way down the slope. At just over 1,228 metres – 'Only four satellites, Richard!' – we stopped for an unnecessary but gratefully accepted *estimulante* stop at a place called Alto del Caldera. It was here, informed Alexis, that a soldier had fallen off a ledge and hadn't been found for seven days. He suggested we dismount and let the mules go on ahead. By now, the vegetation had changed from the eucalyptus, cedars and palms of the lower slopes to the ferns, mosses and lichens of the cloud forest. Straggly beards of what looked like green cotton hung from the trees, many of which supported giant leafy cups on their branches. The air had a musty greenhouse tang to it.

An hour and a half later, after a long stop while Alexis and Melian used the binoculars to check out the smoke from an illegal clearing in a valley below, we finally heard distant voices and the sharp crack of axe on wood. A few more switchbacks and slaps on mules' bottoms and we'd arrived at the Micro Estación Biológica, source of the temperature report the previous night and our sleeping quarters for the next four. The centre – set on a piece of flat cleared ground just below the summit of Pico Cuba – was a single-storey wooden building with a tall radio mast and two old water tanks. Off to one side was a lopsided dunny-style hut with '*El baño*' painted on its side and a couple of old copies of *Granma* stuffed into a hole in the door. All over the surrounding ground, thin strips of chopped wood had been laid out to dry in the sun.

The three residents introduced themselves and showed us where to put our bags. The living conditions were extremely basic and it was clear the Micro bit of the title referred to the station's budget more than its physical size. With exterior walls constructed from a single layer of loosely joined wooden slats, and a roof made from corrugated iron, the Micro Estación offered about as much insulation from the elements as a string vest. It looked as though it had been put up in a day and –

with the first direct hurricane hit – would undoubtedly come down in substantially less. At one end was a cooking room with an iron hearth for a fire. There was a food storage room that contained nothing but a small pile of yucca, some rice and a small sack of black beans. The living area had a couple of uncomfortable wooden chairs, a TV that couldn't receive a signal, and a two-way radio that sporadically squawked into life. In a touching attempt to make the place more homely, one of the men had tried to decorate the room using old soft drink cans. He'd sawn off the tops, peeled the tins like a banana, and then carefully attached little sweet wrappers into each stem. On one shelf there was a picture of Elian Gonzalez and his father and a couple of rusty tins filled with soil and a droopy plant. Off the living room were three small bedrooms with filthy foam mattresses set on top of Heath Robinson wooden bed frames. Melian and I were given one of them to share.

Our new companions were called Armando, Dorangel and Rei. Dorangel seemed pretty nonplussed at our arrival and went straight back to chopping wood. The other two looked pleased to have new company and took a particularly strong interest in the edible element of our luggage. All wore clothes that were totally unsuitable to the conditions they were living in. Dorangel was the only one wearing a jacket and all of them had holes in their shoes. They told us they did fifteen days up the mountain and then another team of three came up and they went down for fifteen days with their families on the coast. They had virtually no food, and apart from making sure the fire didn't go out, had absolutely nothing to do all day. Officially, they were there as Flora y Fauna staff but they weren't conducting any research and, as the days progressed, it became clear they had been given absolutely no training. 'We're here to man the radio and help if someone has a problem on the mountain but most of the time we just chop wood,' said Armando.

Later that afternoon, after a lunch of spaghetti with chopped-up hot dogs followed by a long siesta, I got my first real taste of the buzz that comes with ornithological fieldwork. Returning from a sunset walkabout with the binoculars, Melian asked me whether I had seen anything. I told him I thought I had seen a large object moving in one of the trees and that I had heard a loud repeating birdcall. I did my best impression of the sound and the effect was stunning. Melian jumped off his bed and with the face of a young boy who had been told his lost puppy has been found, shouted, 'Do it again! Do it again!'

I repeated the sound and grabbing his own binoculars and the tape recorder, he quickly put on his boots and told me to show him where I'd heard the noise. 'You just made the sound of a Cuban Pigmy Owl,' he cried as we rushed up the hill. We stayed out until darkness fell and heard lots of interesting noises but sadly nothing that resembled the sound of a Cuban Pigmy Owl. It didn't help matters that I couldn't pinpoint the exact place I had seen the movement – to me all the trees looked exactly the same. Eventually, we decided to call it a day and any lingering disappointment was soon washed away by a more pressing concern about bodily warmth. An hour after dark and with the temperature down to nine degrees and the humidity up to 90 per cent, it was, to put not too fine a word on it, buttock-clenchingly cold.

Having decided the only right thing to do was share out our rations, we all sat down to a delicious Melian creation involving rice, packet soup and tinned ham with a fine five-year-old vintage Havana Club. Armando, Dorangel and Rei ate and drank like men who have just been rescued from a desert island. They said they had no cooking oil and had been living off yucca and boiled beans for a week.

With nothing to do and the only warm room permanently filled with choking smoke, the damp cold soon forced all five occupants of the Micro Estación 'El Cuba' to retreat to their creaky beds. The radio had to be kept on at all times, so as well as Rei's unrestrained flatulence and Melian's snoring, my fitful dozing was regularly interrupted by loud bursts of '*Veintecuatro!*

Veintecuatro!' Somewhere on another hill, number 24 had either fallen asleep or was being savaged by an army of flesh-eating mutant arboreal rodents.

Sometime around midnight, the call of nature forced me to brave the cold and pad out to the dunny. Outside, the wood-strewn clearing had an eerie, almost fairy-tale feel to it. A full moon had risen over the back of Pico Cuba, bathing our mountain refuge in a surreal light and casting ghoulish shadows everywhere. I was just starting to carve wet initials on the ground when I heard the noises. It sounded almost like a human cry, not a cry for help but more a sad, mournful cry, and it was coming from the hill above the hut. I remembered reading somewhere that during their nights in these mountains, one of the regular campfire stories spun by the Revolutionaries was about the 'witch's bird'. According to the myth, a Spaniard tried to shoot the bird and ended up getting shot himself – by the bird. The strange human wailing was, so the legend went, the ghost of the wounded Spaniard. One of the youngest soldiers, Joel Iglesias, didn't believe in the myth but all the others were so superstitious they refused to go on night patrol with him. I didn't fall for any of that mumbo-jumbo, ghouls-in-the-dark stuff either. I just ran back inside because I was cold. Okay?

I did eventually drift off and briefly enjoyed a star-studded dream that involved me playing my double bass around the campfire with Che, Fidel and Camilo Cienfuegos. Unfortunately, my crisply delivered *tumbao* was rudely disturbed by a scary-looking man who was pointing a video recorder at me and muttering something about pigmies and owls. Eventually I recognized the intruder and realized he wasn't part of the dream. It was Melian and he seemed very excited. It turned out he'd also gone to relieve himself and ended up staring with disbelief at a Cuban Pigmy Owl perched on a tree branch barely 20 yards away. All annoyance at being woken up and dragged out of bed again disappeared the second I focused the binoculars on the branch Melian was pointing at. There, caught in the moonlight, motionless apart from the occasional lazy blink of its huge eyes, fluffy-legged just as the book described, was one of the most beautiful birds I have ever seen. When it eventually called out – a single high note followed by an accelerating series of short 'coo' notes – Melian patted me on the back and said, '*Compay!* See how close you were!' I was beaming with pride. Perhaps they'd rename it Pepe's Pigmy Owl, I thought. Perhaps I should ditch this music lark and become an ornithologist. Perhaps we'd have omelette and croissants for breakfast.

On the way back to the hut I casually mentioned the odd cries I'd heard earlier on and Melian laughed and said it was probably just a Black-capped Petrel. 'They sound very human,' he confirmed, 'but it's strange because they normally don't come up this high.'

The following morning we set off for the summit early. The cloud had come down and it felt more like a hike in the Scottish glens than a walk in the Caribbean. The path was greasy with moisture and my trainers slithered like slippers on a polished floor. Along the way, Melian kept stopping to call out for another bird he was trying to find. It was Bicknell's Thrush – after thirty years without a sighting, a bird-watcher had recently reported hearing its distinctive voice in this area. But there was no answer to Melian's repeated whistling. In fact there was virtually no sound at all.

To reach the highest point we had first to descend to a pass between Pico Cuba and Pico Turquino. It was nothing but a narrow ledge with a precipitous drop on both sides. For a brief few minutes the clouds dissolved and an *estimulante*-worthy view unfolded below us. Down to our right lay the ocean, while to our left the flat plain of Granma province stretched off to the port of Manzanillo in the distance. This view alone was worth the hike, or the mule ride, should I say.

The summit was actually a bit of a disappointment, not least because we weren't the first to get there. A group hiking up the route from the other side of the Sierra had obviously set out before dawn and were already unfurling flags to celebrate their ascent and pay homage to the bust of José Martí, martyr of the Cuban struggle for Independence. A few minutes later, a big group of army cadets and MININT (Ministry of the Interior) officials filed into the clearing and before long there were at least forty people surrounding the sculpture. Underneath was a stone plaque inscribed with a piece of Martí's poetic verse. It read: '*Escasos, como los montes, son los hombres que saben mirar desde elles y sienten con entrañas de nación o de humanidad*' ('Few, like the mountains, are the men that know how to look from them and feel with their hearts the spirit of their nation and of humanity'). By the time one of the cadets had delivered an emotional Martí eulogy followed by a spontaneous rendition of the national anthem, the clouds had come down and rain was starting to fall. I'm ashamed to say that at that point the adventurer in me disappeared and I failed to disguise envious glances at the other climbers as they headed back down to sea level. Four days of this sort of weather and I'd be begging to be allowed to go back to warm double bass lessons.

My *estimulante*-fuelled prayers that night were answered. For the rest of our stay, we were not only blessed with beautiful weather but the birds put on their best show, too. Melian said he had never seen so many species in such a short period. We never did hear or see Fernandina's Flicker but there were plenty of compensations. A rare daytime sighting of a Cuban Screech Owl, a huge variety of hummingbirds, a couple of Cuban Solitaires singing a duet, and the extremely rare sight of a hawk dropping and recatching a large white *jutia*, the rat-like rodent found in the Cuban forests. 'The Discovery Channel would pay thousands for footage of what you just saw,' claimed a jubilant Melian after the hawk incident. He was still telling friends in Santiago weeks after we got back.

If it hadn't been for lack of food and my fear of what Pastor would do if I delayed my return, I could have happily stayed up in the mountains for weeks. For all their hardships, I left the Micro Estación convinced that Armando, Dorangel and Rei had one of the best jobs on the island. No stress, no nagging bosses, and a view from the toilet that almost made it worth getting clogged up with yucca.

14. La Bomba

'*Eres loco, compay!* You are crazy!' announced Pastor with an exasperated sigh. Since my return from the boonies, I had made a determined effort to show that I meant business. There would, I had assured him, be no more distracting trips. Pico Turquino had been conquered and I was ready to concentrate on the musical challenge to hand. As well as doubling my practice time (okay, nearly doubling), I'd increased the number of sessions I was having with Yamira to three a week, listened to nothing but *son* in my spare time, and even asked to start having extra bass classes at weekends. Finally, after managing to return British–Cuban relations to a level where PlayStation baseball games were back on again, I reckoned it was time to reveal my master plan for winning the *bomba* battle. There was no tactful way of telling Pastor, so at the end of one of our lessons, after the bricks had been returned to the roof and the coffee poured from the thermos, I just came straight out with it.

'Pastor?'

'*Sí, compay?*'

'I've, um, I've decided to join one of the conga bands.'

I'd prepared myself for a less than enthusiastic reaction and '*loco!*' was, I suppose, not an unreasonable judgement. Given the ridicule I'd received at the baseball stadium during that first game of the season, and given the variety of warnings dished out since (the words '*violenta*' and '*peligrosa*' seemed to crop up a lot in conga conversations), Pastor's assessment was only confirming the widely held view that the conga was a thing to watch and listen but not take part in.

Only I don't think safety was what Pastor was concerned about. I believe he thought I was *loco* because with only three months left before performing on stage with an instrument I hadn't even begun to master, I was proposing to spend vital bass-playing hours embarking on a second musical challenge that could make things worse rather than better. And all because someone, Rene specifically, had told me it was the route to *la bomba*.

'Look, Pastor,' I tried to explain, 'you've tried everything to help sort out this *bomba* problem and . . .'

'And what?' interrupted Pastor, realigning his favourite Michael Jackson poster in the kitchen.

'And I thought that maybe the conga could help.'

There was also the small matter of male pride – I felt obliged to prove to my baseball buddies that I had the *cojones* to do it – but I decided to keep this admission to myself. Pastor disappeared into his bedroom, leaving me to sit in silence. Forced back out by a lack of cigarettes, he stomped around for a few seconds and then suddenly declared, 'All right, go and join the conga, but . . .'

'But what?' I smiled.

'But you must not let the conga affect your double bass lessons.'

'I promise.'

'And, you must not let it affect your double bass practice.'

'I promise that as well.'

'And you must be careful.'

'Pastor . . .'

'I'm serious, *compay*, the conga can be . . .'

'Dangerous?'

'Yes, dangerous.'

When an outbreak of bloody violence brought my first conga lesson to an abrupt halt a few days later, I began to take his warning a little more seriously. The class was being held in a house in Flores, a *barrio* just ten minutes' walk from Chicharrones. I was in a tiny living room hammering away on a metal brake drum – the *campana*, to give it its correct musical name – when a series of loud yells from outside on the street forced us to stop and see what was going on. A crowd of about a hundred had gathered at the bottom of the hill. From where we stood, you couldn't see who was fighting but there was definitely something big going down. Two or three women were screaming loudly and every few seconds the mass of people would scramble away in reaction to the moves made by whatever was lashing out in its centre. It took less than five minutes before the first police siren sounded and immediately, the crowd broke up and a young guy with blood pouring from his arm ran up the hill towards us.

'That looks like a *mocha* wound,' said my teacher, Carlos, as the bleeding man passed by.

'What's a *mocha*?' I asked.

'It's what they use for cutting sugar cane.'

Another man lay injured at the bottom of the hill. He had a nasty head wound and blood was also pouring from his leg.

'Does this happen much?' I asked Carlos.

'No, but when it does the injuries are always bad. People used to fight with fists but now it is always with knives or machetes. It's rare to see a *mocha* being used though.'

When I questioned what would have caused such a brutal fight, his answer was immediate.

'Stress,' he said. 'It usually starts with an argument over nothing. We are all living on top of each other and sometimes the strain breaks out into violence.'

Carlos, or Caletin as everyone called him, ran the Guillermón Moncada conga. It had taken me weeks to pluck up the courage to approach the group of muscle-bound drummers who performed at every game and when I finally did manage it – during an evening televised game that none of the *barrio* wanted to go to – I prepared myself for the sound of mocking laughter or at least a few disbelieving shakes of heads.

'*Como no!*' replied a beaming Carlos after listening to my request for *bomba*-grasping assistance, 'of course I can organize lessons.' His keenness to assist probably had more to do with his rapid calculation of the financial outlay required to achieve said goal than the assessment of the goal itself, but I didn't care. The first difficult move had been made and the response had not been ridicule.

As well as leading the baseball crew, Carlos and his father Lorenzo ran the San Agustín conga, a group that pooled its musicians from a variety of poorer *barrios* including Flores, Asunción and Chicharrones. Carlos was a twenty-two-year-old wiry dude with a big grin, a busted-up nose and a look that was *Boyz in the Hood* on a budget. His hair was cropped and bleached *à la* Denis Rodman, he wore baggy nylon tracksuit bottoms and a shirt with the arms cut off at the shoulder, and his favourite fashion accessory was a pair of spectacles without any lenses in the frames. It was an image that only the leader of a conga band could pull off without causing widespread sniggering.

When I arrived at the family house for the first lesson, it was clear to me that the living conditions in Flores were even worse than at the Damelos' house. There was no running water, no fridge, no TV, no telephone, and very little furniture. Carlos told me that since his parents had divorced, he had become the major source of income for the household (Mum, sister, brother, and Carlos's two-year-old daughter from a previous girlfriend) and yet he was only receiving about 12 dollars a month for playing percussion for one of the city's folkloric groups. The San Agustín conga received a Government fund of 1,300 pesos (52 dollars) a year but all of this was soaked up in paying for instrument repairs, costumes for the carnival and some food for the occasional post-performance *caldoso*.

Carlos started the first lesson by laying out all the instruments on the floor of the tiny living room and explaining the role of each. Leading the band was the instrument most associated with the conga and in particular the Santiago conga. The distinctive improvisational skirl of the Chinese cornet was always the first thing you heard before the drums started up and, when the conga took to the streets to honour San Juan day, it was the distant wail of this Oriental import that brought people out of their homes like drugged followers of some strange religious cult.

Behind the *corneta china* came the *campana* section. A relatively recent addition to the conga line-up, the *campana* was a classic example of Cuban musical invention. To create three different levels of metallic percussion they had simply taken three brake drums from different vehicles. In the San Agustín conga they had a small one from a Lada for the distinctive ding-gadingy-ding sound of the lead *campana*. The middle ding-de-de-dingdingding-de-de-dingdingding pattern was played on a rusty old Chevrolet part. And for the loudest and most improvisational section of the threesome, they used the brake drum from a tractor. Each was held like a waiter's tray with forearm vertical and hand flat against the metal circle, so to play the heaviest *campana* for longer than ten minutes required a Popeye-sized forearm and a very strong wrist.

Immediately behind the *campana* came the big guns. When the first conga bands started they played an instrument called a *bombo*, a giant drum that was a direct imitation of the beat-maintaining monster used by Spanish military bands. It was the heartbeat of the conga, the deep resonant thud that could be heard blocks away from the action. Very few *bombos* were still being played today but the modern equivalent, called the *tambora pilón*, required just as much stamina to carry and play. San Agustín's muscle-bound *pilón* player was called *caña* – in Cuban street dialect, someone who had *caña* had lots of strength. On either side of the *pilón* were two flat, disc-like drums known as *galletas* or *tambores redoblantes*. These were suspended by a shoulder strap and balanced on the player's stomach so that both hands were free to play. The *galleta* was a double-sided drum whose resonance could be altered by pressing or releasing the bare hand on one skin while hitting the other with a thick wooden stick.

And behind this front line of *galletas* and *pilón* came the real rhythm section of the conga. Providing the fast-beating heart of the group was a combination of single-headed funnel-shaped drums called *quintos*, cylindrical drums of Haitian origin called *bocues*, and tall, slim *tumbadoras* that were often confusingly referred to as congas. In all, there were fourteen different instruments in the conga with two players per instrument. Such was the ferocity with which the conga was played, the temperatures in which it was performed, and the hours it lasted, all instruments were played in a relay system. When one player became exhausted, he simply passed it over to his tag partner while the rest of the conga continued pounding away.

Originally, the plan had been for me to share duties with one of the *campana* players but two weeks into my brake-drum sessions, another outbreak of violence caused the plan to veer off into far more nerve-racking, rhythm-testing territory. Within sight of one of the first conga parades of the year, a punch-up left Carlos with one of his *galleta* players in plaster. Revealing a worrying glitch in his ability to run the conga, he decided I should move into the available slot.

'You want to discover *la bomba*, well, this is your chance,' he responded to my shaking head and nervy laugh. 'You can do it, *compay*!' he urged.

Sure, but did I want to do it? The more I dug into the history of the conga and the more I listened to anecdotes of recent conga experiences, the more legitimate the warnings seemed and the more my cowardly side started to consider sticking to HP and leaving the drums to the tough guys. Ever since the first percussive snakes began sliding through Santiago's streets, the musical celebration author Helio Orevio called 'a rich arsenal of noise' had dragged with it a reputation for ugly violence. A reminder of that infamy could be found in an old conga number by Los Compadres called, '*Through the barrios of Santiago*'. The words to the first verse went: '*The people from Los Hoyos go through Tivoli. And those from Tivoli go through Los Hoyos.*

It's no longer like old times when riots happened. Now we wish to live.' Now we wish to live? It made the conga sound like some sort of musical hari-kiri. The riots might have gone, but amongst the white population of Santiago, Orevio's rich arsenal of noise was still perceived as an uncontrolled frenzy best observed from the safety of your balcony.

The origins of the conga can be traced back to the parties held by the *cabildos*, slave associations permitted by the Spanish authorities during colonial times. At first, these were nothing more than meetings where slaves came to hold religious ceremonies and observe cultural traditions. But from them sprang the carnival bands called *comparsas*, and the most musically striking *comparsa* of them all was the conga. Its distinctive dance – three short steps followed by a kick to the side – was supposedly based on the short step shuffle of slaves whose ankles were chained together. Compared to the rather stuffy and elitist dances performed by the whites, the conga was a celebration of the masses. It was music of the streets and it was one of the few musical events where criollos, negroes and blancos could all mix together.

It was only a matter of time before someone latched on to the export potential of conga, or at least a non-violent indoor version of it. The thuggery only really began when the conga was appropriated for political campaigning. Remove the politics and you had a type of music that was perfect for parties and large club audiences. The rhythm was infectious, the dance was easy to master, and you didn't need a partner. In 1928, Elisio Grenet introduced it to Paris audiences and such was the sensation it caused, that for a while jazz and tango suffered a decline in popularity. From there it hit New York, and with suitable commercial spin, the old slave shuffle was soon being copied by wealthy clubbers all around the world.

Like most musical exports, the foreign version soon bore little resemblance to the real thing. Yet in its homeland, and specifically in its spiritual birthplace, santiago, the conga still represented one of the most powerful and magnetic forms of raw musical expression in the world, a piece of street theatre that had the power to *arollar* (overwhelm) all those it sucked up in its path. And it still remained a seedbed of crude violence where anything could, and usually did, happen. Fights were common, particularly during the renowned 'invasions' when conga groups from one *barrio* would weave their human snake through the neighbourhood of another. It was accepted and expected, for example, that when San Agustín invaded the streets of their biggest rivals, Los Hoyos, blood would be spilt somewhere.

Although *barrio* rivalries generated ugly displays of macho posturing, the most feared forms of violence were invisible to all except the poor sod on the receiving end. Closely connected to the conga were the cowardly acts of revenge performed by men wielding long sharp needles called *punzones*. In the confused scrum of a street parade, it was easy to strike your enemy with one of these lethal weapons and then disappear into the crowd without being caught. Often, the victim – fired up on rum and the power of the music – would not realize he had been stabbed until he saw the blood on his shirt.

Carlos had calmly told me all this straight after the *mocha* incident, and seeing the wimpish concern on the face of his student, he tried to allay fears by pointing out that no one in the San Agustín conga had ever been killed. Comforting news but the words, 'or maimed' on the end of that sentence would have provided the full reassurance I was looking for.

'There is always a ring of police around the band,' he explained, 'so you'll be in the safest place in the conga.' Carlos's mum, mixing up *zapoti* milkshakes in an old blender, nodded in agreement and assured me I'd be '*muy seguro*' ('very safe') with her Carlito. Just as she said this, a huge rat scampered out from behind the 10-gallon drum of water and her Carlito proved his manhood by chasing after it with a mop.

Playing out on the streets had never been my original idea.

When conga-joining plans had first been hatched, my dream had been to play with the band at the Guillermón Moncada, ideally during the final that would see Santiago crowned as champions for the fourth year in a row. Unfortunately, I hadn't counted on the road flatteners not sticking to their side of the bargain. Not for one minute had I envisaged them doing a Sheffield United on me. But they did. After creeping into the play-offs by coming a disappointing second in the Oriente group, Santiago inexplicably lost to Villa Clara with barely a whimper of resistance. The day after the defeat, the crowd in the Plaza de Marte was the biggest I had ever seen, and even a few women had come along to voice their grievances. No doubt they were demanding to know how they would get any peace now that their husbands had nothing to do. Explanations for the untimely exit were numerous. Even politics was raised. The city's previous political leader had been a Santiaguero who went to every game. The new one was originally from Las Tunas and was hardly ever seen in the stadium. Blaming a lack of party support seemed to me to be clutching at straws. The truth, of course, was that Santiago had fallen victim to one of the given rules of baseball – you don't win a championship with only one decent pitcher. I obviously kept this opinion to myself. The guys at the Peña could take a lot, but an Englishman telling them what was wrong with their team? The open house policy wasn't that open.

So with no chance of playing in the baseball stadium, I had little option but to accept Carlos's challenge to join a performance in the street. And becoming the fourth *galleta* man was definitely going to be a challenge. It took over a week just to master the basic repeating beat of this heavyweight drum. Not only did it run slightly off-synch from the *pilón* but it required a deft bit of two-handed coordination: the left hand connecting with and releasing from the underside at exactly the right moment. There was no magical formula or clever syncopated trick involved in my eventual mastering of this off-the-beat challenge – just hours and hours of skin bashing in that living room in Flores. The one beneficial side-effect for Carlos's extremely racket-tolerant family was that all the noise and vibrations seemed to cause the rats to disappear.

Sadly, the *galleta* routine was required to stretch beyond just a monotonous single repeating beat. On top of this solid base, the player was expected to paint an elaborate rhythmic picture. For a start there were the '*efectos*', as Carlos called them. Every conga band created its own signature patterns where – on a signal from the leader – the whole fourteen-strong outfit came together to perform little synchronized sequences. These were given different numbers, so in the heat and frenzy of a performance all Carlos had to do was raise the required number of fingers, and with a nod of the head, everyone would come together for a loud ensemble, crowd-motivating burst of noise. Having mastered the core *efectos* I faced the far trickier task of creating my own improvised moves, my own '*comida*', as Pastor would have put it. Out on the street I would be required to execute a double act with the other *galleta* player. While one did his improvised solo, the other maintained the steady basic beat and vice versa. And yes, a solo did require a demonstration of *bomba*, that natural internal instinct for rhythm that allowed you to weave your own creation around the other instruments and then slide back into the beat without a hiccup.

'Just give it a go, do whatever comes into your head,' said Carlos after rather defeating the object of the exercise by showing me a few examples of what I could do. Aborted attempt followed aborted attempt, but just as I was about to admit defeat and ask for my brake drum back, a miracle happened. At first I didn't even notice I had done it, but the jubilant reaction from Carlos confirmed that I had somehow tapped into some as yet untouched source of musical fertility and concocted my own little arrangement. Carlos was used to male bonding but even he was a bit ruffled by the enormous bear-hug he received.

'Careful, *compay*, people will talk,' he said, straightening his shirt and glancing nervously out of the open door to check no one had been watching. I'd be lying if I said this small moment of creativity was the Vicks Vapour that unblocked my musical sinuses. I didn't suddenly switch into the John Bonham of Cuban drumming. But it was a start and, from this tiny germ of newfound confidence, the first shoots of self-belief began to spring.

And they continued to flourish right up until the afternoon when Carlos made two surprise announcements. News item number one was that instead of a normal lesson we were going straight round to the team practice area (called the *foco*) to test out my *galleta* moves in a real live conga scenario. And next, after an ominous pause and a nervous scratch of the peroxide top, came the revelation that none of the other members of the conga knew about this.

'You mean, you haven't told anyone else that I'm joining the band?' I spluttered theatrically. 'Not even your dad?' Carlos grinned back and ignoring the question simply picked up his Chinese cornet and said, '*Vamos a tocar!* Let's go and play!'

The *foco* was nothing more than a small abandoned wooden building. It was easy to spot because a big crowd of groupies were milling around outside listening to the chaotic cacophony that I presumed was a conga warm-up. Some were hovering around the doorway while others were peering through the cracks in the walls. Carlos had conveniently neglected to warn me there would be spectators. The strange glances I got as I squeezed past were nothing compared to the bemused line of faces that greeted me on the inside. Imagine Vanilla Ice turning up to open-mic night at Detroit's meanest venue and you'll have some idea of how tight and fast my sphincter closed up. If I could have walked straight back out I would have done, but all retreat possibilities disappeared the moment Carlos introduced me to his father, Lorenzo. It had been Lorenzo's grandfather, Victoriano Palacio, who had set up the San Agustín conga in 1922 – it used to be called, rather more grandly, 'The Sons of Asunción' – and although Carlos was increasingly taking control, Dad still had the final say on important decisions. Decisions such as whether a white guy with minimal experience should be allowed to receive a wild-card entry into a team with a reputation to uphold.

'This is Richard – he's going to be playing the *galleta* with Osmari,' shouted Carlos over the din. Somewhat disconcertingly, his father appeared totally unfazed by this announcement. He just smiled and replied, '*Con fuerza!* With power!'

With all escape routes blocked and Carlos busy rallying the troops, I slunk off to one of the back walls and tried to hide behind one of the carnival props. Skin colour, nationality, dress sense, even the way I stood felt like it was setting off the intruder alarms. A few minutes later, Carlos came over and introduced me to a serious-looking gym-toned guy who I'd seen carrying in a *galleta*. He was wearing wraparound shades, a Bacardi bat logo pendant hung from his neck, and each of the fingers of his right hand had been wrapped in boxer's tape.

'This is Osmari – you'll be teaming up with him,' announced Carlos.

We shook hands, but Osmari, first impressions no doubt confirmed by the lack of force to my handshake, looked distinctly unimpressed.

'Osmari will start first and when he gives you the signal, you'll take over.'

As I watched everyone strip down to bare chests and lift their instruments into place, I knew that any fear I felt about standing on stage in a blue suit paled into insignificance compared to the testicle-retracting intensity of what I was going through right now. Was finding my *bomba* really worth this much humiliation?

To start the conga, Carlos had created a complicated and highly syncopated entry routine. It was clearly a form of San Agustín password – if you couldn't get through the first door you weren't up for the challenge. On the first attempt, one of the *campana* players screwed up, and the howls of derision he received from the others left little doubt about tolerance for mistakes. Suitably chastised, the offender got it right the second time. This was my first experience of a conga at close quarters and the intensity and physicality of the performance were startling. Such was the level of noise being produced, the vibrations were causing a fine precipitation of dust to fall from the ceiling.

Previous reservations about physical readiness now switched to unequivocal confirmations. The longest I had played in any one stretch at Carlos's house was ten minutes and the cause of stoppage was usually either a dead arm or a slipping drum. Actually, it was always a dead arm, the slipping drum was just a handy excuse. With only a thin shoulder strap made from various strips of material knotted together, there was a particular knack to balancing the drum so that it rested at a suitable playing angle. Even standing still, with no sweat, and with no one jostling me, I didn't have the knack.

Come the changeover moment, the reaction of the San Agustín team suggested the tall white man had just taken all his clothes off and was now moondancing across the floor. All I remember was this room full of teeth as everyone in the room started grinning. With all the noise it was hard to tell whether there were laughs behind the grins and if so whether they were of ridicule, disbelief or just plain amusement. Probably all three, I guessed. Focusing on the beat of the other *galleta* and aided by the closest *campana* player who chivalrously broke off from his brake-drum duties to give me life-saving signals, I managed somehow to slide into the groove. It didn't quite deserve a Rocky at the top of the steps punch the air moment but a Timmy Henman fist clench wouldn't have been out of place. When Cana, the *pilón* player – drenched in sweat, veins bulging with the exertion, underarms visibly foaming – sidled over and nodded his head in encouragement, I knew everything was

going to be okay. Today, no *pepes* were going to die. I sailed
through the first *efecto* without a hitch and when I successfully
pulled off a couple of my *bomba* manoeuvres, the look on
Carlos's face spelt out just how important this had been for
him, too. Had it all gone wrong, the man with the lensless
spectacles would have been the butt of *barrio* jokes long after
I had left town.

Such was my concentration on keeping the beat and playing '*con fuerza*' I didn't even notice that I was grazing the bottom
of my fingers on the skin of the drum with every hit. When,
after twenty minutes, Osmari signalled he would take over, I
was shocked to discover there were red stains all over the *galleta*'s
goatskin and my knuckles were a raw bleeding mess. In my
desperation to become a musician I had now managed the
dubious feat of removing skin on both sides of my fingers.

'If I'd known you were going to hit it that hard I'd have
told you to tape up your fingers like Osmari,' laughed Carlos
back at his house. 'My father couldn't believe it – he said he'd
never seen a foreigner play the *galleta*.'

Later that evening, after a medicinal and celebratory drink
or three, I cycled home in a strange kind of triumph with blood
on my clothes, one hand wrapped up in toilet paper, and rum
on my breath. Persuading Tania and Braulio that they'd got the
wrong impression of the conga was going to be a struggle.

The chance to lose my *galleta*-thumping virginity came a
few weeks later in the San Pedro Day celebrations. With fingers
taped up and sun cream slathered all over my bare shoulders
and neck, I prepared to make the trek up the hill to Flores.
Looking in the mirror before heading out, I was not overly
convinced by my conga outfit. Staring back at me was a tall
man wearing one of Pastor's singlets – T-shirts were considered
too much clothing for the conga – a wide-brimmed, straw
cane-cutter's hat, Miu-Miu sunglasses, and the same pair of
bloodstained shorts. I looked like some sort of camp *machetero*
who'd had a nasty accident while trying to sharpen his *mocha*.

Unrestrained giggles from Liana and Tanita confirmed the worst, but at least I knew there was no chance of being stabbed for reasons of mistaken identity.

In a group pep talk the previous day, Carlos had set down the rules. There was to be no inviting friends inside the police cordon, any provocation from '*locos o borrachos*' (madmen or drunks) was to be ignored, and anyone turning up drunk before the conga started would be sent home. Clearly, the definition of inebriation was a little hazy because he subsequently suggested a bottle of rum would be a wise investment. '*Dos*,' Osmari chipped in, overhearing our conversation. '*Hay que poner gasolina en la máquina* – you've got to put fuel in the machine,' he added, to which Carlos quickly nodded in agreement. 'Yes, you'd better bring two – it's going to be hot.'

Hot was an understatement. San Pedro had been honoured with a cloudless count-your-moles skin fryer of a day. Even the vultures had decided to take a siesta. The scene at the *foco* was bedlam. The surrounding streets were already heaving with people waiting for the head of the snake to emerge. Police armed with long rubber riot sticks were trying to clear a way for the traffic but pedestrian power seemed to be winning.

Thankfully, my ridiculous attire was at least partially overshadowed by the bizarre conga accessories being modelled by the San Agustín crew. One was wearing a woman's shawl in the style of a pirate's headscarf, another had laughed in the face of public ridicule by placing a large lace doily on his head. One of the *bocue* players was sporting a giant pair of women's sunglasses. All three *campana* players were dressed up in full-length, bright turquoise Arabic-style gowns and each had sprigs of *vencedor* leaves tucked behind his ears. Carlos, in comparison, looked rather conservative in black combats, white T-shirt and black woollen beanie.

A fire had been lit in one corner of the room and a huge pot of *caldoso* was bubbling away violently. Every so often someone came and lifted the lid and gave the grey liquid a stir.

Various unidentifiable ingredients bobbed to the surface. A couple of old socks? A few bones? It was hard to tell. Judging by the quantity of rum being consumed, we had clearly gone past the official start time. I unscrewed the top of one of the two bottles and after wetting the dust for the *santos*, took a big swig and passed the bottle to Osmari. He then passed it to Cana who necked a third of the contents and handed it on to an already visibly drunk Lorenzo. The entire bottle was drained in less than five minutes. Lorenzo came and put his arm around my shoulder and, eyes moistened by alcohol and smoke, slurred something into my right ear about me taking on the role of new European agent for the San Agustín conga. I told him it would be an honour.

Just before the appointed hour of departure, a policeman came inside and gave strict instructions as to what was and wasn't permitted. Absolutely no women were allowed inside the ring of police protecting the band, the conga was to stop and start when ordered by the police, and there was to be no retaliation if someone outside the conga tried to start a fight. After that there was a quick pre-match huddle and then we slowly filed out on to the street.

As soon as Carlos raised his Chinese cornet a huge cheer went up. The crowd had at least tripled in size during our time inside the *foco* and all traffic had long since given up trying to pass. Instead of the expected arrangement of a conga head dragging a long tail behind it, we found ourselves in the middle of the snake with equal numbers in front and behind. Twelve policemen formed a protective square around the group and pushed away anyone crossing the line. For about the first half-hour all seemed to be going relatively smoothly. There were certainly a few characters worth keeping an eye on – a mad-looking, barefooted bloke wearing a wig kept trying to sneak into the playing area – but generally it was everything I imagined a conga would be. Whistles, twisting umbrellas, people cheering on balconies, provocative bum movements, that sort of thing.

But then we turned down one of the narrower side streets, and a relatively orderly human snake suddenly became a tightly squeezed chaotic tide of flesh with a wave maker in the middle. From being fairly restrained with their conga-protecting duties, the police suddenly switched to riot mode (in fairness, it did actually feel a bit like a riot) and rubber batons were lashed out with a level of aggression that was frightening. Being in the eye of the storm and dependent on the police, I was torn between being grateful for being on the inside and distinctly uncomfortable about the brutality of some of the blows being landed. In many cases, there was simply nowhere for people to move, but this didn't stop the batons from being swiped across the backs of legs. Old men, women, teenagers; it didn't make any difference to the men in blue. Carlos had been right about being in the safest place. It was like travelling in the eye of a hurricane, a hurricane whose intensity you controlled and whose bad weather you could watch with a cool detachment. I saw a man with what looked like a sharpened screwdriver getting dragged away by two cops, a woman being hit over the head with a large stick, and endless scuffles as people got pushed into one another. This was Santiago at its wildest, its most anarchic, its most rhythmic, its most exciting and its most frightening.

In one respect, it was easier playing in these conditions. I was so pumped up I hardly noticed the weight of the drum. But in another, it was a far bigger challenge. Sticking to the beat while moving and being moved was not something I found easy, and a couple of times I received worried glances from Cana as I slipped out of rhythm. Occasional shouts of '*Pepe!*' and '*Yuma!*' could be heard from passing balconies but I was concentrating so hard I couldn't afford to look up.

At some point, the police signalled to Carlos and, raising his arm in the air, he brought the conga to a halt. Instruments were off-loaded, fingers rewrapped with tape, rum guzzled as if it were a refreshing soft drink, and congratulatory hugs exchanged. Then with a change of players it was off once more. Down the hill towards the sea, left along Felix Peña, back up the hill to Villalón, and across to Asunción. The aggro started up again close to our return to the *foco*. It was now getting dark, and with the pushing and shoving becoming more aggressive, the atmosphere had unquestionably grown more menacing. I'm not exactly sure what triggered things off, but one minute we had a police presence and some semblance of control, the next there were no police and a full-on street fight had broken out. A good journalist would have stood his ground and watched, risking injury to bring back a full report of conga bloodshed. A good wine writer, on the other hand, knows the value of making a discreet but hasty withdrawal down the nearest available safe-looking side street. I'd joined the conga for a variety of reasons but testing out the Cuban emergency services was not one of them. With *bomba* glimpsed if not convincingly seized, and my conga virginity lost without my singlet receiving additional unwanted perforations, it was time to head back to the safety of 101.

15. Singing through Stockings

Sometime during the late 1930s, while Miguel Matamoros was at the height of his fame, a man called Martin Valiente Ramos ('Chichi' to his friends) quietly set up a Santiago-based *sexteto* called Sones de Oriente.

'I know I'm biased, but Chichi was a brilliant composer and Sones de Oriente were one of the best bands this city ever produced,' said Chichi's wife (now widow), Conchita, one Sunday morning.

I had managed to track down Conchita after repeatedly pestering Pastor about the history of Sones de Oriente, the band in whose company I was about to record a CD. Apart from digging out an old vinyl recording from the 1950s, he hadn't been much help. All the original members were now dead, he said, and the usual aural tradition that helped maintain records of a band's memoirs seemed to have come unstuck somewhere.

'You could try Chichi's wife – she might be able to tell you something,' suggested Pastor in a final attempt to appease his nagging student. He was clearly more interested in discovering the origins of Lara Croft than those of his own band.

Conchita lived alone in a small house in Reparto Mariana de la Torre, just off the road to the airport. Even though it was eleven in the morning and I'd phoned to warn I was coming, she was still wearing her nightdress and a bright red net covered the halo of hair rollers stuck to her head.

I immediately warmed to her. She was a bubbly seventy-one-year-old with a cheeky sense of humour and an endearing habit of breaking into song to illustrate her stream of anecdotes. I also surmised very early on that under those curlers was a very tough woman who wouldn't suffer fools gladly. On a shelf in her tidy living room sat a trophy for services rendered in the *zafra*, the sugar-cane harvest. Conchita had cut cane with the best of them.

She told me she had met Chichi when she was singing for a group called the Quarteto Harmonia and before long she was married and a full-time member of Sones de Oriente. She sang in the group for fourteen years. 'We toured all over Cuba,' she answered when I asked how successful the band was. 'People knew Chichi's songs by heart.' Bringing out a large photo album, she showed me a mouldy black and white portrait of the 1938 line-up. It looked as if it had been taken outside the Casa Grande hotel and they were all dressed in elegant well-cut suits (carefully folded white hankies poking out of pockets) and looking very serious about what they were doing. Flicking through the other photos, I stopped at a picture of Conchita with a man whose face I recognized from a portrait in the Casa de la Trova.

'Is that Sindo Garay?' I asked.

'*Sí, es Sindo*,' she smiled with obvious affection. Sindo, full name Antonio Gumersindo Garay y Garcia, was another Santiago legend. Born in 1867, he grew up with guitar-playing parents in a small house next to the rum distillery. He was a fast learner. By the age of ten he had already displayed a talent for songwriting (and an eye for the ladies) by composing his first song, 'Quiereme Triguena' ('Love Me, Mulatta'). During his teenage years he became actively involved in the Independence movement and for some time worked as a messenger for the Mambi freedom fighters. Legend had it that the young Sindo swam across Santiago Bay a total of fourteen times to deliver various secret messages, the bay back then being far cleaner though far more likely to have contained large, hungry predators. As a songwriter, he continued expressing his strong political views, and when the Americans took possession of Guantanamo Bay he wrote a *bolero* entitled, 'You can't live here.'

As well as being one of the greatest of Cuban *trovadores*, a prolific songwriter and talented guitar player, he was one of the
few Cubans (perhaps the only one) who could claim to have
shaken hands with both José Martí and Fidel Castro. I was very
impressed that Conchita had met and sung with him. When I
asked her what he was like – Sindo died in 1968 at the age of
101 – she sighed and traced a finger delicately over his face.
'He was such a gentleman,' she replied quietly, 'and very charismatic – we all loved him.'

Returning to the subject of Sones de Oriente, I told Conchita
about my connection with the band and, as soon as I mentioned Pastor's name, the smile melted and the head shook.
'That Pastor Panes,' she muttered, dark pencilled eyebrows
levitating towards the rim of her hair net, 'he never comes to
see me and he never asks me to come and sing with him.' The
rapid return of the smile suggested she was only half serious
but nevertheless, I decided it would be prudent not to inform
her that Pastor had just taken on a new female singer. Before
leaving, she made me promise to come back soon and to remind
Pastor she still had a great voice. To emphasize the point she
began to bellow out a beautiful *bolero* and I could still hear her
voice as I turned the corner at the end of her street.

In Cuba they don't allow great bands to disappear. That's
why Sones de Oriente was still performing, some sixty-odd
years after the band had been formed. Obviously the Cuban
Government couldn't stop band members from retiring, giving
up or dying, but by giving the band a protected status (almost
like a national park) with subsidized salary and strict monitoring of musical output, they managed to protect and maintain
those symbols of cultural identity that would otherwise disappear into the music vaults. It was a bit like having official tribute bands, only they didn't call themselves a tribute band, and
unlike Bjorn Again and The Australian Doors, they weren't
trying to copy, but simply to maintain a particular style of
traditional Cuban music. I tried to imagine the British

Government doing the same thing, but the idea of prolonging the life of bands like the Bay City Rollers and Spandau Ballet didn't seem to have quite the same appeal.

In between conga adventures and my own increasingly intense double bass regime, I was trying to hang out with the band as much as possible. These were the people I would be joining in the recording studio, and assuming that all went without a hitch, they would also be the people I stood on stage with for my live performance. I wanted them on my side, and if that meant buying rum for seven instead of one, so be it.

Hanging out with Sones de Oriente didn't actually require much effort. We both practised in the same front room in Chicharrones, so I simply moved the timing of my lessons so that they overlapped with the group's daily *ensayo*. During the first I sat in on, the session was broken up by a particularly heated discussion. This, I discovered during subsequent visits, was not unusual. If there was one thing that Cuban musicians liked more than playing, it was having a heated debate about it. On this occasion, it turned out that the *tres* player, Yuri, had written a new song about (and I promise I'm not making this up) the delights of eating yucca, the starchy root crop that filled Cuban stomachs on a daily basis. Somewhat unexpectedly, the argument was not about the lyrical content – all the others seemed perfectly comfortable singing about a vegetable – but rather the notes attached to the words. According to Pastor, the song didn't have the traditional rhythmic structure of *son* and therefore couldn't be sung in the Casa de la Trova. According to Yuri, it did and therefore could. As a Government-subsidized band, the seven members of Sones de Oriente had the benefit of a guaranteed monthly income (even if someone was ill and the band couldn't play) but their repertoire had to stick to strict 'traditional music' guidelines. Pastor couldn't, for example, just add a pianist to his line-up because the band's Government contract had them down as a '*sexteto tradicional*' and a *sexteto* did not, under the official definition, have a pianist. Pastor argued that if they played the yucca song as Yuri had written it, they'd be in trouble with the local Centro de Música and could lose their contract. Amazingly, these playing constrictions went right down to the specific way in which each instrument was played. For instance, the bass player could improvise and garnish his lines with his own *bomba* but only up to a certain point. If you strayed too much outside the classic tonic-dominant pattern of bass lines, you'd be hauled up in front of the style police and have your knuckles rapped. In the end, the changes were agreed and Yuri's song joined their set.

Pastor's concern about keeping the bosses happy was understandable. In the time since I'd been in Santiago his band had suffered a series of personnel setbacks. Angel, the square-jawed, maracas-playing lead singer, had briefly been rehospitalized for a long running battle with paranoid schizophrenia, the guitar player Pici – a Rasta with a habit of being just a little too happy on stage – had been forced to stand down due to not having his mind on the job, and they were now on their third bongo player in six months. Being a Government-subsidized band meant it wasn't hard to find new recruits, but each new member had to be sanctioned by officials in the Centro de Música, and their tolerance of multiple changes only stretched so far.

Sones de Oriente were certainly no Buena Vista Social Club. This was just your average journeyman band whose immediate goals went no further than selling a couple of CDs a day and making sure they all swayed in the same direction on stage. Like all the other journeyman bands in Santiago, they had one set of threadbare, smart clothes for festivals, a set list of tourist-pleasing covers, and a curious fondness for wearing large money belts that appeared to have nothing in them. The most talented member, musically, was José Luis, the guitarist who had taken the place of Pici. If there was a music problem to be solved, José Luis was the one who inevitably sorted it out. Having sung for many years in Santiago's Choral Group, he also had the best voice. We called him Mr Flexible because he could do the weirdest things with his joints – his favourite trick was playing his guitar with one foot facing forward and the other back. Most important of all, though, José Luis knew all the words to 'Hotel California' and together – over yoga sessions on the roof of his house – we began to hatch a cunning plan to restore my honour in Calle Santa Lucia. Yuri, the yucca-inspired, thirty-three-year-old *tres* player, was the musician I had had most contact with. In an attempt to help me get used to playing with others, Pastor had started bringing him to lessons, and while I liked having Yuri around I soon built a huge dislike for his instrument. In my ongoing battle with tempo maintenance, the various instruments which my bass was meant to accompany had quickly been divided into friends and foes. The bongos and guitar – both delivering nice steady repeating rhythms – were the good guys while the *clave* and *tres* (the latter with its jangling staccato rhythm and fondness for distracting improvisational diversions) were the bad guys. As far as I could see, the *tres* had been created simply to piss the bass player off and, much to the enormous amusement of the man doing the distracting, it only took a small *tres* solo to trip me out of my already delicately balanced *tumbao* stride. Yuri was the troublemaker in the group. He always turned up late to *ensayos*, always took longer than anyone else to tune his instrument, and always continued tinkling away when Pastor tried to hold a discussion. He lived with his parents in a little urban *finca* near the university and divided his time (and earnings) between his first wife and two children and his pregnant second wife who, since impregnation, had become an ex-wife.

On lead vocals and *clave* was Jonas, a fifty-six-year-old ex-dock worker from El Caney, a small satellite town on the outskirts of Santiago, famous for its fruit. As well as being one of the longest-serving members of the current line-up, he was Pastor's closest friend. For twenty-one years, Jonas had been loading and unloading Soviet ships for 114 pesos a month until eventually he got a job singing for a *septeto* called Los Portuarios, and that had eventually led to a full-time job with Sones de Oriente in the mid-1980s. Things were not going well for Jonas, however. Years of singing without microphones had damaged his vocal chords to the extent that many of the higher notes were out of reach. Even to scale the foothills now required the sort of vein-bulging facial contortion you associate with a severe dose of constipation. Poor old Pastor was faced with the cruel director's dilemma of knowing that a younger, more flexible singer would be better for the band, but also realizing he couldn't sack his best friend.

At least Jonas had his sanity. Angelito was back in the *hospital para locos* having had a fit in the Casa de la Trova one night. According to Pastor, he'd once spent three months in the psychiatric hospital and for most of his stay he'd been strapped down in a straitjacket. Ironically, and rather tragically for his career, his biggest problem was facing audiences. His personality changes were triggered by crowds, so the bigger the audience, the higher the risk of a fit. Once, on a short tour in Colombia, they'd had to play at one massive outdoor event in Cartagena, and Pastor had walked onstage knowing that at any moment his lead singer could lose the plot and lash out wildly with his maracas.

The other two members of the group were the quietest. Felito's wife, Vivian, had been recruited as a new singer and although shyness caused her to hover nervously at the edge of the stage, her voice was beautiful. And finally, there was Marco on bongos and *campana*. Pastor was worried that Marco wasn't integrating with the others – an inability to strike up a conversation seemed to be the crux of the problem. As quiet percussionists go, he made Charlie Watts look like a chatterbox. But at least he turned up on time, didn't argue, and always got a cheer from the crowd when he did his nightly bongo solo. And a cheer for a bongo solo is no mean feat.

The more I hung out with the group, the more I got to

learn about the bureaucracy that underpinned the Cuban music scene. Most musicians started their careers by becoming members of the Movimiento de Aficionados de la Música. Then, if they wanted to become professional musicians on a state salary, they had to perform an audition in front of a Commission of Evaluation. In the early years of the Revolution, there used to be just one national commission that toured the country doing auditions, and if you missed one round you'd have to wait another year to try again. Now each province had a commission and assessments were more regular. There were two stages of tests. The first was a basic audition, and if you passed and managed to obtain a contract with a group, you were guaranteed a basic salary of 138 pesos (just over 5 dollars a month). The second evaluation was tougher and grouped musicians into three levels of proficiency: A, B and C. Pastor, an A-level musician and director, was walking home with 440 pesos a month – just under 17 dollars. In theory, this was for a minimum of eight performances a month, but in reality, Sones de Oriente played at least four nights a week and on some nights that would involve playing for up to three hours.

Faced with such small wages, musicians inevitably targeted tourists to earn extra dollars. Although strictly speaking it was illegal to sell CDs, a blind eye was turned and after every gig, band members would grab a pile of CDs and quickly work the room before the next act came on. The proceeds would then be shared equally. On top of this they would try to give lessons or look for someone wanting to buy an instrument. On two occasions I was dragged into Pastor's little side deals and given an insider's look at the economics of such transactions. The first time, he asked me to lend him 20 dollars so he could buy a *tres* guitar to sell to a tourist for 100 dollars. I knew I was becoming a bit Cubano when I lent him the money without hesitation, but on condition he gave me 25 dollars back if the deal went through. The second time, Pastor had managed to hook in a Dutch tourist who was looking to buy a double bass but the Dutchman (who hardly spoke a word of Spanish) had wavered on hearing the one thing he did understand – 'it costs 800 dollars.' 'Tell him what a good bass it is and I'll give you a cut,' whispered Pastor as the wavering client took a close inspection of his Russian veteran. Fortunately, I didn't have to lie. In the end, despite Pastor's insistence that he always got his bass inside the cabin of the plane, worries over transportation meant the deal fell through.

It was hard to feel too disappointed for Pastor. Compared to many musicians in the city he was in an enviable position. He had a Government contract and he played in a place that was always heaving with tourists. For others, life was not nearly so easy. Just getting a contract with the Centro de Música was difficult and without that contract you were a musical nobody. Part of the squeeze on new contracts was simply related to supply and demand – too many musicians and not enough places where they could play. But there was also the selectivity of the contract-giving process. In its determination to cherish and protect traditional music forms like *son* and *trova*, the Government made it almost impossible for new, young innovative bands to break into the scene.

One of the best examples of the many disheartened young musicians in Santiago was a rap artist who went by the stage name of Candyman. Amongst the younger population, Candyman – no one seemed to know his real name – was probably the most popular musician in the city and yet because he couldn't get a contract, he either had to do unpaid guest slots with bands that had one or perform semi-illegal spontaneous concerts that were announced by word of mouth. For a brief period, Candyman was going out with one of the Damelos and a buzz went around our street every time the rapper was spotted coming in or out of the house.

'I don't sing about politics – it's not worth the hassle,' he told me over a pizza one evening. 'Most of the time I just sing about love, relationships, and things that go on in the street.'

He told me that there used to be a place where Santiago's rappers were allowed to perform but the recent stabbing of the director of the venue meant the police had clamped down on all rap. Not only were the authorities being very shortsighted – Candyman's highly original fusion of rap with reggae and salsa was just as worthy of a tourist audience as *son* – but by forcing rap underground, they were increasing rather than decreasing its popularity. He said if things didn't improve, he would have to move to Havana where rap artists were given more freedom. At least in the capital there was an annual rap festival that gave *raperos* the chance to showcase their talent.

Another musician, Juan Manuel Villy or 'El Villy' as he was known, didn't really want a contract, preferring instead to wander the streets with his *tres* and perform like one of the roving *trovadores* of the old days. With his trademark Stetson, sharp suits and big bushy moustache, Villy's image was as instantly recognizable as his powerful tenor voice. Every day he would drift around the city – he claimed he sang up to 100 songs a day – and judging by the sixteen suits he owned, the busking was certainly lucrative. Villy lived only a few blocks away from 101 and one day he invited me around to his house for lunch. Turning up at the appointed hour, I was welcomed at the door by a dripping Villy wearing just a towel around his waist. He was almost unrecognizable without his suit and hat. '*Venga!* Come in!' he smiled, after a brief delay trying to remember who I was. The ensuing heated conversation with his wife confirmed he had completely forgotten about our appointment. On the wall was a line of burnt hats. Villy was a magician as well as musician and one of his favourite tricks was taking a 10-dollar bill off a tourist, lighting it, putting it inside his hat and then bringing it out again totally untouched. His price for the trick was the note he'd miraculously saved and the cost was a lot of wrecked hats.

'I could have been a great magician,' he announced grandly, now dried off and dressed. 'I could have made cars disappear.

I could have made people disappear.' I nodded in agreement while poking my finger through the singed hole in one of the hats. 'I just never had the budget, that's all.'

Villy was extremely disdainful of local musicians who left Santiago to further their careers. 'People in the street keep asking when El Villy is going to get his fame – the barber, the construction workers, the women in the market, they all ask – and I tell them I will not leave Santiago to find my fame. This is my land and I will wait for my triumph here.'

I asked him why he liked Santiago so much and without pausing he fired off his reasons. 'The happiness, the hospitality, the mountains, the sun that burns my skin, the *son*, the sound of the conga – these are the things that I love. If I left Santiago I would die.' And with that, El Villy picked up his *tres*, grabbed a hat, and told me he had to go to work. 'El Villy must walk the streets,' he announced grandly. 'If El Villy isn't on the street, El Villy don't eat!'

Staying in Santiago certainly made the climb up the musical career ladder harder, but there were exceptions. One of them was right on my doorstep. I first met José Aquiles Virelles the day after my arrival in the Hero City. As part of her meet-the-neighbours tour, Tania had introduced me to an incredibly hairy, soft-voiced man washing his car just off the first team football pitch. I remember he had a serious air about him and, at the time, seemed far more interested in cleaning his hubcaps than talking to strangers. It took me nearly a month to pluck up the courage to go across and see him again, but when I eventually walked into his basement studio, I found a totally different person. Aquiles, as he preferred to be called, turned out to be very funny, incredibly generous, and endearingly modest about his talent.

A budding guitarist by the age of fifteen, Aquiles grew up with the *Nueva Trova* movement that sprang up during the Sixties. Cuban singer-songwriters like Pablo Milanes and Silvio Rodríguez were his obvious role models but Aquiles was also influenced by the music of the Beatles, Bob Dylan and the great Chilean guitarist, Victor Jara. In the end, though, it was milk that drove him into a music career. After studying 'Mechanization and Automation of the Milk Industry' in Havana ('The Revolution led us down some strange paths,' he explained with a wry smile), boredom with udder clamps and self-cleaning churning devices pushed him into setting up a vocal quartet called Proposición Cuatro.

His big break finally came in an annual televised singing and songwriting competition called the Concurso Adolfo Guzman; a kind of Cuban Eurovision with far better songs. It was hugely popular – the final night always drew one of the biggest TV audience figures of the year – and as well as the cash prize (10,000 pesos for the 2001 competition) the winner was guaranteed huge publicity and real kudos within the Cuban musical community.

Aquiles had reached the final twice before in the Eighties, coming second and winning the critics' choice in 2000. In 2001, with two of his songs in the final stage, he reckoned he had his best ever chance at winning. In a city full of talented musical families, the Virelles clan had hogged the button more than most. Mercedes, Aquiles's wife, played flute in the Santiago orchestra. The oldest son, David, was considered to be one of the greatest young jazz pianists the country had ever seen. His younger brother, Alejandro, was top in his year at the National Ballet School and little Abelito was tipped to become a superb violinist if only he would stop playing so much football on the street.

Shakespeare, their lively cross between a poodle and a Pekinese, had yet to take up an instrument but barked perfectly in a high G sharp.

On the big night of the Adolfo Guzman finals, practically every member of the *barrio* was huddled around their respective TV sets as the presenter opened the judges' envelope. 'And that the winner of the Gran Premio is . . . José Aquiles with his song "Mira"'. You could hear the street erupt. This wasn't just a case of local boy done good. This was Santiago 1 Havana 0.

For the first week after our hero's return it was impossible to get five minutes with the man. In between the local hacks and the camera crews, a constant stream of friends, fellow musicians and general hangers-on kept filing into his kitchen to shake the composer's hand and admire the two kitsch trophies he had been given.

While Aquiles basked in musical glory, I was feverishly preparing for my moment in front of the microphones in his tiny basement recording studio. Confidence boosted by my successful conga outing, I had returned to bass-playing duties with enthusiasm restored. Which was just as well, because if I wasn't doing brutal Rocky-style finger workouts, I was enduring gruelling practice sessions with Pastor, and if I wasn't suffering those I was battling through nerve-shredding *ensayos* with the rest of Sones de Oriente. Aquiles's little studio was a model of Cuban invention. His basement had been divided into two parts – one side was the performing area, the other the recording and mixing room – with a glass partition allowing one to see the other and a double set of doors for sound insulation. At a push, you could squeeze a *septeto* inside but with seven musicians tucked into the little sealed room, it soon felt like playing *son* in a sauna. For acoustic enhancement, the walls had simply been lined with old egg containers and foam padding. The voice-softening filters in front of the microphones were nothing more than women's stockings stretched tight over wire frames. And the technological side was equally basic. There was an old piece of software on a PC that took at least a minute to warm up and a small mixing desk that looked impressive to me but which Aquiles claimed was a dinosaur.

The studio was his den, the place he felt most comfortable in. Filling one wall was a montage of photographs of his family, friends and musical heroes: Frank Sinatra, John Lennon, a poster for a piano recital by Amanda Virelles, his daughter from a previous marriage, David with the great jazz pianist Chucho Valdez, a moustachioed Aquiles playing in Argentina. It was also the only part of the house that didn't resemble a building site. Like all Cubans, Aquiles was trying to extend his house, and like all Cubans he was faced with the problem of finding building materials. Ever since Hurricane Michelle had blasted across the centre of the country, all cement being made at Santiago's dust-belching factory had been directed towards the urgent rebuilding programme. Only black-market cement was available and such were the risks of selling it, prices were running at fourteen times the norm. The whole city was in a state of construction freeze.

None of which offered any respite to me. The leap from playing scales and practising *tumbaos* to actually playing whole songs with a group of other musicians was, I soon discovered, a substantial one. It was about as wide as the gulf between learning salsa steps in front of Rafael's blind mum and actually dancing with a stranger in front of a big crowd of onlookers. My biggest problem – well, the largest of the biggest problems – was stamina. Performing a five-minute song left me with throbbing fingertips and a left arm that felt as if it had been injected with lead. Often we'd have to repeat a song four or five times in a row to get it right and I soon had to invent delaying tactics (coffee breaks, deliberate loosening of tuning keys, unnecessarily convoluted questions about rhythmic structures) to give me a breather before the inevitable 'da capo' announcement and more pain.

Keeping tempo on the double bass, despite my success in the conga, was also still proving a headache. It was easy to tell when I was starting to slip off the beat because either José Luis started frowning slightly or Yuri, rather less subtly, would shout '*Cuidado!* Watch out!' and begin sniggering. Sometimes, things would fall apart to such an extent that Pastor would call out, '*Mareado!*' and everyone would stop like it was a game of musical chairs. In Spanish, *mareado* means 'seasick' and in Cuban muso-speak it means someone's rhythm (more specifically, my rhythm) was acting a bit green about the gills. Sadly, this wasn't a form of seasickness that could be cured by simply looking at the horizon and breathing deeply. In a naïve attempt to find a solution, I asked Pastor whether I could stand closer to José Luis (friendly, steady guitar rhythm) and further away from Yuri (unfriendly, bass-tripping *tres*). Poor old Pastor just gave an exasperated sigh and, pulling me to one side, spelt out the cold cruel facts. 'Look, Richard, you can't base your rhythm off another instrument because they are relying on *you* to keep them in rhythm. It has to come from inside you.' With all my other tempo-keeping tics (tapping feet, clicking the tongue, general swaying) already outlawed by Pastor on the grounds of being bad bass-playing habits, there was nothing else to do but close my eyes and try to feel the force.

Recent trials in the White House had already proved the eyes-shut approach was a dangerous tactic. Exasperated by his student's inability to stop peering round at the fingerboard, Pastor had finally forced me to go and practise *tumbaos* in the pitch-black confines of his son's bedroom. 'Instinct, not eye sight, is what a good bassist needs,' came the muffled advice from the other side of the door. Incoherent muttering and a strange form of sliding *tumbao* was the reply from my side.

As if all that wasn't enough to cope with, I also discovered another fatal and very humiliating flaw in my musical circuit board. No matter how hard I tried, I just couldn't play and sing at the same time. Now, I know bass players aren't expected to do much on the vocal front – the unplugged bassist's microphone is a standard joke – but this was still a bitter blow. My Spanish was now good enough, and for me, the ability to sing with the group was an important signal of my reduced *pepe* status. Sadly, it was not to be. If ever I needed proof that the men working the buttons down on my musical shop floor were not going to accept multi-tasking, the results from the first few lines of 'Chan Chan' were enough. Total *mareado* melt-down.

It might have been a cliché to record Compay Segundo's famous ode to shaking female bottoms and their effect on the surface tension of male swimming trunks (amazing what you can get away with when no one understands the lyrics), but sometimes necessity demands cliché. For the beginner bassist, 'Chan Chan' was a four-note breeze that could be played even after the eight shots of rum required to kill your pre-performance nerves. 'Chan Chan' was a musical Sure Thing. Pastor said I was doing 'Chan Chan'. After this opening nerve settler, I then planned to tackle a rather trickier Miguel Matamoros track called 'Yo sí, tu no' and then sail into my *pièce de résistance*, 'Hotel California', Cubano style. What had started as a bit of a joke between José Luis and me had now transformed into a cracking version of the Eagles classic complete with syncopated bass lines and a *son*-style call and response section (in Spanish) in place of the usual guitar solo. Yuri sang out the improvised call and the band responded with a chorus of '*Bienvenidos al Hotel California, Pero no te puedes ir*'. Unfortunately, the original 'But you can never leave' line didn't fit our salsa-style arrangement so we had to make do with the not so snappy, 'Welcome to the Hotel California, But you can't go'. I could only hope that the purists in the *barrio* would not take offence.

Before my big moment arrived, I had to wait until Sones de Oriente had completed its own recording session. For any Cuban band, having your own CD was crucial to economic survival, and with so many changes to the line-up, the band needed some up-to-date merchandise.

On Day Four of the Sones de Oriente recording I popped round to see how things were going. The mood was extremely tense and Pastor looked in desperate need of some of his moonshine. The reasons soon became clear. As well as waking up to find his video machine had broken (broken video equalled no *telenovelas*, which in turn equalled acute emotional turbulence at the White House), he was now trying to complete a recording with a paranoid schizophrenic whose exit from hospital had clearly been far too hasty. Angelito was still an official member of Sones de Oriente and so Pastor couldn't release a Sones de Oriente CD without his presence on it. At least three songs had to be sung by a man who clearly had no idea where he was or what he was doing. When I first arrived, Angelito seemed to be acting fairly normally. He was standing alone in front of the microphone and, apart from not appearing to recognize me, didn't display any obvious signs of mental instability. 'Believe me, he's not well,' whispered Pastor, proof of which was delivered the moment the music started up.

In any recording studio there are two choices. You can either record all the voices and instruments at the same time – as if it were a normal live performance – or you can break it down into individual parts ('*por pista*', as Aquiles called it) and then mix them all together later. The latter was far more time-consuming but the advantage was that armed with all the various components, the studio engineer had much more flexibility to tinker with the overall sound. Sones de Oriente were recording this CD '*por pista*' and with most of the instrument parts now completed, it was time to lay the vocal parts over the top. Normally, it should have taken Angelito no more than a couple of hours to do the three songs, but already he had been in the studio for three hours and they were still not through the second song. On reflection, putting a recuperating schizo into a claustrophobic space with felt-padded walls and a group of people gawping at him through a thick glass partition was probably not the best of ideas.

Watching Pastor trying to deliver calming instructions into Angelito's headphones was like witnessing an air traffic controller attempting to bring in a plane whose pilot has just smoked an enormous joint. The biggest problem was that Angelito was dancing around so much when he sang that it was impossible to pick up a steady vocal. 'That's great stuff, Angelito,' tried a soothing Pastor after yet another failed take. 'Let's see if we can do it again, but this time with you a little closer to the microphone.'

Then, just when it seemed as if they were going to get as good a version as they would ever get, Angelito suddenly got the proverbial frog in his throat. The popular method for clearing said amphibian was to call out the word '*Jaime*', the proper guttural pronunciation of the 'J' helping to release any residual mucus, phlegm or other tone-snagging obstruction. 'Give me a big *Jaime*,' instructed Pastor, to which Angelito answered with a spittoon-filling series of tube-clearing noises straight into the microphone.

'Okay, let's go from the top again,' announced Aquiles wearily. 'Silence everyone, recording.'

On went the backing track for the umpteenth time, and in came Angelito with his freshly cleared, rich tenor voice. It was perfect. Not a note wrong, not a lyric misplaced – this was the one. Pastor had his eyes closed. Aquiles had his hand on the mouse ready to click save as soon as the track finally faded. And then it happened.

'*JAIME!!!!*' shouted Angelito right in the middle of the last chorus. It was the hoick that broke Mr Panes's back. Grabbing the communication microphone, Pastor could no longer disguise his exasperation.

'*Qué pasa, compay?*' he pleaded. 'We nearly had it!'

Angelito evidently had no idea he had done something wrong. 'I was just clearing my throat like you told me to,' he replied with almost childlike innocence.

'But not during the song, *compay*, not when we're recording.'

Watching all this from the sidelines was extremely painful. On the one hand, I was distinctly ill at ease watching a grown man being humiliated in front of his peers. And on the other, I felt a growing dread at what would be in store when I was the one standing on the other side of the glass partition. One thing was abundantly clear; in a Cuban recording studio, fools (even mentally ill fools) were not suffered gladly. If you were singing out of tune, they'd tell you. If your rhythm sucked, the people watching you through the window would start making strange mocking faces. A bass player who asked for his teacher to come and tap out the rhythm for him would doubtless be ejected with accompanying howls of derision. And while all this wouldn't have been quite so bad if the only witnesses on hand were the members of Sones de Oriente, I now knew that Aquiles's studio was a magnet for bored musicians who had nothing better to do than watch another band record.

News that a *pepe* was having a go would probably generate a queue down the street with ticket touts offering ringside seats to the highest bidders, and as the big day approached, attempts to relegate this vanity project (I couldn't deny that recording my own CD was driven in part by ego) to 'just enjoy it' status disintegrated as swiftly as Angelito's composure.

The morning I was due to record, the whole gamut of pre-performance reactions was on display. Butterflies in stomach, sweaty palms, uneven breathing, heart flutters – and that was just Pastor. To crank up the pressure a few more notches, he'd announced that Melian would be coming along to film the action with his trusty video camera. Either this was a sign that, post-Angelito saga, Pastor no longer cared about high-risk studio antics or it was an ingenious ruse to distract his trembling student's mind from the bass-playing heebie-jeebies. After eight months of hard work, I was now poised for my first big double bass test. A lot had changed in those eight months. The Dobermann had refound its coat, the White House had gained another room, Tanita had started wearing a bra, and Roberto had sold four bits of unidentifiable plumbing equipment. More important, a thirty-five-year-old English bass student had passed through a series of torture chambers and was now about to prove whether the knife-brandishing, the spoon-tapping, the vinegar-soaking, the do-re-me-ing and *galleta*-smashing had all been worth it. Could I at last begin to call myself a bass player?

The answer to this question was, somewhat distressingly, put on hold as the cruel whims of the man behind the control panel demanded I first test out my voice. Much to the delight of the attendant hangers-on, the first recording session of the day would involve putting down the vocals for our Latino-style version of 'Hotel California'. I think deep down we all like to fancy ourselves as lead singers. From the hairbrush in front of the mirror antics of teenage years to singing along to the radio in the car, it isn't hard to delude yourself of vocal prowess when either the acoustics are friendly or you just can't hear yourself. But standing in front of a proper microphone – albeit one masked by a pair of stockings – with a bunch of real musicians staring at you, all pretence disappears. I was about as ready to do a Don Henley impression as Fidel was to display a series of salsa moves.

'I think I'd better go low and you go high,' I suggested nervously to José Luis.

'You just go where you want,' responded Mr Flexible, who was trying to lighten the mood by bending his fingers back to touch his arm. Miraculously, we did it in three takes, although I think this might have had more to do with the sneaky lowering of output from my microphone and the fact that Aquiles was fully aware that my bass playing would be a far more time-consuming recording challenge.

It was an astute prediction. On about the twentieth attempt to complete our new syncopated bass line to 'Hotel California', a voice in my headphones suggested a break and Pastor came in to have a little pep talk.

'*Relax, compay!*' were his first words on seeing the sweat-covered wreck formerly known as Richard. Aquiles had a separate little foam-padded booth where bass lines were recorded, and the combination of nerves and lack of ventilation was causing perspiration beyond the services of even a jumbo-sized *panuelo*. To make matters worse, Melian had decided there wasn't enough lighting in the booth (he was filming this painful scene through a glass panel in the door) and insisted on laying a bright temperature-boosting arc light on the floor. What with Pastor fluttering around like a mother hen, Melian wiping my head with toilet paper to remove the shine, and Aquiles rapidly losing his sense of humour, I was getting dangerously close to doing an Angelito. I'm sure this studio had seen its share of tearful moments but none I'd venture would have been caused by an inability to play a simple *tumbao*.

If I got a dollar for every time I heard the word '*mareado*' in my headphones, I could have bought a boat and taken them all on a proper seasick joyride. Those eight months might have seemed like a decent investment, but in musical terms – as this humiliating shirt-soaker was revealing all too clearly – it was nothing. Perhaps the most brutal evidence of musical deficiency was my inability to recognize the notes I was hearing on the playbacks relayed through my headphones. Desperately trying to clear up the *mareado* sections, Aquiles would start re-recording a few bars ahead of the problem part, the idea being that I began playing as soon as I heard the instruction, 'Recording!' But by the time I worked out the right note to get me back in the loop, we, or rather I, had inevitably run past the start of the screw-up I was trying to unscrew.

Much as it pains me to reveal this, the only way we managed to complete that recording before Melian ran out of tapes was by having Pastor call out the opening notes and then tap out the rhythm on my shoulder at the first sign of seasickness. None of this, however, made any difference at all to the pride I felt when, ten days and some nifty mixing work later, I was the owner of my very own CD, signed by the winner of the 2001 Adolfo Guzman. And by the time Pastor had started playing our version of 'Hotel California' over the PA in the Casa de la Trova – people were actually dancing to music I had made

– I had completely forgotten about the pain behind the gain. Now all I had to do was iron out the mistakes, put on the blue suit, and repeat the process without a safety net. It was time to replenish the rum stocks.

16. Live and in Blue

In golf there is a well-known psychological condition called the yips. Essentially a nerves-related affliction, it can turn even some of the world's best players into jelly-legged disasters on the putting green.

With two weeks to go before my appearance at the Casa de la Trova, I was starting to suffer a horrible recurring nightmare that suggested I was going to have the bass-playing yips. In this dream I'd be standing on stage looking suitably Kid Creole-ish in my blue suit. Everything would appear normal: Yuri tinkering away at his habitually over-extended *tres* warm-up, José Luis fooling around with his leg-twisting exercises, and HP propped up in the corner ready to be played. But then when Pastor gave the *un, dos, un, dos, tres y* . . . starting sequence I would find I couldn't remember a single note. Instead of waiting for me, the band continued to play while I just stood there holding HP.

Now, I'm not generally a dream-reading type, but the clarity with which this nightly show kept repeating started to freak me out. What if I did have the musical version of a fluffed putt? What if I froze? The conga experience might have settled some nerves but I knew there was a big difference between thrashing a drum among people who didn't know me (and with an audience so stoked up on rum they'd barely register a mistake) and playing an instrument in front of a stationary audience of friends and musicians, an instrument whose rhythm was crucial to the performance. A missed note in the conga and you could always fall back on your *galleta* partner to get you back in synch. A missed note, or worse still, a whole raft of forgotten notes, in the Casa de la Trova and Sones de Oriente could be the first group to lose their Government contract due to a bass player breakdown.

For a musician whose future earning capacity was about to have its make-or-break moment, Pastor seemed disconcertingly unflustered. Part of this could be put down to the completion of a new White House roof and the recent arrival of a new consignment of Mexican *telenovelas*, but I believe the real reason for his distraction was a global event happening thousands of miles away. With the Road Flatteners knocked out of the baseball championships, Pastor, like the majority of Santiago's male population, had decided to switch allegiance from one type of *pelota* to another. Just as I was approaching the climax to my year of tortured fingers, football World Cup fever hit Santiago.

Astutely sensing it would be politically advantageous to keep the masses happy, Fidel had coughed up the funds to allow fifty-nine of the sixty-four games to be transmitted live. Announcing this decision a week before the competition began, the following piece of editorial appeared in the sports pages of *Granma*. In a country where stealing a base in baseball was once decreed as contravening revolutionary principles, not mixing sport with politics was unlikely. '*Despite the difficult economic situation provoked by the brutal blockade that the US Government has maintained for the last forty years,*' began the rather clunky first paragraph, '*the Cuban state will be transmitting the majority of the World Cup.*' The writer finished with a stirring addendum. '*The enjoyment of this event will be accompanied by the demolition of all the fibs and lies that the President of the USA has declared against our Revolution. Seguimos en Combate!*' Enjoy the football was the message, but don't forget to stick pins in your Dubya dolls after every match.

Delighted by this news, Pastor decided to get in some pre-World Cup training by renting out the Chicharrones PlayStation and plugging in the FIFA 2000 programme. Despite having never played the game before, he took to the task of skills acquisition with exactly the same self-help determination and dogged dedication he'd employed to learn the bass. Day after day I'd walk into his living room and find him practising free kicks and corners in every type of weather condition the PlayStation could throw at him.

For Pastor, the World Cup coverage was a novelty. For me, it was a welcome distraction at a time when a veritable *caldoso* of emotions was threatening to bubble over. Apart from the obvious build-up of stage nerves, I was also dreading the good-byes that would follow a few days after the big gig. My bus ticket back to Havana had been booked and the date for my return to Europe was now just a couple of lines away on Tania's kitchen calendar. I didn't need to hear Liana and Tanita tell me how much they were going to miss me to realize my year in Santiago had left an indelible emotional mark. As well as all the things that El Villy had listed about his beloved city, I had built up my own collection of sensory snapshots of my adopted home. The daily clatter of the trolley traders with their high-pitched sales calls, the street Olympians of Santa Lucia, Sandra's *pru*, the Padre Pico social centre, the haggling with Roberto over unrecognizable appliances, the '*Qué vola aceres?*' and '*Hola compays*', the queues and their associated calls of '*Quién es el ultimo?*', the mangoes at a dozen a dollar, the sight of cakes being carried around the city at all hours of the day and the sound of *son* and salsa on every corner. But in prime position in the memory bank, ingrained from months of visits, was that garish living room in Chicharrones, the unchanging backdrop to my 36 Chambers of Double Bass-playing.

Life without Mr Panes was going to be strange. The man who had coaxed, encouraged, bullied, but above all inspired me to find an intelligent fingering had become more than just my musical mentor. Brought together by a large lump of wood and a busker with bad teeth, a professional student–teacher relationship had quickly developed into firm friendship. Whatever happened at my big gig, I would remember Pastor for much more than just his bizarre teaching methods. This was the man who had shown me how to carry a double bass while riding a motorbike and taught me how to re-attach a sound-post with nothing more than a piece of string and patience. This was the man who had educated me on the culinary delights of fried eggs and crispy plantain chips, enlightened me on the joys of computer-generated baseball and introduced me to the sounds of bass-playing legend Oscar de León. And he was the man who had taught me to speak like a Cuban, drink like a Cuban, and appreciate bad B-grade action movies like a Cuban.

Now only one last piece of shepherding duty was left. All he had to do to earn a signed copy of my Simandl book (signed by me, not Simandl) and the promise to bring him a PlayStation machine the next time I visited Santiago was somehow to guide me successfully through the last phase of Operation Beat those Dastardly Dutchmen. For the last month I had been rigorously practising the three songs I had chosen to play – two Matamoros compositions and a regular Sones de Oriente number called 'El Florero' – and bar some lingering jitters about a tricky triple-*tumbao* combo in the latter I reckoned I was as ready as I would ever be to perform. As a warm-up and nerves-settler before the big night, Pastor decided it would be a good idea to have a mini-gig with a few selected friends as the mock audience. It was a sensible if not particularly attractive plan. Apart from the recording studio, I could claim precious little experience of playing in front of people and I needed to see how I would cope with stage fright. Running with the dress rehearsal idea, I asked Tania whether she would mind having a few people round to watch us play. To say she loved the idea would be a massive understatement. A few people soon ballooned into a large lunch party and as the doorbell kept ringing and the patio filled to capacity, I got the distinct impression that this had been Pastor's idea all along. This was his way of testing my nerves, his chance to find an excuse to cancel the concert proper. Such speculation was heightened when I opened the door to find Santiago, the manager of the Casa de la Trova, standing there with a big smile on his face.

'What did you invite Santiago for?' I hissed at Pastor a few seconds later.

'He said he wanted to see you play,' he shrugged back.

'But what happens if I screw up?'

'You won't screw up.'

'What makes you so sure?'

'Because I know you really want to play at the Trova.'

Muttering a select choice of expletives from my now expansive repertoire of Cuban swear words, I disappeared into the kitchen to find the rum. After everyone had finished eating lunch, Pastor stood up and explained the purpose of this gathering and asked everyone to be respectful of the fact that this was my first performance in front of an audience.

'Richard has worked very hard to get this far so please give him a big round of applause.' Whichever idiot came up with the expression 'dry run' clearly had a strange sense of humour. The only dry part of my body was my throat – the rest was dripping in sweat.

The first song was a complete and utter mess. I blamed it on the fact my sweaty fingers kept slipping on the strings, but a bad case of rampant butterflies was nearer the mark. In the middle of the first *tumbao*, Pastor called a halt and suggested we start again. The second attempt we (sorry, I) made it through the entire song. Admittedly, Pastor had briefly to employ some hidden back-tapping assistance to get me through some of the trickier syncopated rapids but the thunderous applause from the assembled spectators helped removed the worst of the jitters. To my relief, I managed to get through the other two songs without too many stray notes and Santiago was the first person to come over and offer congratulations.

'I think we'll have to organize more seats for Saturday night,' he chirped before disappearing.

This small bubble of confidence quickly burst when, later

that day, I watched Melian's video recording of our dress rehearsal. Having not yet seen his coverage of my recording studio debut, this was the first time I had actually watched myself play and it wasn't comfortable viewing. As the image locked on to the man behind the wood, a chorus of sniggers came from a huddle of people trying to get a glimpse of the action on the small video display. Under the job description of double bassist, I was fully aware there were certain criteria that any hopeful applicant had to be able to demonstrate. First, there were handling skills. For this I gave myself a reasonable grade. My left hand, the crucial judge-impressing left hand, had poise and grace, albeit with a little finger that still poked out in the teacup-holding position. The right hand had a tendency to creep up the fingerboard but at last I seemed to have got the hang of the friction-not-traction conundrum. Second, there was rhythm-maintenance, and while I had to humbly admit to using occasional outside assistance, it was still a vast improvement on the uncoordinated drumstick display of a few months back. Third, there were improvisational skills. Even post-conga with its brief glimpses of *la bomba*, I accepted the likelihood that some improvisation on the big night was extremely slim and by now I had woken up to the reality that full *bomba* extraction was a long-term mining proposition. And fourth and finally, there was what could loosely be called artistic delivery. When they weren't tucked away in the corner bouncing vibrations off the wall, double bass players were meant to be the showmen of the band. Armed with the biggest and sexiest prop on stage, a double bassist was expected to provide plenty of razzle-dazzle with his performance. One look at Melian's recording and I could see I was to razzle-dazzle what Ian Duncan-Smith was to charismatic political leadership. Whereas Pastor always appeared to be having the time of his life every time he played, I wore the facial expression of a mine-defusing expert in mid-job. Pastor could play the bass and have a conversation with someone at the same time. I had to concentrate so hard on not screwing up that even talking to myself was banned.

'You've got to try and loosen up a bit,' said Rafael when I told him about my performance a couple of days later. 'You don't have to grin like Pastor when you play but if you're tense there's more chance of you losing the rhythm.'

Although grateful for his advice, I wasn't in Asunción looking for some *un-dos-tres* therapy. I was back at my dance teacher's house to sort out a few unresolved spiritual matters. Ever since learning that personal possessions could be given a protective blessing from the *santos*, I'd decided it would be best to go on stage with all my bases (and one bass in particular) covered. HP might not have revealed any signs of lingering bad spirits so far but after all the recent bad dreams the time had come to remove all doubt.

Obviously the cleansing process didn't come without a price. Rafael agreed to sort out HP on the proviso that I visited a *babalao* and undertook the basic *santeria* ceremony to find out who my chosen *santo* was. 'This is important to me,' said the man whose little baby already wore a *santeria* amulet. 'I can't let you leave Cuba without the protection of a *santo*.' Expecting yet another large dip into my now desperately meagre resources, I was amazed to be told I would only need two candles, two coconuts and 124 pesos. 'If you want to leave a tip for the *babalao*, that's up to you,' Rafael added. A discretionary service charge – now this was a *babalao* I could work with.

The instrument-cleansing ritual didn't take long. In fact, the hardest part involved lugging HP up the hill to Asunción. Once inside, Rafael went into his kitchen and after a lot of rummaging around emerged with a jam jar full of what looked like spiritual haberdashery. Two chicken's feet were sticking out of the top at a comical angle. Candles were then lit and, taking a big mouthful of aguardiente, my host sprayed the jar and most of his kitchen surfaces with a fine mist of spirit and spittle. Three small discs were then extracted from the jar. They were made of coconut shell. One side was smooth while the other had been etched with some sort of linear markings. A one-way conversation started, one that involved Rafael talking very fast in the same unintelligible dialect I recognized from my pigeon and honey ceremony. The only words I could identify were '*inglés*' and '*contrabajo*'. After every piece of dialogue, he'd throw the discs on the floor and, as if reading an answer from the way in which they fell, he would pause for a second and then continue with his monologue. Finally, all three discs landed signs up and picking them off the floor, he announced that it was all done.

'Sometime before you leave, I will put something small inside the bass. You must not try and take it out.'

I asked him what he'd been saying to the *santos*. 'I was telling them this *pepe* needs some help with rhythm,' he laughed. 'And that they must fill this bass with a relaxing energy that loosens up the man who plays it.'

I went over and took hold of HP, keen to see if I could feel any new tingle of divine intervention. Nothing. HP felt like HP always felt; a stubborn sixty-year-old with absolutely no intention of helping out the poor sod given the task of coaxing coherent messages out of her vocal cords.

Sticking to my side of the deal, I then walked with Rafael to the house of the local *babalao*. He wasn't there but his mother told us to sit and wait. Assuming the wise old man had been delayed by some important saintly business – an animal sacrifice, perhaps – it was a bit disappointing when a thirty-something, casually dressed man turned up and explained he'd been delayed by a phone call with his French girlfriend. If it weren't for the brightly coloured beads hanging around his neck, I'd never have guessed this was a *santeria* priest. Getting straight down to business, he told me to take off my watch, shoes and glasses and join him in the adjoining room. I did as he said and walked through. Without my glasses, it was all a bit of a blur but with a lot of squinting I managed to identify various items set out on the floor. There was a small pair of antlers, a horse's tail fly-swisher, a round tray covered with a fine layer of gritty material ('magic sediment', corrected Rafael later), and a bowl full of palm nuts. I handed over the candles, coconuts and money and the *babalao* lit the first, smashed the second into pieces, and pocketed the third.

Rafael explained that to begin with the *babalao* had to call on the *santos*. This involved a lot of chanting in Yoruba, much tapping on the floor with the antlers and the touching of my forehead and shoulders with one of the broken pieces of coconut. After about ten minutes, connection appeared to be established and the ceremony proper began. Guided by Rafael, I was asked to perform a series of complicated arm-crossing, joint-touching manoeuvres. Then the *babalao* began scrunching the palm nuts in his hands and after dropping them on the floor he traced linear markings in the sediment on the tray. While all this went on, Rafael wrote down columns of zeros and ones on a piece of paper. He later explained that this was the process of divination, or *ifa*. By reading the apparently haphazard pattern displayed by the nuts, a well-trained *santeria* priest could discover the destiny of the person undertaking the ceremony.

It all lasted about half an hour and then the *babalao* said something to Rafael and Rafael in turn put the question to me.

'Which *santo* have you chosen?'

There had been a crucial breakdown in communication.

'I thought I was here to find out my *santo*,' I whispered back.

'No, you have to say which *santo* you want and then the *babalao* finds out whether your choice has been accepted or not.'

Unused to indecisive visitors and clearly keen to get on with business, the *babalao* fiddled with his beads with undisguised impatience. Looking at the rainbow of colours on display, I picked one out at random.

'The blue and white beads — which *santo* is that?' I hissed into Rafael's ear.

'Yemaya — the goddess of the sea — that's Amber's *santo* — a good choice,' he answered.

'Yemaya,' I announced confidently to the *babalao* who in return gave me two small stones — one black, one white — and told me to put one in each fist behind my back. As requested, I then held out both arms in front of me and opened the clenched fist chosen by the *babalao*. It contained the white stone.

'Your choice has been accepted,' beamed Rafael. Judging this to be a somewhat arbitrary method for confirming a saintly partnership, I nevertheless silently thanked the gambling gods for their timely cooperation. Not only had they saved me from further steps in the potentially *babalao*-baiting, colour-decoding process, but I would also now be certain of having saintly support on my shoulder (in fact on both shoulders) come Saturday night. Ruocco's fine piece of electric blue tailoring had just transformed itself into a well-cut homage to my protective saint.

I had just completed the first and most basic step towards *santeria* induction. To be allowed to wear a blue and white amulet, however, I would need to take things to the next stage, a three-day session with animal sacrifices and a substantially larger financial investment. Obviously keen to keep the funds rolling in, the *babalao* stressed that it was important to complete this second phase as soon as possible. My budget and time restrictions suggested that amulets were unlikely to be secured before my departure.

'And there are a few things I must advise you on,' he added while tidying up the spiritual paraphernalia, 'things I have been told to tell you.'

I nodded for him to continue. The list was a strange one. I was told to be careful to protect my eyes, to watch out for people who wanted to blame me for things I hadn't done, to not go to bed straight after eating (hardly visionary advice there), and that it was time to find a partner who would let my intelligence shine. I assumed here we were talking about human rather than wooden partners. Asked if I had any questions, I chose to ignore potentially vital details on what I should be protecting my eyes from and instead pushed for divine information on future musical performances.

'Did you see anything about music or musical instruments?' The *babalao* fiddled with his beads again and after a long pause asked, '*Eres un musico?*' I told him I was trying to be one.

'You have chosen a good *santo* – Yemaya loves music.' Quite how this music-loving *santo* of the sea would react when one of her subjects suffered a bad case of rhythmical seasickness was clearly not going to be answered today. My time was up. The *babalao* had other fish to fry, or should I say coconuts to crack. I left a modest discretionary service charge and headed back down towards the bay happy in the knowledge that my instrument was blessed, my concert costume was appropriate in colour (if not cut), and my spiritual support team would be there for me, come the moment of truth. As one of Ruocco's most famous clients once advised while dressed in tight jeans and a studded leather jacket, 'You gotta have faith, faith, faith.'

D–Day dawned just like any other. The usual sound of ablutions from the Damelos' bathroom, the usual frustrated attempt to hear the BBC World Service news through the interrupting signal from some bizarre Catholic station, and the same breakfast battle with the Cuban bread roll. Hearing the newscaster announce the date, I realized that by some quirk of timing, my big gig – my big, three-song set – was happening exactly one year on from the day I arrived in Santiago. After 365 days in the Hero City, I was about to celebrate my first anniversary with the biggest musical moment of my life. Just as I'd done on that first day at 101, I went up to the roof after breakfast and sat down to soak up the view and contemplate the day ahead. For a second, it was as if nothing separated the two days. The thermal-riding vultures were still wheeling around in search of a meal, the boatless bay was just as ghostly quiet, not a single new building project broke the same cluttered, clay-roofed vista, and the sky was filled with that familiar parade of towering chef's hats and bleached Afros. The only visual break in an otherwise surreally perfect *déjà vu* was the bright green canopy above my head. When I'd stood here with Tania the previous summer, the tiny vine they'd planted for shade was only a few feet tall. Now it covered the entire metal frame and thick bunches of grapes hung everywhere.

Feeling a sudden on-rush of pre-performance stress – despite still being a good ten hours away from suit unwrapping – I decided an hour of relaxing yoga might be a good idea. Returning to my room, I rolled out the purple mat, stripped down to a pair of shorts, and slotted one of my two yoga tapes into the cassette player.

'Bring your right heel into the perineum,' came the familiar opening command on the tape, 'and then earth your sitting bones, and establish an aligned balanced position.'

Following the orders, I sat down in the middle of the mat, bent my right knee and drew the ball of my foot in towards my groin. Then, with sitting bones earthed – on a strategically placed cushion – I brought the left leg in front of the right and attempted to establish a position that was at least aligned if not totally balanced. It was just after 10 a.m. and already the heat in my room was such that even wearing next to nothing, the small exertion required to bring about this most basic of yogic manoeuvres had caused small beads of sweat to erupt along my forehead and top lip. I licked at the salty skin under my nose, closed my eyes, and prepared for the next move.

For the last twelve months I had been listening to the same soothing voice, following the same commands, and executing the same sequence of sweaty manoeuvres in my room at number 101 Calle Santa Lucia. After so many repetitions, I now knew the tape so well I could pre-empt the instructions before they arrived. I had memorized every cough, giggle and extraneous background noise and had even built up an imaginary picture of all my invisible classmates.

'Loud cough followed by distant hum of lawn mower,' I muttered silently to myself, 'relax the body while maintaining a long spine . . .' Right on cue, in cut the cough, the lawn mower, and then the teacher's voice. 'Relax the body while maintaining a long spine, an open chest, and . . .'

'*COJONES!!*' screamed a female voice outside my window. Oblivious to the interruption, my yoga teacher calmly continued with his next command. It too was smothered, this time by a longer, more drawn-out '*CO. . . JO . . . NES!!*' followed up by a shorter but equally furious '*VEN ACA!!*' I leaned over to the tape recorder, pressed pause, and waited for the inevitable follow-up. Sure enough, another neighbourhood-shaking '*DAMELO COJONES!!*' segued immediately into an unintelligible volley of Cuban Spanish, a clearly audible slap of palm on bare backside, and after a short pause for pain recognition to set in, the predictable wail of a child. Five minutes of crying and a few more *cojones* later, and tranquillity was once more restored. Releasing the pause button, I sat back down on the mat.

'Feel a gentle extension up through the neck, your breastbone lifting away from the groin, shoulder blades dropping down, and now take your attention to . . .'

'*HIJO DE PUTA! VOY A MATARLE!*' screamed a male voice this time. Normally, I would have ignored it. I'd got used to doing my yoga to the accompaniment of testicles, pricks, and sons of bitches. But today I couldn't. Today was different. Today I needed peace and quiet.

I pressed the stop button and ejected the tape. Maybe another shower might help, I thought. Grabbing a towel, I opened the door to my room and stepped out into the long corridor that ran along the length of the house. By now the family had got used to seeing me padding around half naked and Marcela smiled but said nothing when she looked up from her rocking chair. Turning on the light inside the bathroom, I found Chiri splayed out on the wet tiles under the showerhead. Chiri was not the most intelligent of dogs but he certainly knew where the coolest sleeping spots were.

'*Vamos, Chiri. Afuera!*' I ordered, nudging his backside with my foot. Clearly disgruntled at being disturbed, he ambled slowly out of the shower, then stopped at the door and turned to give me a knowing stare. 'You never take showers at this time,' he seemed to be saying, 'you must be in a mess.'

'Out!' I said again, and with tongue lolling out of a half-panting, half-grinning mouth, off he loped. I shut the door, turned on the single shower tap and, after quickly stripping off, stepped under the weak dribble of water. Even this early in the day, the sun had already penetrated the tank on the roof and what had been refreshing two hours ago was now lukewarm. The water wouldn't be cold again for at least another sixteen hours. And by then it would all be over.

Chiri was right. I was a mess. I was a clammy-handed, nervous wreck. I couldn't concentrate on anything. I felt nauseous. I had bags under my eyes from lack of sleep the previous night. I had no appetite. I couldn't face talking to anyone. And now I'd just failed to complete a single sun salutation. Here I was standing under a shower, thousands of miles from home, plucking stray clumps of wet dog hair out of the plughole, and feeling so nervous I was seriously considering breaking the 'not before midday' rum rule.

For the second time in less than an hour, my mind raced back to the advert I'd placed in *Time Out* over eighteen months ago, the simple three-line announcement that had kick-started this whole bizarre chain of events. The ridiculousness of it all made me let out an involuntary snort of laughter. To think I actually wanted this to happen. To think I gave up a career to feel like this.

'*Loco, loco, loco!*' I repeated, while rather over-dramatically slapping the wall with a wet palm. And then, just as abruptly, I was brought to my senses by the vision of the task ahead – the grand finale, the *pièce de résistance*, the big white-knuckle climax – and amusement quickly dissolved back to fear. Whichever way I tried to spin it, the reality of what was about to happen looked horrible.

This evening, a thirty-five-year-old Englishman would walk across the centre of Santiago de Cuba wearing a ridiculously bright piece of clothing and carrying an unfeasibly large instrument. The same man would then take the stage in one of the most famous music venues in Cuba and play bass in front of an unsuspecting audience of music lovers. Yes, a musical oaf who not so long ago thought syncopated was something you sorted out by eating figs would be taking responsibility for striking out a steady rhythm to hold together six other band members in one tight unit. Just saying all this to myself made me feel ill. I let out an audible groan and slowly sat down on the floor of the shower with the water still running down my back. '*Cojones!*' I cursed to the wall. 'Great big Y-front filling, whose idea was this *COJONES!*'

After managing to pull myself together to do an hour of practice and finger exercises, I went for a walk, and on the way past the Casa de la Trova, stopped off to confirm timings and try to remove any of the extra chairs that Santiago might have added. Just inside the entrance, the usual handwritten sign listed the bands due to appear over the course of the day. First up were José Luis's old group, Guitarras y Trovadores, followed by the Duo Hermanas Ferrin, a Santiago sister act that had been performing *boleros* and *canciones romanticas* since 1963. The evening slot began with Changui de Santiago, continued with Estudiantina Invasora and finished with Sones de Oriente. Underneath the last entry, someone (Pastor, I presumed) had handwritten '*con Richard en el bajo*'.

Having your name spelt out in red marker pen isn't quite the same as having it up in lights but it was good enough for me. I stared at the sign again and tried to suppress a panic attack.

'Jesus,' I muttered, 'I'm going to be coming on stage straight after Roberto Napoli.' The most experienced bassist in town was going to be the warm-up act for the most inexperienced. It was not the dream support act.

Walking inside the small hall, I climbed up on to the small raised stage and paced around the square of ruffled green felt like a football player testing the pitch before a big game. I was alone apart from the nine men staring out from the left-hand wall. These were the guardians of quality control at the Casa de la Trova, the reminder, if such a thing was needed, of the importance of the venue and the weight of musical history pressing down on every performer's shoulders. Nearest to me was Pablo Armaignan Castellanos – guitarist, composer, singer – born 17 August 1895, died Christmas Day 1991. Next to him was Virgilio Palais, the guitarist and composer whose café formed the original Casa de la Trova. Along to the right was José 'Pepe' Sanchez, father of the *trova* movement and author of what was widely considered to be the first *bolero*, and then further down, staring out impassively from their canvases, hovered the distinctive profiles of Miguel Matamoros and Sindo Garay. If the live audience were going to put a few butterflies in my stomach, the ghosts in the VIP section were sure to make them flap around more energetically than normal.

With a seemingly prescient sense of timing, Pastor appeared at the door just as I stepped back off the stage. 'You're a bit early aren't you, *compay*?' he chuckled.

'Just getting the feel of the place,' I replied, 'and you?' If he was feeling the pressure too, he was doing a good job at hiding it. Apart from a very soggy *pañuelo*, there was little evidence of pre-battle panic from the ex-army engineer. He said he was here to give a lesson to one of his Cuban students, a twenty-year-old who had started at about the same time as me but who was already, much to my disgruntlement, playing with a band. Taking a seat out on the patio, we went over the arrangements for the evening. 'The band will meet at seven-thirty in the backstage room,' he confirmed in a tone that had abruptly switched from civvy jokiness to precise army mode. 'Make sure you do half an hour of warm-up before you come and don't forget to bring your tuner.' Usually, he never wrote anything down but I noticed he was half hiding a scrap of paper with a list of spidery instructions on it. The man from Crackling, the supposedly unflappable Mr Panes, was suffering the colly-wobbles as well.

'And bring a couple of dry *pañuelos*. You are going to sweat a lot,' he continued.

Luckily, his student arrived just as I feared we were getting into 'Wear clean underwear' territory and the conversation was steered into calmer waters. As well as diverting attention away from the dreaded checklist, my young Cuban counterpart unex-pectedly provided a morale-boosting tonic just when I needed it most. Not only had he got plasters around the tips of three fingers, a glance at his fingerboard revealed the heart-lifting sight of little pieces of sticky tape all the way from the first position down to, well, a long way down. Here was evidence that Cubans (some Cubans at least) were just as human as us *pepes*. Sure, he probably didn't have to use Ted Reed's drum-ming book to improve his syncopation, and I doubted he'd need to risk a performance in the conga to find his *bomba*, but here was encouraging proof that in at least some departments we were equals.

The afternoon dragged by interminably slowly. I tried every-thing to take my mind off my musical High Noon but nothing worked. Eventually, after another two showers, a walk up to Padre Pico, and so many cups of Marcela's coffee that I was in danger of getting the caffeine shakes, I ended up in front of the TV watching *Billy Elliot* with Liana and Tanita. I'll freely admit to being a sucker for these sorts of triumph-over-tragedy movies but with all the added emotional baggage I was carry-ing around that afternoon, I'm afraid I was in a terrible lip-quivering state by the time Billy got to dance in front of the

Ballet School judges. 'Billy, what do you feel like when you dance?' came the question from one of the panel. 'I sort of disappear,' replied Billy. How I wish I had the power to 'sort of disappear'.

At approximately six-thirty, after the slowest ten hours in my life, I showered for the fourth and final time, and then, after a pause to take in mentally what was about to happen, carefully unhooked the now dusty protective suit cover from its position on the wall. The moment had come. It was time to put on Ruocco's linen masterpiece. The good news was that even after a year of fried chicken and rice, the trousers miraculously still fitted. Standing in front of the mirror with HP in the playing position, I tried a few bass-twirling moves, shook a leg, and doffed an imaginary cap at the audience. We looked quite a pair. For five minutes, I strutted proudly around the room returning to the mirror every few seconds to give a wave to the imaginary crowd and strike the sort of poses I hadn't practised since my air-playing days. And five minutes moving around was all it took to feel my shirt starting to stick to my back. For all the points it was doubtless going to score me on the image front, there was absolutely no doubt that a paisley-lined suit, in the height of a Santiago summer, was right up there in the Wombles league of inappropriate stage dress.

Pañuelo deployment had to be activated far earlier than expected and, deducing it would be hazardous to carry HP in the comfortable but sweaty rucksack position, I ditched the carrying case, hooked my jacket over her head and went for the traditional Cuban-style bass man's lift – fingers hooked around the bottom of the fingerboard, hips resting against hips. With the rest of the household getting dressed to come to the gig – and me keen not to show them my stage outfit – I slipped quietly out the door and into the soft mango glow of a stunning Caribbean sunset.

It was like walking into a surprise party. The entire Damelo household was out waiting for my departure and I had to suppress another eye-moistening moment as kind words of encouragement rained down. Looking up the street, I could see it was going to be an emotional walk up the hill. Everyone was out waiting to see me off. Francisco and his gossipy mum shouted, '*Buena suerte!*' from their doorway, Angel broke off from his pile of shoes to shake my hand, Roberto and the rest of the Padre Pico crowd briefly suspended play on the lower table – a move unprecedented in Santiago dominoes history – to wish me luck. Roberto apologized for not being able to come but touchingly explained that he no longer had suitable clothes for such an event. I told him not to worry. 'It's only three songs, Roberto.'

Rene was away having medical treatment in Havana but Sandra and little Frank came out to wish me well. I could have done with a few gulps of *pru* but lack of funds to buy the ingredients meant production had recently ground to a halt. Probably just as well. Gassy *pru* and butterflies would have been a potentially lethal combination.

With all the stops and starts, it took me over forty minutes to complete the normal ten-minute walk to the Trova. By the time I arrived, Pastor, perhaps thinking I had done a runner, was wearing the face of a man whose video has broken for a second time. '*Compay*, you were meant to be here fifteen minutes ago,' he chastened, the sweat beading visibly across his forehead. I'd never seen him looking so stressed. 'Marco hasn't turned up and no one can find him,' he added quickly. No bongo player, a rookie bass player; the poor man was watching his Government contract dissolve in front of his eyes. The room was already nearly full and, as I walked down the central aisle, familiar faces popped up in every row. I spotted Rafael in his crispest, cleanest whites, Ivan my flute-playing friend, Ernesto whom I hadn't seen for months, Conchita almost unrecognizable in a wig, and Carlos with his trademark lensless specs and best conga outfit. He grinned and raised his fist in salute. Aquiles, probably the musician I admired the most, was sadly in Canada visiting his son, David, but his middle son, Alejandro the ballet prodigy, whom I had only met once, had come along in his place. Failure in front of all these people was not something I could contemplate.

Estudiantina Invasora were coming to the end of their set and, as I tuned up the bass in the backstage area, I stole a glance at Napoli pecking away contentedly at his three strings. His eyes were closed and he had a big grin on his face. How I wished for his calmness. With God Damned African Elephants all setting off the required green lights, I went through my customary digit-warming routine and practised each of the first few bars of the three songs. Somehow, Pastor had found a replacement bongo player, and we all got into a pre-match huddle in the middle of the room.

'Whatever happens out there tonight,' he began, 'I want everyone to just keep going.' Even Yuri looked serious for once. 'If anyone makes a mistake, everyone else keeps playing like nothing has happened.' I could have hugged him for saying 'anyone' rather than 'Richard'. By changing that one word he'd made me feel part of the group rather than some hazardous intruder. A bottle of rum appeared.

'*Para los santos y Richard,*' said José Luis, sprinkling a few drops on to the floor. I took a big gulp of spirit and passed the bottle on. '*Listo?*' said Pastor. 'Ready!' I replied.

Just before Santiago headed out to announce the band, Liana came running through the backstage door with a worried expression on her face. Wearing her best white dress with frilly socks and shiny black shoes, she was only a wand short of winning a fairy lookalike competition. 'Are you going to sing?' she asked in a tone of great concern.

'No, I'm just going to play the bass,' I answered, 'I can't play bass and sing at the same time.' This seemed to be the answer she was looking for. 'Good,' she clucked, putting her tiny hand inside my big and by now very clammy palm. And with that, she ran off back to her seat.

The next twenty minutes went by in a fast, fear-smudged blur. I watched the band walk out on stage leaving me in the wings. Pastor had insisted I come out alone. I remember catching snatches of Santiago's speech about an Englishman arriving off a train with a double bass and a grand plan. I recall cringing as Pastor delivered a heartfelt eulogy to his longest-serving foreign student. And I dimly recollect whispering a little prayer to Yemaya as I walked out to face the clapping ranks of friends, tourists, *jineteras* and musicians. As Yuri began strumming the jangling intro to 'Yo sí, tu no' – one of my favourite Miguel Matamoros songs – I didn't disappear like Billy Elliot but I did focus on HP like my life depended on it. I don't think I even glanced at the audience once during the first song and, when the last bar finished, there was a small circle of wet green felt between my feet where sweat had been dripping off my chin. Underneath Ruocco's suit, things had got so damp that when Pastor gave me a congratulatory pat on the back it was like hearing someone slap a wet flannel.

Relative calm quickly turned to heart pumping panic on the second song, 'El Florero'. For some inexplicable reason, Yuri ignored everything we'd done in the practice sessions and set off at a tempo that was much faster than normal. Supposedly, the bass player sets the speed limit but, having not yet mastered the art of tweaking with musical velocity, I didn't dare risk slowing down only to find that no one else had followed me. That would unquestionably lead to a *mareado* moment, an embarrassment I refused to contemplate. Pastor was right at my shoulder and with a broad grin on my face so as not to give away signs that the ship was in trouble, I hissed, '*Demasiado rapido* – too fast!!' in his general direction. I knew I could get through the easy first half of the song, but at this speed the second and trickiest of the three *tumbaos* would require the sort of finger speed my motor-neurones would never cope with. Keeping up the grin game, Pastor simply sidled over to Yuri and whatever he said, it worked. The foot immediately came off the *tres* accelerator and we cruised through the rest of the number with only the occasional rhythm-holding tap on the back from my sidekick.

By the third and final song, the blinding fear had receded enough for me to be able to take in the significance of what was happening. I was living the moment I had dreamed of ever since thrashing those air instruments as a teenager. I was at the end of a road that had involved substantial sacrifices (my bank balance and wine rack were equally empty) but also a catalogue of experiences whose value I would doubtless only appreciate properly in years to come. That first journey back from Foote's music store, my 'Stand by Me' fiasco at the Contrabasse Shoppe, Jennifer's 'Do you hear it?' tuning queries, lumping HP down a deserted Camaguey siding in the middle of the night, the knife-wielding horrors of that first day at the White House, singing scales with Yamira, salsa lessons in front of blind mums, blood-stained goat skins in the conga: these were not your average musical mileposts.

And now I was finally at the Casa de la Trova, a venue that over the decades had hosted the biggest names in Cuban music, playing the same Cuban *son* that had brought a smile to my face while driving through the New Zealand countryside four years previously. Here I was in the strange and not just a little ego-buffing position of being the one looking down on the audience, rather than the one looking up at the musicians. Here I was playing bass lines that were supposed to be *pepe*-resistant. Where, I pondered, was the ghost of failed piano exams now? Where was the Richard Neill who had cowered behind his instrument at Camden Town Tube station a year ago?

Given that I had only performed three songs and stood on stage for little more than fifteen minutes in total, some might argue that the post-performance scenes of suit-grabbing mayhem were unjustified. Some might like to take their arguments elsewhere. I had just scaled a very high mountain wearing no oxygen mask and totally inappropriate clothes. I make no apologies about milking the adulation, posing for the cameras, slapping the high fives, taking the free drinks, and, on at least two occasions, wiping away the odd tear. Standing there in the middle of the scrum, feeling like I'd been magically transplanted into a scene from that Wim Wenders movie, my one regret was that my own family had not been here. This last hour was the best explanation I could ever have given for resigning from the wine job and leaving behind the people I loved, and none of them were around to witness it.

Such grey thoughts were not allowed to linger for long. '*Compay*, I have some good news and some bad news,' announced a breathless Pastor, pushing his way through the mêlée to speak to the man in the once electric, now dark wet marine blue suit. 'Let's have the good news first,' I laughed, convinced there could be no real bad news on a night like this. 'Marco has turned up,' he grinned. 'And the bad news?' There was a sinister pause as Panes bit his bottom lip and gave a preparatory wince. 'The bad news is I've told everyone you're going to sing "Hotel California".'

17. Quivering Bottom Lips

'All I want is your CD player,' announced Pastor the morning after my sweaty triumph, the 'all' suggesting he had at some stage considered asking for a few other leaving presents.

'But you've already got a CD player,' I replied with clear indignation. 'What happened to the one I gave you for your birthday?'

'It broke,' he shrugged.

'But it had a guarantee, didn't it?'

'*Compay*, this is Cuba! The guarantee was for two weeks!'

As with all the other requests he had filed during our twelve months together, his timing was perfect. He knew I was still basking in the afterglow of the previous night's activities, a night that had seen me sing 'Hotel California' to a packed house and leave impressive sweat rings on a bespoke suit. In short, a night that had seen all my musical fantasies fulfilled, right down to the autograph I signed for a tourist who mistook me for a famous bass player.

'The CD player is yours,' I caved in.

Pastor was not the only one eyeing up my belongings. Rafael wanted my condoms and candles. José Luis said the yoga mat would be useful and Alexis, the overweight nurse, promised to start losing pounds if he could have my size twelve Nikes. Such was the intimate knowledge of my wardrobe ('Can I have the shorts with the stain on the back pocket?' one of the *barrio* football team had asked), I sensed that somewhere in circulation there was probably a detailed list of my possessions with names next to every item. The Italian mountain bike received the greatest number of offers, and when I told one interested party that there were already quite a few people ahead of him, he simply shot back with the standard Cuban queue-forming response of, '*Quién es el ultimo?* Who's the last in line?'

After experiencing the emotional high of live performance, a post-gig, pre-departure bout of blues was inevitable. Released from the pressure of preparing for a performance and with days no longer organized around lessons and *ensayos*, I found myself drifting around in a bit of a structureless daze. Even in my last few days in Santiago I still cycled around to Chicharrones but it wasn't the same as before. Pastor was happy to keep giving me lessons but we both knew that our mutual adventure was over. I hadn't even left yet and already I was missing the place. Like dog years, time spent in a Cuban community seemed to have been worth (in terms of emotional attachment, at least) about seven times the value of an average London year. Of course I knew that a *pepe* would always be considered a *pepe* no matter how long he stayed in Cuba, but for the first time in my life I'd been made to feel part of a community. Talking to the neighbours every day, visiting the same market every day, hanging out with the same cast of *barrio* odd-bods every day: these were simple pleasures I would miss once back in Europe. Of course, there were also plenty of things I couldn't wait to see the back of. After a year on a Cuban diet I was starting to hallucinate about spicy food, vegetables, a decent cup of tea, and bread rolls that didn't require a jack hammer to break open. After living for so long in an ovenless house, I was salivating over all the cooking possibilities I had missed out on. Even the non-cooking possibilities seemed tantalizing. A year ago, the thought of pricking holes in the top of one of those Marks & Spencer bung-in-the-oven TV dinners had stirred me into life-changing action. Now, the same thought simply stirred up strange pangs of anticipation. But poor food was not the main reason I was ready to leave. I wanted to turn on the TV at 7 p.m. and not see Randy Alonso and his one-sided *Mesa Redonda* team of pundits. I looked forward to returning to a place where you didn't need a permit to stay in a friend's house, where it wasn't illegal to travel in a friend's car, where the best beaches were open to everyone, and where buying some fish didn't require breaking the law. I'd had enough of road checks, housing inspectors, and police on every corner.

'So you like Cuba, then?' asked Manuel during the last of what had been a long-running series of journalist head-to-heads. 'I love this country,' I answered, fully aware that 'Yes and no' (the more legitimate answer) would cause our conversation to be extended at least another two hours with endless shots of rum.

The real answer was that my twelve-month stay had left me more confused about Cuba than before I'd arrived. Wherever I'd gone looking for neat conclusions, I'd found only contradictions and an endless series of frustratingly unsolvable mental equations involving the trading off of positives and negatives, pros and cons, ups and downs. For example, on the one hand I was totally inspired by the extraordinarily high levels of literacy in what was a country with Third World resources, but on the other, frustrated at the lack of freedom to use all that literacy to express opinions. Similarly, it was hard not to applaud Fidel's campaign to install computers in every school in the land, even those with just two pupils in remote rural settlements. And yet I didn't agree with the block on Cubans using the Internet.

Here you had a small nation battling with enormous dignity against the biggest superpower on the planet for nearly half a century, a tiny island defending its right not to conform to the capitalist norms surrounding it. But at the same time, here was a country that refused to give its citizens the same rights to be different. In the end, like most visitors who have tried to separate Cuba's greys into neat black and whites, I ended up cheering and criticizing the Revolution in equal amounts. And after all the debate and intellectualizing about good communism, bad communism, my abiding memory of Cuba would always be the inextinguishable spirit of ordinary Cubans whose generosity, energy and wonderful sense of humour had remained untouched despite all the economic hardships, the family separations, the hurricanes, the waiting lists, and the hour after crappy hour of political speeches on the TV.

For me, Cuba would always be Pastor's never-ending search for the next *telenovela*, Melian stomping through the Sierra Maestra in search of Fernandina's Flicker, Braulio pulling a pig out of the back of his Moskovich, Napoli and his three-string bass, and Carlos beaming with pleasure as he led his San Agustín conga past the carnival judges. Those were the images of Cuba I wanted to keep.

On the day of departure I went around and knocked on doors, delivered last-minute hugs and kisses (or pats on stomachs in Roberto's case), and shimmied awkwardly through the inevitable questions about when I would be coming back. '*Hasta pronto* – See you soon,' I promised to everyone, knowing full well that I had no idea when I'd be back in Santiago. By the time I returned to 101, the Moskovich was parked in readiness. Braulio had said he'd take me to the bus station, an offer I had accepted without questioning how exactly HP would make the trip. Looking at the rackless roof of the car and then at my watch, I went in hurried search of my driver. 'Braulio?' I called to the figure lying flat out on one of the beds. '*Sí?*' a sleepy voice grunted back. 'I, er, I was just wondering whether you might need a hand getting the roof rack ready?' His head remained flat on the pillow. 'What roof rack?' came the muffled reply. 'The one you'll need to carry the double bass?' Half an hour later I was shaking my head ruefully as HP's belly was gently lowered on to two blocks of wood strategically placed on either side of the Moskovich's wobble-board of a roof. A long piece of rope was tied around the front engine grille, wound through the handles on one side of the carrying case, wrapped around the rear bumper, back through the handle on the other side and on to the front again. To my somewhat pessimistic eye, the chances of me making a last-minute debut in

Sierra Maestra's *Camera en la Calle* slot were looking extremely promising. 'Don't worry, it'll be fine,' reassured Braulio, wedging a piece of foam in the gap between the case and the car. With a top cruising speed of 30 m.p.h., the reliable Russian was unlikely to be able to generate the sort of centrifugal forces required to dislodge the case.

The good news was that with all the worries over bumper strength, rope tension and missing buses, there was little time to get too emotional come the final hugs with Marcela, Manuel, Antonio and Carlos. Pastor seemed disconcertingly cheerful – maybe it was his way of dealing with things – and his carefully chosen final words revealed a stoic refusal to see this as a last goodbye. 'Remember the PlayStation, *compay*!' he shouted as Braulio turned the ignition. And without waiting to wave, the man from Crackling turned and headed off up the hill.

We made it to the station with minutes to spare and by the time I'd finished arguing with the Viazul bus manager about the cost of putting HP on board the bus – a discreet 10 dollars in the palm did the trick – there was only enough time to give each member of the family a quick hug as the driver repeatedly pressed the horn. Just as I was climbing up the stairs, Liana called out and, running up to the door, she pressed an envelope into my hand.

'You promise to come back soon?' she asked as the door hissed shut.

'I promise,' I mouthed back through the glass as we nudged forward. And then they were gone. My surrogate family, the Hero City, Chicharrones, Pastor Panes, Sones de Oriente, the beautiful Sierra Maestra; all slipped away behind us as the bus turned on to the runway-wide, traffic-less Autopista and headed west on the fifteen-hour journey back to Havana.

I sat down and opened the envelope Liana had given me. Inside were two small pieces of paper. The first was from Tanita. 'Richard, thank you for your friendship and love, we will never forget you.' The other was from Liana. 'Richard, I love you a lot. I will never forget you because you are like one of the family. Come back soon.' Yes, that was a bottom lip quivering in seat 5B.

Three days later, I was back in Camden reacquainting myself with the taste of London Pride and the new layout of the Marks & Spencer food hall. The initial culture shock was enormous. Suddenly, there were mobile phones again, a choice of newspapers, and pedestrians who didn't have time to stop for a chat. In place of having nothing to choose from in the shops, there was now a mind-boggling variety of ways to fill your basket. On my first trip to the supermarket, it was over twenty minutes before I managed to put something in my trolley, such was my sense of wonderment at the aisles and aisles of groceries. The once depressing Camden branch of Sainsburys was now an Aladdin's Cave of luxury items. Walking back to my brother's flat with bags laden with groceries, I stopped at a bus stop and stared at the dot matrix display flashing out the number of minutes until the next three buses arrived. I remembered Pastor and his excitement over motorway signs and smiled at the thought of what his reaction would be to such up-to-the-minute travel information. What would any Cuban's reaction be to a bus stop that told you when the bus would arrive?

A week later, I went to pick up HP at a cargo depot somewhere near Heathrow. It had cost me nearly £200 to fly my partner home, but after a week of feeling totally dislocated and more than a bit homesick for 101, I was overjoyed to see the familiar fibreglass outline at the back of the storage shed. This was my connection with Santiago, my physical reminder of an incredible year in the Caribbean.

'You wanna get y'self a smaller instrument, mate,' joked the man behind the Customs desk, sliding over a bundle of release forms for signing. 'Why'dya choose to play such a biggun then? No violins left in the shop?'

For a moment, I considered giving him a quick lecture. I desperately wanted to tell him how I came to be standing here picking up a large piece of German maple, tell him about the great Cachaito Lopez and that amazing gig at the Festival Hall, about my bond with a sixty-year-old German that Peter Tyler had written off as 'not an investment buy'. But this was no time for a cathartic storytelling session. The queue behind me was growing restless and I had to get my mum's car back to her as quickly as possible. So I scrawled my signature on the dotted line, smiled and told him the simple truth. 'I chose it,' I answered, 'because some idiot friend of mine told me it was a forgiving instrument.' And with those words I grabbed the case, tipped it on to its wheels and zigzagged my partner out the door.

Postscript
Barcelona – August 2003

It's now been over a year since I boarded that bus in Santiago. A couple of weeks in London were enough to convince me that a return to the old life couldn't happen and, with HP in tow, I moved to Barcelona, a city that seemed to offer the perfect blend of Mediterranean lifestyle, cheaper living and bags of culture, a city with enough Latinos to help stop me getting homesick for salsa and badly-spoken Spanish and enough gastronomic news to keep a freelance journalist in work.

For the first few months, I rang 101 every couple of weeks. I'd sit in the Pakistani-run phone centre near my flat in the Gothic Quarter and, for an hour or more, dial and redial until finally I got through and heard the excited squeals of Tania or Liana in my ear. Even after such a short time in Spain, the sound of strong Cuban accents made me laugh. '*Qué pasa, compay?*' asked Braulio when I started sniggering in the middle of one of his rapid-fire monologues. 'It's your accent,' I replied. 'Hearing it makes me miss Cuba even more.' And every time, the phone calls would end with the same question ('When are you coming back?') and evasion ('Soon', 'In a couple of months', 'After Christmas') routine. The truth was I didn't have the money to take a two-week Cuban holiday. Occasionally, I tried getting in touch with Pastor. This was a complicated procedure that involved ringing the nearest community phone to Pastor's house (Chicharrones had few connections), persuading the owner to walk down the hill to the White House, and then ringing back five minutes later hoping that a) I could get through and b) that the man I wanted was there. The first few times I failed, but on the third attempt I nearly choked up when I heard the familiar voice on the end of a very crackly line. I asked him how things were and he laughed, and replied, '*Luchando, compay, siempre luchando.*' The last thing he said before hanging up was that he hoped to be in Europe soon.

Some months later, I received an email from a strange Dutch-sounding address. Opening it up I found a short message saying, 'Pastor is here in Amsterdam, please ring the following number.' Those damn Dutchmen had obviously got together and paid the money required to get Pastor the exit visa, the official letter of invitation, the return flight, the insurance, and the packets of filterless Cuban cigarettes their music teacher would need to survive two weeks in Europe. I tried ringing a couple of times but we never did manage to make contact. Pastor was always out, and each time I rang and one of the Dutchmen answered the phone, I felt a nagging annoyance that my bass teacher was gazing at Dutch rather than Spanish motorway signs.

More months went by and I followed the occasional bits of Cuban news that appeared in the main Barcelona newspaper, *La Vanguardia*. Three men were executed for attempting to hijack a ferry and over seventy dissidents were rounded up and given long jail sentences. Diplomatic relations between the EU and Cuba deteriorated as a result, and with Fidcl saying that Cuba didn't need European funds, it looked increasingly as though the island was heading towards total isolation and economic meltdown. Then came the announcement that the great Compay Segundo had died and, as I read all the obituaries, I imagined the huge crowds that would have turned up for the burial ceremony in Santiago. Maybe they would have held a special concert in the Casa de la Trova, the place where Segundo had played both with the duo Los Compadres and later as a guest singer with Eliades Ochoa's band. Maybe the tatty old poster would finally be taken down and a proper portrait of the Siboney-born musician would join the ranks of the greats up on the wall. The man who wrote 'Chan Chan' deserved nothing less.

Segundo's death brought with it a stream of elegies to the power and beauty of *son*, and with each one I read, the feeling of guilt kept rising. I had arrived in Barcelona with great intentions. I was going to find a new bass teacher, practise every day, maybe even try to join a band. And of course, none of these things happened. There was never enough money to afford the lessons (Pastor's reducing price system sadly didn't exist in Europe) and, as the weeks had drifted by, so the layer of dust on HP's shoulders and hips had thickened. One day I was strolling down the Ramblas when I heard the distinctive scraping sound of a Cuban *guiro*, the elongated calabash with ribs cut into its side. Seeking out the source of the noise, I spotted a man striking out a salsa rhythm on a section of the ridged plastic tubing the Catalan builders wrapped around scaffolding. I knew immediately from the way he was playing – and his ingenious use of building materials – that this man was Cuban and I went straight up, put out my hand, and with my best Cuban accent said, '*Qué vola acere?*' He dropped the plastic and with a huge grin on his face, embraced me with an enormous bear-hug.

Five minutes later, we were chatting and laughing like old friends, one homesick Habanero trying to sort out his Spanish immigration papers and one homesick Englishman struggling to get to grips with his new life in Spain. When I told him about my double bass, his eyes lit up and just for a second I saw Pastor's mischievous face looking at me. 'We have to start a band!' he burbled excitedly. 'We can make lots of money here in the street.' We agreed to meet again the following day to talk about it, and after shaking hands I turned and left my new friend to return to his improvised *guiro*. I'd only gone 10 yards when a voice called out behind me, '*Oye, compay, tienes la bomba, no?*' I smiled back and tipping my hand from side to side, gave the answer I knew Pastor would have given. '*Más o menos,*' I replied, '*más o menos.*'